^{THE}Anglo-Indians

THE
Anglo-Indians
A 500-Year History

S. Muthiah

and

Harry MacLure

with inputs from
Richard O'Connor

NIYOGI
BOOKS

Published by

NIYOGI BOOKS

D-78, Okhla Industrial Area, Phase-I
New Delhi-110 020, INDIA
Tel: 91-11-26816301, 49327000
Fax: 91-11-26810483, 26813830
email: niyogibooks@gmail.com
website: www.niyogibooksindia.com

Text © S. Muthiah
Photographs © As acknowledged

Editor: Shaurya Shaukat Sircar
Design: Shashi Bhushan Prasad

ISBN: 978-93-81523-76-6
Publication: 2017

Printed at: Niyogi Offset Pvt. Ltd., New Delhi, India

Contents

A bridal couple leads their guests through an arch that the groomsmen and bridesmaids form during the Grand March, a grand Anglo-Indian tradition that survives to this day. (Photograph: Raghuraman Radhakrishnan)

Foreword

Some years ago, in the early 1990s, Prof. Lionel Caplan, of the School of Oriental and African Studies in London, was in Madras in connection with a book he was writing on the Anglo-Indian community. He interviewed a few of us. Wary of outsiders with their preconceived and rigid notions of the community, I asked him whether he was researching us as "a vanishing tribe".

I was being unnecessarily facetious. In his mild way the British scholar replied that he was attempting to discover the reasons for the Anglo-Indian community surviving for more than 500 years, since its origins in the 16th century.

To survive is to be a part of history. Down the years, the community has attracted the attention of historians and research scholars, writers of fiction and producers of films. The works of authors writing in the 1900s, before and after Independence, reflect the shifting fortunes of the community, revealing uncertainty, angst and a sense of betrayal.

The more important writers are: Herbert A. Stark (*Hostages to India,* 1926. *The Call of the Blood,* 1932); Cedric Dover (*Cimmerii or Eurasians and their Future,* 1929. *Half Caste,* 1937); K.E. Wallace (*The Eurasian Problem,* 1930); and Frank Anthony (*Britain's Betrayal in India,* 1969). These books are valuable as records of the changing times and are classics of their genre.

Writers like Khushwant Singh (*The Times of India Magazine,* 1969), called the community "a historical anachronism" and viewed with dismay the time when "the sponge of oblivion be passed on the slate of Anglo-Indian history". Blair Williams in *Anglo-Indians: Vanishing Remnants of a Bygone Era* (2002) looks at his community from the point of view of the emigrant Anglo-Indian. British and Indian novelists and film producers, who even today view the community from the single standpoint of 'mixed-blood', have been prejudiced and judgmental.

It was left to Gloria Jean Moore in *The Anglo-Indian Vision* (1986) to reclaim Anglo-Indian history from, in her words "the encrusted literary and academic conventional attitudes which ... ignored a people who achieved so much with so little aggression and so much good grace ... a transitional group who challenged prejudice ... and made the unity of diverse peoples a reality." She is the community's first woman historian. With the easy intimacy and style of the raconteur, through recorded interviews and photographs, she allowed Anglo-Indians in India and abroad to participate in the telling of their own history.

It is our privilege that one of India's leading chroniclers of the historical, S. Muthiah of Madras, should conceptualise what is the first pictorial history of the community. In the narrative that forms the first part of the book, Muthiah explores the encounter between European and Indian and the origins and growth of the Anglo-Indian community, in the context of colonialism and empire-building. By further adopting a post-colonial perspective, Muthiah has acquired a retrospective overview that encapsulates more that 500 years of chronological linear history. In the 21st century, in a post-Independence "New India", Muthiah is in a position to see the community not piecemeal but whole. Further, an empathy born out of a close interaction with the community, frees the narrative from the stereotyping that marred earlier writings.

Muthiah traces the origins and growth of four generations of Anglo-Indians. He combines meticulous research and a descriptive-analytical approach with a style enlivened by personal anecdote and imagery. One is pleasantly waylaid by quaint expressions like "for the nonce". There is the delightful image of "the pagoda tree being shaken successfully", which causes us to imagine gold coins raining down on the heads of the plundering Warren Hastings et al! Also characteristic of his style is an almost text-book use of summary and capitals for emphasis.

While elaborating on the definition of 'Anglo-Indian' enshrined in the Constitution of India (1949), Muthiah is careful to point out when a person is NOT an Anglo-Indian! Muthiah himself prefers the term "Euro-Indian", which he uses in the course of his narrative. In a significant remark he points out: "It is the search for the Anglo-Indian and not the Euro-Indian, which often misses the roots of the community," which is European and not British alone.

Throughout the narrative Muthiah stresses the fact that the Anglo-Indians are a distinct Indian community. The phrase "joining the mainstream" is often used even by Anglo-Indians to suggest its desirability. Muthiah makes it clear when a merging, or joining the mainstream, in sections of the community occurred in Britain and India.

William Dalrymple, who acknowledges and names an Indian forebear in the maternal line, writes in *White Mughals* (2002): "The Portuguese in India and their Indo-Portuguese descendants did not leave one culture to inhabit another, so much as live in both at the same time, accommodating in outlook and lifestyle rival ways of living and looking at the world."

In the post-colonial discourse, the community is seen as modern and its "mixed-blood" indicative of modern multicultural societies. Irwin Allan Sealy, the Anglo-Indian writer, calls Anglo-Indians "the first modern Indians".

It has not always been so. While we were always comfortable in our own skin, others saw us differently, looking at us through the lens of "mixed-blood". We were called "half-caste" and to quote the title of a research paper published as late as 1994, 'Neither Fish nor Flesh ...'.

Reams have been written on promiscuity in the Anglo-Indian woman and what Muthiah calls the perceived "lack of focus" in the man. British writers in colonial times, with no scientific basis whatsoever, attribute lack of moral fibre and a diminished intellect to mixed-blood and "malformation of the hybrid brain".

Muthiah stays clear of any mention of mixed-blood, except while commenting on a Company directive in 1786, that stopped East Indian orphans from being sent to England for higher education. It was felt their eventual inter-marriage would "debase generations of Englishmen". As Muthiah says, it was "the first sign of discrimination against those of mixed blood in India" and, what is significant, "stated as national policy".

His definition of 'Anglo-Indian' extends to and includes what he calls "a sub-culture", which "offers a generally accepted picture of the community". An Anglo-Indian is defined by his language, English; his religion, Christianity; his Western lifestyle and dress; a cuisine that is Western, influenced by regional Indian cuisine, and a love of Western music and dance. Muthiah has even mentioned the Grand March at Anglo-Indian weddings, which we do not know the origin of and is probably no longer observed in other Western societies.

Unlike other writers, Muthiah has noticed that the greatest virtues of the community are our strong family ties and equally strong religious ties. He also makes the point that the love of Western song and dance and the intermingling of the sexes, which shocked the conservative Indian in the past, is descriptive of the Europeanised Indian today. I would like to add that as the only casteless Christian community in India, we are free of caste-ridden considerations, such as the giving and taking of dowry, which afflict other communities in India.

Muthiah remarks that the "most truly literate community in India is perhaps the Anglo-Indian community". He devotes an entire chapter to the

'Legacy of Anglo-Indian Schools'. Allan Sealy in *The Anglo-Indians* (Dileep Prakash, 2008) says:

"It is a clouded fact that up to and beyond Independence, English was diffused through the country not officially by the Raj, in spite of Macaulay's famous Minute, but unofficially by the Anglo-Indians ... A whole century before Macaulay there are records of 'Dame Schools' run by formidable women from their homes ... who taught English and elocution under a mofussil sky." In the established Anglo-Indian schools, Sealy goes on to say, "Anglo-Indian teachers outnumbered the British. We forget that is their demotic that is spoken in the country today."

The community has often been seen as answering "the call of the blood" and rallying to the support of the British. Khushwant Singh writing in 1969 (*The Times of India Magazine*), points out: "Too late in the course of history did it occur to the Anglo-Indians that they would have got a better deal from the Indians. Indian resentment against the Anglo-Indian was not because of what he was, but because of what he did or was made to do by the English."

Muthiah too finds it difficult to understand the Anglo-Indian "offer of armed support" to the British in the Non-Cooperation Movement in 1920 and the Quit India Movement in 1942, which "weakened their relations with the Indians". Anglo-Indian railwaymen are proud of their service in the AF(I)—Auxiliary Force (India)—which, while admitting it was a condition of Railway service, Muthiah still maintains "failed to win friends among the Indians". At this stage of their history, Anglo-Indians were not answering "the call of the blood" but the call to duty as members of the armed forces and the police.

Anglo-Indians were later to exhibit the same sense of duty in the Indo-Pakistan wars, with air aces, the Keelor brothers, and Brigadier Desmond Hayde, decorated for bravery. A little known fact is that Anglo-Indians displayed the same sense of loyalty fighting for Pakistan.

There are Anglo-Indians who still rue the cessation of reservations in Central Government jobs. Muthiah with the clarity of hindsight argues convincingly that focus on job reservation, particularly in the Railways that had become virtually a heritage occupation, had led to railway families "not pushing the talented upwards".

With Anglo-Indians forced to seek other avenues of employment, higher education became necessary. After liberalisation in the 1990s, Anglo-Indians are employed in "every profession other young Indians are making headway in".

The poverty index in the community, according to Muthiah, is less than the national average. Unemployment, underemployment and other factors are dependent on market forces and the state of the national economy. I believe that with India on an upward graph and the community's youth—educated, talented, ambitious and unafraid, our future can only be bright.

Muthiah calls the Anglo-Indians of today the fourth generation and "closest to Anglo-Celtic roots". It was in this group that many saw themselves 'as culturally British' and who post-Independence emigrated to " 'White' countries of the English speaking world". Muthiah, however, is fair in considering the various factors that led to half the Anglo-Indian population leaving India.

Large scale emigration has been linked with doomsday predictions of the eventual demise of the Anglo-Indian community in the next fifty years. The Anglo-Indian children of today who will inhabit the future are growing up in Anglo-Indian homes. Their parents who belong to a generation which has moved away from the traditional service-oriented jobs, have not moved away from their inherited culture.

The upwardly mobile Indians, including the Anglo-Indian and the Indian who has 'arrived' while belonging to a cosmopolitan workforce and adhering to the workplace culture it imposes, are in their homes, rooted and comfortable in their own cultures—customs, food, religion, mother-tongue, all of which define and reinforce identity.

Muthiah has given the Anglo-Indian community its rightful place as a modern community in 21st century India. I believe that the unrelenting forces of history will further propel it not in dying out but in reinventing itself. Muthiah himself believes that the fate of the community is linked with that of other Indian communities.

If one had to choose just two books on the Anglo-Indian community, one would be this magnum opus of Muthiah's, brilliantly conceptualised and executed. The other would be what has been called the Great Anglo-Indian Novel, Allan Sealy's *The Trotter-Nama* (1988) subtitled 'A Chronicle' and dedicated "To the Other Anglo-Indians". While historically valid, it is a work of art.

While Muthiah has erected the scaffolding as it were, Sealy has filled the spaces with the colour, romance and adventure of the Anglo-Indian story. He "has done for his community what Joyce did for the Irish, illuminating its soul through sheer poetry and imagination," in the words of Tony Jesudasen in an issue of the *Indian Express Magazine* in January 1989.

A pictorial history follows the narrative in the second half of the book. The immediacy of visual portraiture effectively highlights the political, social and cultural ethos of a people who lived their lives with courage and grace. A people's history is often lifted above its everyday ordinariness by exceptional men and women, who rise from within it, a product of their times, to distinguish themselves, each in his or her own field.

Every community has its share of achievers, but as Frank Anthony often remarked, the microscopic Anglo-Indian community has made contributions to the country of its birth far in excess of its numbers. It is not just a matter of achievement but achievement that has been found worthy of recognition and has secured a place in the history books.

The portrait gallery is a roll call of honour, immortalising for all time, heroes and heroines in every age and century, as well as ordinary men and women, who in their lives and their achievements have exemplified what it is to be Anglo-Indian. Unfortunately, we as a community have never known our own history. We have never had the know-how or the aggression to challenge the stereotypes that reduced our men and women to figures of derision.

S. Muthiah has chronicled our history, a legacy we can bequeath to our children and our children's children. As a comprehensive and definitive history of the community it is a valuable book for research scholars and should find pride of place in a home library. This history will rekindle in Anglo-Indians wherever they are, pride in themselves and pride in our extraordinary community. It is our story, a history we have reason to celebrate.

Dr. Beatrix D'Souza
Former Member of Parliament

Chennai

PART I

Harry MacLure and Richard O'Connor who have teamed with me on this book are Anglo-Indians. I am not. Making many a person who'd heard I was working on this pictorial history of the Anglo-Indian community wonder what my connection with it is.

In the first instance, the European period in South India, particularly the British era, is a special interest of mine and of which I've written much. Very much part of that post-1498 history is the Anglo-Indian story. But my connections with the Anglo-Indians are very much more personal than that.

As far back as I can remember, I was taught by a Mrs. Smith from Madras. I learnt the three Rs, my English and table manners from her. To all in the family, she was 'Nanny', reflecting Indian society of the 1930s when affluent Indian families demonstrated their Westernisation or their affinity to the Raj by having their children brought up or taught by British, European or Anglo-Indian governesses. For years afterwards, I kept in touch with 'Nanny', calling on her whenever I was in Madras; she would always be helping at her son-in-law's pharmacy in Vepery, Wilfred Pereira's.

When I joined Kindergarten in Colombo, a Mrs. Sanger from Bangalore entered the family to look after my sisters till they joined school. Meanwhile, in school, I caught up with glamorous Miss Mavis Sansoni. Petite, lively, and, as I was later to discover, heavily rouged. More motherly but sterner was Mrs. de Kretser. The two Kindergarten teachers were Burghers, the Ceylon equivalent of the Anglo-Indian. The Burghers were to be part of my daily life in the school years that followed. That was a Colombo where in its 'public schools' Sinhalese, Tamils, Burghers and Moors scarcely recognised ethnic diversity, were bound together by English and the 'old school tie', and spent time in each other's homes, interdining, as the anthropologists would say, and socialising.

The next three years were to be spent at Montfort School in the Shevaroy Hills of South India and at Lawrence College, Ghora Gali, near Murree, the hill station of the then undivided Punjab. In both, the Indian student strength was less than ten per cent; the rest was Anglo-Indian. The six years that followed were in the U.S., discovering that the Negroes, as they were then called ('Black' was to become correct usage only some years later), had as mixed-blooded a heritage as any Anglo-Indian or Burgher and ranged in colour from the palest *café au lait* to ebony. They were as out of place on the American campuses of the 1940s as the handful of foreign students. More significantly from the point of view of the background to this book, they shared many of the characteristics, uncertainties and concerns of the Anglo-Indian and the Burgher.

Back in Colombo, I was once again among the Burghers. *The Times of Ceylon*'s editorial staff was a third Burgher and its press room was half Burgher. And finding me a bachelor, more often than not at a loose end, almost every one of them wanted me home for a meal or a party. Thus, for nearly the first forty years of my life, I spent much time with those of a mixed ethnic heritage.

In Madras, from the late 1960s, the Anglo-Indian connection diminished considerably. There were just three or four Anglo-Indians in the large printing and publishing house I managed, working as printers or editorial and secretarial staff. Much later, I caught up with Dr. Beatrix D'Souza, M.P. and Professor of English, and through her a few members of the Anglo-Indian community like Harry and Richard.

In the years that followed, I met several Burgher colleagues in the U.K. whenever I visited that country and, then, from the new Millennium, others in Australia when one of my daughters settled there. There, I spent time with many of them in Canberra, Melbourne or Sydney, going down memory lane and remembering what a great team we were at *The Times*. In these cities, I also got the opportunity to meet several Anglo-Indians at one gathering or another.

By then the 'British in South India' period had me in thrall and one aspect of that history was discovering the moving story of a community in search of itself. The community of people of mixed ethnic heritage, those whom Kumari Jayawardena, the eminent Sri Lankan social scientist, now calls the Euro-Asians, is one I've been in fairly close touch with longer than most of its members alive today. Some of those insights the decades have provided and what the history books and archives tell me are what you will find in the pages that follow. They will, I hope, present a vibrant community that's had more than its share of ups and downs and NOT be seen as an epitaph to what many in the community feel is a vanishing "tribe".

This book owes much to:

Harry MacLure and his team at *Anglos In The Wind*, a quarterly journal that over the last fifteen years has done much to link a community now spread around the world;

Richard O'Connor of Indian Customs who sheds officialdom with his uniform and adopts scholarship at one end of the scale and emceeing concerts with blazing guitars at the other;

The numerous Anglo-Indian authors round the world who over the last couple of decades have begun to tell the story of their community and its members, adding to what others had written a few generations ago;

Dr. Beatrix D'Souza who has written a perceptive and candid Foreword to the book;

All those who have contributed the photographs that have enriched this volume and who are individually acknowledged with the pictures;

V. Srinivasan, Pushpa Dhanavandan and Krishna Prasad, G. Shankar and the rest of the team at PACE systems graphic communications, Chennai, who have provided all the secretarial assistance I needed to put this book together;

And Bikash D. Niyogi of Niyogi Books, New Delhi, who commissioned this work and who has ensured its excellent production.

Chennai   S. MUTHIAH

During the 9th Anglo-Indian Reunion, held in Kolkotta, in January 2013, Anglo-Indian identity received further recognition when 'The Derozio Anglo-Indian Research Collection' was inaugurated in the Central Library of the University of Calcutta. (Photo: AITW)

Who are the Anglo-Indians?

Till 1911, 'Anglo-Indian' was the term used by the British to describe themselves, Anglo-Celtics for the most part, who spent most of their lives in India in the civil and military services, and who held senior positions in government departments, or spent years in the country as merchants and professionals, traders and planters. They were men like Thomas Munro, 'Boy' Malcolm and Charles Metcalfe, on the one hand, and William Jones, Colin Mackenzie and William Lambton, on the other. Many, like Munro and Lambton, died during a lifetime of service in India and lie buried here. Some, like David Ochterlony and William Fraser, lived like Indian princes, with opulent harems in tow. Others, like William Kirkpatrick, married into well-to-do Indian families. Still others, like that pioneering Madras merchant Thomas Parry, had an Indian "bibi", or mistress, wherever he had a home. And, of course, there were the many who were faithful to their British or European wives, like Warren Hastings to his 'Maid Marian' and Robert Clive to his Margaret Maskelyne. The essence of the description was that though the pre-1911 Anglo-Indian was British, he spent most, if not all, of his working life in India, loyal to Britain but committed to governing or developing India, in the process losing some of his Britishness and gaining some Indianness.

It was in the 1911 census that the government of Lord Hardinge officially termed those of mixed blood, children born of European fathers and Indian mothers and children born of their offspring, as 'Anglo-Indians'. Till then they had been called—ignoring such derogatory terms as 'half caste', 'half-and-half' and 'eight annas'—Eurasians (a term they thought disparaging, though it was well accepted in Singapore, Malaya and Hong Kong), Indo-Britons, and what was, curiously, for long commonly used, East Indians.

What was proclaimed by executive order was included in the Government of India Act of 1919 which described Anglo-Indians as follows:

"Every person, being a British subject and resident in British India, of

(a) European descent in the male line…

(b) Mixed Asiatic descent, whose father, grandfather or remote ancestor in the male line was born in the continent of Europe, Canada, Newfoundland, Australia, New Zealand, the Union of South Africa or the United States of America, and who is not entered in the European electoral roll."

This was further amplified in the Act of 1935 and, later, repeated in the 1949 Constitution of India. In the Constitution, Article 366(2) states:

"An Anglo-Indian means a person whose father or any other of whose male progenitors in the male line is or was of European descent but who is domiciled within the territories of India and is or was born within such territory of parents habitually resident therein and not established there for temporary purposes only."

A careful look at that definition of one community[1] in India enshrined in the Constitution makes several long-debated issues clearer.

Firstly, to be considered Anglo-Indian, a person must descend from a European forefather, NOT from a European maternal line. The child of an Indian father "habitually resident" in India and a European mother is NOT Anglo-Indian; he or she is 'Indian'. On the other hand, the child of an Anglo-Indian father "habitually resident" in India and a mother who is Anglo-Indian or not is an Anglo-Indian.

The second important point is the emphasis of the male line being European and NOT British. Thus, in the Indian context, this would mean that the descendants of Portuguese, Dutch, French and British forefathers would all be considered Anglo-Indians. Further, the armies of all these major powers in colonial India as well as those of Indian potentates included up to the late 18th century, thousands of mercenaries from Sweden to Sicily, Spain to Russia and even men of European descent from North America and Australia. If these soldiers, like Thomas, Raymond, and Reinhardt, among the legendary ones— and there were also numerous others who worked in the trading posts of the major powers in India—had put down roots in India, their children too would be Anglo-Indian. But the children born abroad of Anglo-Indians now settled overseas and who have become citizens there are NOT Anglo-Indian. They are persons of Indian origin and Anglo-Indian heritage but are British, Australian, Canadian or whatever, depending on the country they now call 'Home'.

---

1.   Six communities are listed as minorities in the constitution. They are the Scheduled Castes and Tribes, Muslims, Christians, Sikhs, Anglo-Indians, and Parsis.

It should also be noted that the 1911 definition covered those of European descent settled in the subcontinent from Baluchistan to Burma, Kashmir to Cape Comorin. In 1935, Burma was no longer a part of India and Anglo-Burman became preferred usage there. And under the 1949 definition in the Indian Constitution, those of European descent living in Pakistan (and, later, Bangladesh) would not be considered Anglo-Indian, their "habitual domicile" excluding them from the definition. In any event, there is hardly anyone left of European descent in Pakistan or Bangladesh these days.

This stress on male European lineage is responsible for the fact that Anglo-Indian surnames can be traced to almost every country in Europe. Besides Portuguese and Dutch names like Madeiros and D'Souza, van Geyzel and van Hefton, and Anglo-Celtic names like Smith, Jones, O'Brien and Macdonald, Anglo-Indians include among their numbers La Fontaine (French) and Schmidt (German), Reghelini (Italian) and Micetich (Croatian), Muhldorff (Danish) and Lopez (Spanish), to give just a sampling.

Given this background, a more correct description of those of mixed descent would be Euro-Indians, a term I will use from time to time in these pages. In fact, taking into consideration descent from either the male or the female European lines, and the spread of the mixed community from the Indian subcontinent to the Philippines, leading Sri Lankan social scientist Kumari Jayawardena prefers the term Euro-Asian. Indeed, Kumari Jayawardena's focus on the female line is something few Anglo-Indians share.

Herbert Stark of the Indian Educational Service and the Bengal Legislative Council, one of the early leaders and documenters of the community, stated in 1936, "If Europe is the land of our fathers, India is the land of our mothers." Strangely, few Anglo-Indians show any interest in the maternal line. Geraldine Charles, Trustee of the Families in British India Society, is one of the few who traces her own ancestry

Geraldine Charles, settled in the U.K., says "Susan Harvey was the great granddaughter of Mootamah aka Sarah and I am the great granddaughter of Susan which makes me the great great great great granddaughter of Mootamah." Charles is one of the few of Anglo-Indian descent who has spent time on tracing the maternal Indian ancestor—and recorded it in this picture. (Photo: Geraldine Charles)

Marriages between Britons & Indians

Robert & Sarah's
Grand-daughter Susan

- Baptised before marriage or simply adopted a British Christian name
- 23 November 1788 marriage of **Robert Harvey** (Sgt. of Supernumeraries) to **Mootamah**
- Mootamah adopted the name of **Sarah after birth of first child**
- Sarah died 1830 aged 65 having had 6 children
  Robert died 1805
- Both Buried at St Mary's, Fort St George

The Bradbury family c.1896 in Bellary where William Henry Bradbury (centre in picture) was Prison Superintendent. Bradbury married an Anglo-Indian from Bangalore, Catharine Williams, and their son Herbert (Bertie), seated extreme right on the floor, was the grandfather of Geraldine Charles. (Photo: Geraldine Charles)

Top: *The Harvey family c. 1894 in Madras. Mootamah married Robert Harvey in November 1788 and descended from them are the two men standing (John and Alexander Harvey) and their two sisters on the right, Grace and Susan Harvey. Their mother Anne Edwina Harvey is seated centre. Next to Susan on the floor is her fiancée Robert Johnson. (Photo: Geraldine Charles)*

to a 1788 marriage of Robert Harvey to a Sarah (Mootamah), an Indian, on one side and, on the other, to a James Bradbury who was married to a Catharine Williams (an Anglo-Indian). Willam Dalrymple, the well-known author, is another who mentions by name an Indian forebear in the maternal line.

Anglo-Indians tracing lineage through old church records will find male forebears marrying brides with no names recorded or just a Christian name such as Mary. In the former case, the bride had, usually, NOT converted to Christianity, like the wife of Job Charnock, the founder of Calcutta, or, as in the latter instance, if she had converted to Christianity, only the baptismal name was recorded, her family having washed its hands off both her and the proceedings. But if a European name like Catharine Williams was recorded, there was no way of knowing whether she was Anglo-Indian or 'pure' European. Which is why you can still find an occasional family, like a prominent one that I know, that claims to remain 'pure' European after 200 and more years in India. The forefather in this family, stated to be European, was an orphan who spent most of his early years in a Christian orphanage that hosted both European and Anglo-Indian orphans[2] and trained them for middle level supervisory work or as skilled artisans. For a family descended from such a background, and given the comparatively low numbers of 'pure' Europeans in such services at the time, it would have been well-nigh impossible for the family to have remained 'pure' over 200 years.

The 'pure' European settler was called a 'Domiciled European', a description that lingered on with diehards till

---

2.   Orphan was a term that was often also used for the child of a widow or the child of a deserted mother who entrusted the child to the orphanage.

well into the 20th century and was more likely a person who was truly so only in the latter half of the 19th century. But by the definitions of 1911, 1919, 1935 and 1949, no matter how 'pure' the line, the family would be Anglo-Indian. In the defining statement there is no mention at all of female lineage; all that it states is descent from a European male progenitor who was domiciled in India and whose progeny "habitually lives" in India. That makes the family I mentioned earlier clearly Anglo-Indian in terms of the Indian Constitution.

In sum, then, in terms of the official definition, an Anglo-Indian is a person descended from a European male line whose family is permanently resident in India. This reflects the general Anglo-Indian sentiment that it was immaterial who the first mother in the family was.

In the eyes of the general public, however, Anglo-Indians are of mixed descent, born of relationships in or out of wedlock between European males and Indian women and have, through this union of two different ethnicities, developed into a distinct community in India. The Anglo-Indians themselves today, while accepting that historical concept, see themselves as having in practice grown through marriage with their own, marrying less and less outside the community (till recent times), and nurturing an identifiably distinct subculture in India.

That subculture offers another generally accepted picture of the community. The Anglo-Indian is a person with a European forefather, whose native tongue is English, who is educated and who is a Christian (Protestant or Roman Catholic). Generally an urban resident, the Anglo-Indian dresses in Western fashion (though in recent years more and more Anglo-Indian women wear Indian clothes, particularly to work) and keeps a home strongly influenced by the West in

A Christian upringing from childhood and a deep commitment to religion from childhood to death is a characteristic of the Anglo-Indians. Here Anglo-Indian children in Jolarpet are seen after their First Holy Communion in the 1950s. (Photo: AITW)

Pilgrimages are another feature of the Anglo-Indian commitment to Christianity. Here, Anglo-Indian pilgrims take Our Lady of Mount Carmel in procession during the Annual Feast in Covelong to where they go on pilgrimage from the Madras area. (Photo: AITW)

Right: *Eating with spoons, forks and knives has been very much part of Anglo-Indian culture as seen in this family dinner in Calcutta. (Photo: Cynthia Clark)*

Top Right: *Western clothes were another identifier of the community, particularly of the women who till recently favoured dresses or frocks, as they were called, in the early 1940s when this picture was taken at the Lillooah Railway Colony. (Photo: AITW)*

aesthetics, furnishing and table practices, with spoons, forks and knives used while eating. Anglo-Indian cuisine offers both Western and Indian dishes, but each tweaked by the seasoning of the other cuisine; the Indian element will, however, vary, being dependent on which part of India the homemaker learnt cooking in.

Virtually every home has a tradition of popular Western and church song and music, many own a piano and today's youth favour guitars and harmonicas. A corollary is learning Western (ballroom) dancing from a young age, foxtrots, waltzes and jive the favoured forms. This, together with a more informal relationship with parents, has long led to an ease in conversation and a greater inter-mingling of the sexes. In conservative Indian eyes, this enjoyment of song and dance has long been seen as promiscuity in the women and a lack of serious focus in the men. The British view was not very different. These views were magnified when many Anglo-Indian women were seen on the arms of American soldiers and British officers in Indian cities during World War II—the *Bhowani Junction* view. Which is a rather biased view, given that a couple of the greatest virtues of the community, especially in its erstwhile 'colonies'[3], were the

---

3.   Enclaves in India that were predominantly Anglo-Indian.

All: Whether it's a young teenagers' party, a wedding or a family get-together at home, music and dance are what Anglo-Indians enjoy greatly from childhood. (Photos: AITW and wedding photograph from Elaine Roach)

strong family ties and equally strong ties with their churches. Curiously, much of what has been said in this paragraph (except religion and the War years) is descriptive also of the post-Millennium young Indian! There is a Westernisation of much of India taking place, the growth of the Europeanised Indian!

A part of this subculture, however, has, sadly, been for years an Anglo-Indian divide over colour and origin. Anglo-Indians can range from fair of skin colour and blonde of hair to near black in skin pigmentation and with crinkly black hair. It is not unusual for skin colour to vary sharply even in the same family—often confusing immigration officers from the U.K., the U.S. and Australia.

A well-researched recent article by a Burgher[4], Earl Forbes, settled in Australia on how Australia looked at Euro-Asian migrants only emphasises this—and at the same time makes a point about Euro-Asian heritage that Anglo-Indians and others should not forget. Genes have a way of playing tricks. The article says, inter alia, between late 1946 and 1951, migration from Asia to Australia was rigidly scrutinised and limited to a comparatively small number of Euro-Asians who met the tests of *'European ancestry, appearance, upbringing and outlook'*.

Migration of Euro-Asians to Australia only became possible when the concept of 'Predominantly European' ancestry was accepted by Australia. But what, in practical terms, was "Predominantly European' ancestry? Australian bureaucrats of this period ruled, *"The Regulations are that the immigrants must be more than 50% European and in addition must be European in appearance."*

But this was often not enough for Australian Immigration officers. Among the Euro-Asian migrants in the post-World War II era there was a wide range of 'appearances'. Some were blue-eyed and very fair in complexion. Others were dark skinned. And others had features, like eyes, that indicated Southeast Asian or Northeast Indian ancestry. Those passed by Australian missions in Asian countries were often stopped at the port of landing and sent back. Apparently, in Canberra, politicians and bureaucrats were concerned that the appearance aspect of the migration test was not being applied as rigorously as required overseas.

The Australian preoccupation with *European appearance* persisted long after migrants arrived in Australia. In the 1950s, the typical Naturalisation Application form contained 17 questions. The questions were quite innocuous. However, after the 17th question there was a blank space on the application form termed 'General'. In the 1950s, there is evidence to show that most cases favourably approved for naturalisation carried the handwritten notation by the interviewing officer: *'Appearance predominantly European'*.

---

4.   The Sri Lankan equivalent of the Anglo-Indian.

The fact that more and more persons of non-European appearance were being admitted as migrants from Asia to Australia led in 1950 to a tightening of the migration approval criteria. In October 1950, an official Canberra Memo to its Asian missions stated,

"The Minister has decided that eligibility for admission to Australia of persons of mixed race shall depend upon compliance with the following conditions...

1. *A person must be 75% or more European (as regards origin). Documentary evidence of this must be furnished;*
2. *He must be fully European in upbringing and outlook;*
3. *He tends to be European rather than non-European in appearance."*

Now there were, in addition to the *European ancestry* and *European appearance*, further requirements that the applicant must be *'fully European in upbringing and outlook'*.

It was to be a long time before Australia began to take a more liberal view towards Euro-Asian migration, particularly with regard to Euro-Asian appearance. And that's really when the Euro-Asian numbers in Australia began growing substantially.

What needs remembering in this context is that those descended from the Portuguese and from mothers from the coasts south of the Vindhyas or from the East Indian coast are likely to be considerably darker than those descended from Anglo-Celtic and similar European stock and mothers from North India. There has, in fact, for long existed a colour divide within the community itself. This has been so even at the leadership level of the latter group, which often tended to consider the darker Anglo-Indians as not belonging to the community, particularly if they spoke in the mother's tongue—Konkani, Malayalam, Tamil or Bengali. They were Feringhis, not only to themselves but to the fairer Anglo-Indians, especially those whose names did not reflect Portuguese heritage. Happily, this has been resolved to a great degree in the post-Independence years and colour consciousness is now no different from what most Indians exhibit, perhaps even less with a greater bonding in a diminishing community.

There has in the past been a rather similar divide based on class. The Domiciled Europeans and some Anglo-Indians, generally those employed at the top or middle-level positions, were not averse to considering many of the majority as being of 'Tommy Stock' or 'Railway Stock'. By 'Tommy Stock' was meant those descended from the lowest ranks serving in the British or the Company's European regiments. 'Railway Stock' referred to descent from firemen, fitters, cleaners and even upper grade engine drivers. These again are distinctions that have vanished since Independence and are reflected in the same fashion as in any other community where the divide now is between affluence of some level and poverty.

The Company's and later the Raj's attitude to the Anglo-Indians post the 1880s 'liberalisation' was ambivalent. Europeans and Domiciled Europeans were preferred till well into the 1920s for employment in the senior middle-level and higher levels by Government and British mercantile interests. At the lower middle-levels, Anglo-Indians were preferred to Indians. But once Indians became better educated and proficient in English, the Anglo-Indians and Domiciled Europeans began to feel the challenge. In the early 1920s, two Anglo-Indian deputations went to London to seek reservations in employment for the community. The Crown's response was intriguing, to say the least: "For the purposes of employment under Government and inclusion in schemes of Indianisation, members of the Anglo-Indian and Domiciled European community are statutory natives of India. For the purposes of education and internal security, their status, as so far as it admits of definition, approximates to that of European British subjects."

One foot in each world and with little acceptance by either side forced the Euro-Indians to develop their own lifestyle in their virtually isolated enclaves till Independence. Post-Independence there was an exodus of at least half the community to the 'White' nations of the English-speaking world. But those who stayed on in India after a period of uncertainty are finding themselves from the 1990s in a country where they are just another of its 4635 communities and not one looked at with any dubious focus. They're Indians today, whose community is Anglo-Indian, religion Christianity and language English. And the last-named characteristic is certainly an advantage in 21st century India.

The Birth of a Community

If 1498 is considered the dawn of a new world, it is also the year when the soil was first tilled for the birth of a new international community: the Eurasians or, as Sri Lankan social scientist Kumari Jayawardena would have it, the Euro-Asians. It was a community that was to grow in numbers from the Punjab to the Philippines. Fathers from a dozen European nations sired the community in wedlock and out with mothers from every country of the region where a European flag was planted. Perhaps the largest of the Eurasian sub-communities was India's Anglo-Indian community, numbering about 500,000 at its peak in India and around 150,000 today. There are about another 250,000 of Anglo-Indian heritage elsewhere in the world, mainly in Australia, Canada, the U.K. and the U.S. The numbers in India are themselves open to debate; those with a drop of paternal European blood in them are likely to be very many more given the history of the community from its beginnings on the Malabar and Konkan Coasts where thousands have, abandoned by their fathers, passed into the mainstream.

*

It was on that western coastal stretch that the first Eurasians in Asia were born to Portuguese fathers and mothers from different Indian communities. The Portuguese came to India with sword and cross in hand. As much as they sought the riches of India, they sought permanent settlement and the spread of Roman Catholicism. It was a policy expounded by King Manoel who, to this end, urged his soldiers to marry "fair women of good family" in India. In the early 1500s, Governor Alfonso de Albuquerque encouraged his soldiers to marry locally.

This applied to *soldados* too, young Portuguese men who came to India—and later to the *Estado da India* which stretched from Hormuz in the Persian Gulf to

Japan and Timor—to serve the Crown and who could return to Portugal after ten years of service provided they could pay their passage. Marriage to Indians was a much more attractive proposition in their straitened circumstances. And when many an unmarried soldier or *soldado* chose to settle in India and was given the opportunity to leave the service of the Crown and to provide services to the government, the military and to businessmen, as well as become landowners in rural areas, he was categorised as a *casado*. The *casados,* who nurtured their families as Roman Catholic, were generally farmers, traders, skilled and unskilled artisans and craftsmen.

The early Portuguese settlements were Cochin, Calicut, Goa, Daman and Diu on India's west coast. By 1522, they had established themselves on the east coast in what was to be called San Thomé de Meliapore, now a part of Madras/ Chennai, and then in coastal settlements further north all

The Basilica of St. Thomas in San Thomé, Madras. It was in search of the remains of Thomas Dydimus, one day to be the Apostle of India, that the Portuguese first came to the coast of Coromandel in the 1520s and forty years later began to establish themselves there and raise Fort San Thomé. Some of the relics of St. Thomas are in a crypt beneath what is now the Co-Cathedral of the Mylapore-Madras Diocese. (Photo: SM Collection)

the way to Calcutta, Dacca and Chittagong. In every settlement the policy was the same, the *casados* and the soldiers being encouraged to marry local women; the more affluent, on the other hand, generally took them as mistresses. Of these relationships were born the first Anglo-Indians, the Luso-Indians. As the Luso-Indian community grew through marriage within it or through further relationships, more often than not illicit, with Indian women, the offspring of the latter became known as the *descendentes*, *mestizos* or *topasses*[5], while the offspring of Luso-Indian marriages with other Luso-Indians, few and far between, continued to consider themselves Luso-Indians and a cut above the *mestizos*.

Even though it may be spinning a tall tale, a letter from a priest in Goa dating to 1550—quoted by C.R. Boxer, an authority on the Portuguese Empire— provides an insight into how the numbers of *mestizos* burgeoned. Referring to the Portuguese in the *Estado da India*, Padre Lancillotto recorded: "There are innumerable married settlers who have four, eight or ten female slaves and sleep with all of them." Virtually all this *mestizo* population would have passed into the mainstream. But there were also many who would have been looked after by the fathers, the church or orphanages.

Given that the maximum number of Portuguese settlements were in South India, where the population was darker skinned than in the north, and given the tinging of Portuguese European ethnicity for nearly eight hundred years during Moorish rule with every shade from that of the Semitic of the North African coast to that of Saharan Africa—which itself had been toned for centuries with that of sub-Saharan tribes—Luso-Indians/*mestizos*/*topasses* were almost inevitably darker-skinned than the later descendants of Anglo-Celtic and other northern European fathers. Search in any erstwhile Portuguese settlement in India and you will be hard put to find a fair Luso-Indian or *mestizo*. In fact, in Goa there could well be even fewer Luso-Indians of any pigmentation; the territory's record-keepers say that the Luso-Indians from early times migrated to Portugal or to serve Portugal in its colonies like Brazil. Even as late as 1917, Goa reported the presence of only 2200 Luso-Indians in a population of about 500,000. This is undoubtedly because the Luso-Indians were either of only the first generation, or descendants through marriages among those of the first generation, and kept emigrating.

Early Luso-Indian immigration was to serve Portugal in *Estado da India* as an educated supervisory cadre. Ceylon, Penang, Malacca, Singapore, parts of

---

5.   Topee (hat)-wearers. But it is also stated that this was a description first used by the Dutch, deriving from the word dubash (from dho bhasha = two langauges = interpreter or middleman, but in this context mestizo soldiers).

Indonesia (the East Indies), Timor and Macau all benefitted from this migration and the Eurasian community of South and Southeast Asia was born. There were some who went westwards to Portuguese Africa and Brazil. Most of this migration was from Goa; Luso-Indians and *casados* on the Malabar Coast and the Indian East Coast, from San Thomé to Chittagong, on the other hand, appeared to have found greater opportunities teaming with the English East India Company and prospering. Then, between 1800 and 1900, more left for East Africa and the fast-growing prosperous cities of India's west coast like Bombay and Karachi, leaving few Luso-Indians and *casados* in Portuguese settlements in India, but many thousands in other parts of urban India and in several countries in South and Southeast Asia, as far as Macau and Timor.

Given the history of the Portuguese in India, there must have been from the late 16th century and into the middle of the 17th century, thousands of *casados* and *mestizos* in Portugal's Indian settlements as well as those serving in other European settlements and in the armies of local rulers. Fort St. George alone, the seat of Government in Madras, reported in the 17th century that there were 3000 'Portugee' living outside the Fort, many of them wage-earners working in the Fort[6]. In fact, in 1679, a jury of six Luso-Indians[7] and six Englishmen, including Elihu Yale, sitting in Madras, convicted Manoel De Lima for the murder of his servant Pedro Rangell on September 18, 1678. De Lima, presumably a Luso-Indian, was the first in the British settlements in India to go in appeal to the Privy Council in London.

J. Talboys Wheeler, a 19th century compiler of the history of the Madras Presidency from the official records, states that the Portuguese comprised 60 per cent of the Christian population of Madras—and they were mainly *mestizos/castees/topasses,* the Portuguese-speaking Indian slaves of *casados,* and a small population of affluent Portuguese white settlers (*indiaticos)* and visiting Portuguese traders (*reinos).* This was virtually true of every other coastal European settlement in India.

Joseph François Dupleix's dream of an empire in the 1740s and the British response to it saw a period of unremitting war south of the Vindhyas involving the French, English, Marathas, Hyder Ali and Tippu Sultan of Mysore, the Nizams of Hyderabad, and the Nawabs of the Carnatic from the mid-1700s till the early 1800s. And not only did all of them employ large numbers of *topasse* mercenaries in their armies but the camp followers included, besides Indian women, large numbers of 'Portugee' women and female slaves. Their children, sired by European

---

6.   For almost the entire first 100 years of Fort St. George, the greater part of the garrison were *topasses.*
7.   A number indicative of the community's strength or recognition by the British.

and *topasse* soldiers, passed into the Indian mainstream on the death or desertion of their fathers. But there were also many exceptions that kept the Portuguese-Indian line alive.

Portuguese hierarchy recognised noblemen (*fidalgos*) from Portugual (Doms as they were addressed) and Senhors, as 'pure' Portuguese nationals and wealthy settlers (*casados)* were addressed. But a *topasse* who became wealthy enough, particularly through Luso-Indian or *casado* connections, could become a Senhor—like Domingo Rodriguez of Tellicherry (Tangasseri) did in the mid-18th century. Or there is the remarkable story of Senhora Mequinez who, on the death of her husband, was made Colonel of his *topasse* regiment by Hyder Ali in the 1780s!

Given the paltry number of 'pure' Portuguese in San Thomé, the other 'Portugee' in San Thomé and neighbouring Madras must undoubtedly have been *casados* and *mestizos*. If the Portuguese paternal line returned to Portugal or died in India, many of its offspring would have passed into the mainstream and become Indian. As Christovam Pinto, a Goan Member of Portugal's Parliament, said in 1923, "the Mesticos[8] of Portuguese India, as a class, have already disappeared almost all by their entrance by marriage into that of the *descendentes* of the Portuguese or into the indigenous." That, and emigration as already mentioned, would account for the near absence of Luso-Indians as an

Both: Tangasseri in Kerala was once a major Portuguese settlement and then a Dutch one. Most of its Euro-Indians descend from those days and Portuguese names are the more common ones. In a 1930s picture are seen some of the Anglo-Indian children near Tangasseri's beach and in the 1960s picture is a gathering of Tangasseri's Anglo-Indians. (Photos: Joseph Fernandez)

---

8.   Here likely to mean Luso-Indians.

Both top: Typical homes of Anglo-Indians in Tangasseri where education has helped many families attain a level of prosperity. *(Photos: Joseph Fernandez)*

Once, San Thomé was a major settlement of the descendants of the Portuguese. Today, many of those families are scattered in different parts of Madras and elsewhere. One such family with long connections with San Thomé is the Mascarenhas family seen here in 1934. (Photo: Simeon Mascarenhas)

identifiable community in erstwhile Portuguese settlements. But where the Portuguese-Indians maintained close ties with each other and the British in a few settlements, like Cochin, Tellicherry (Tangasseri), San Thomé, Calcutta, Dacca and Chittagong, their numbers were not insignificant. In fact, Calcutta reported 3181 Luso-Indians in 1837 and Eastern Bengal reported 10,000 "Luso-Indians or Feringhis" in 1919, including 6000 in Dacca District and 1000 in Chittagong District. These Portuguese-Indians have flourished after having had to, at one time, virtually fight to be recognised as Anglo-Indians, their colour and the type of low level jobs/ trades many were in having had a lot to do with this need to assert themselves.

Christovam Pinto's acknowledgement that the *mestizos* "as a class" have almost all disappeared into the indigenous is an

acceptance of a fact that most Goans do not appear to agree with today. In fact, most of them, like Robert de Souza, who critiqued Nirad Chaudhuri's *Continent of Circe*, claim that only a few Portuguese married Indians and these women were widows of Muslim or Rajput warriors vanquished by the Portuguese. They further state that, given the proud heritage of these women, their Luso-Indian offspring had "a certain nobility of character and aptitude for constructive activity ... unlike the Anglo-Indians." There has been in this blinkered attitude an unwillingness to consider the Portuguese-Indians and the Malayalam-speaking Feringhis of the Malabar coast today and the thousands of *topasses* who once lived on the Coromandel coast and in Bengal, particularly in the Dacca and Chittagong Districts[9], as Luso-Indians.

There have over the years been shining examples of Luso-Indian excellence, like Saint Gonsalo Garcia from Bassein who died a martyr's death in Japan in the 16th century, Donna Juliana Dias da Costa (1658-1733) from Cochin who was the harem queen of Bahadur Shah and whose intercession in affairs of state were sought by numerous envoys of European powers, and Henry Derozio, the nationalist poet from Calcutta who equally ardently championed the Anglo-Indian cause. But they are generally ignored by Goan writers who cite excellence only in Luso-Indians of Goa, like the early 20th century anthropologist Dr. Germane Correia, late 19th century literary critic Moniz Barretto, and a Foreign Minister in Portugal in the 1920s, Dr. Bettencourt Rodrigues, focused as they are on Portuguese Goan lineage.

In fact, most Goan Luso-Indians do not appear to accept the Constitutional definition of Anglo-Indians and consider themselves a community distinct and separate from the Anglo-Indians or even other Portuguese Indians. Yet the largest part of India's Anglo-Indian population today is from the South and the greater part of it is of Portuguese heritage or has links with that heritage through marriage with Portuguese-Indians.

The contribution of the 'Portugee' or the 'Black Portuguese' to the success of the other European powers in India, particularly the British, has long been little recognised. In fact, it was forgotten once the British started raising Indian regiments, beginning with the Madras Regiment. By the 19th century, the *topasses* and European mercenaries were history as far as the English were concerned, though Indian potentates used them till the late 18th century.

✳

9.   It is of interest to note that W.H. Thompson, in his 1927 Census Report, referred to the Chittagong Feringhis and said "some of them have in recent years adopted the class designation 'Luso-Indians'."

The Dutch presence on both coasts—especially the southern coasts of India—was particularly noticeable from 1602 to 1781, their major presence being in Pulicat and Nagapattinam on the east coast and Cochin on the west coast. But by the 1650s, their focus was more on the East Indies (Indonesia, today) and Ceylon (now Sri Lanka) and anyone who was anyone in a Dutch settlement in India moved on to Indonesia or to Ceylon. This included the Ollandaise/Wallandaise, most of whom were descended, from Dutch/German soldiers, traders and craftsmen married to Indo-Portuguese women, leaving very few of mixed descent in India.

Before that migration, it had in fact been Dutch policy in India and Ceylon, from the 1660s, to encourage its lower cadres to marry Euro-Asians rather than native women and thereby produce *castizos* and *mestizos* to reduce the "degenerations of our Neitherlanders" and give "our nation strength and vigour". By educating these children in the Dutch language and manners, having them worship in Dutch churches, and with Dutch blood being in them, it was thought that if such girls married those they grew up with or newcomers from Holland, a strong local 'Dutch' community would evolve. It certainly did in the East Indies and Ceylon. Ceylon's Dutch Burgher community prospered through service it offered the British after the Dutch were ousted. And in the early days of British rule in Ceylon (post-1795) there were several educated Burghers who moved to India and merged, through marriage, with the Anglo-Indian community accounting for such names as van Geyzel and van Hefton.

The first to introduce the 'other' North European lineage in this part of the world were the Danes at Tranquebar (1620-1845) who employed a large number of German mercenaries to supplement their own strength. Then there arrived from Switzerland Charles de Meuron's regiment of mainly central European mercenaries, initially hired by the Dutch but then, in the last quarter of the 18th century, by the British. And so were sired the Anglo-Indians with central European names.

It was the travelling conditions of the day, the long sea voyages in the few cramped spaces available for passengers aboard small sailing vessels dependent entirely on the winds, and the cost of the voyage as well as the lack of the wherewithal to support themselves in an alien land that kept women from Europe going out to India and beyond. They also needed permission—never easy to get— from the respective European East India Companies to live in their settlements. And had they been able to manage this, they would have had to be able to cope with the rigours of the climate in the Tropics. All this meant few women from Europe going out to the eastern settlements of the various European East India Companies and, with only few sailings in a year, it also meant long stints abroad for the Companies' all-male personnel, particularly in the lower echelons.

In these circumstances, it was only to be expected that the men would seek the companionship of Indian women through marriage, partnerships or mere liaisons, especially at a time when the Companies' employees generally enjoyed cordial relationships with Indians during a period when the focus was on business and trade and not on empire-building. The Portuguese, as we have already seen, officially encouraged its soldiers and settlers to marry Indian women. So did the Dutch. The English East India Company was to follow this example no sooner it decided it was in India to stay.

*

It was on the last day of 1600 that the English East India Company came into existence and it was on the first day of 1601 that it got down to business. After establishing trading posts (called factories) in Surat on the west coast and Masulipatam on the east coast, at both of which they were pushed around by the Portuguese and Dutch, Company representative Francis Day in 1639 successfully negotiated with the *Naiks* (Governors) of Tondaimandalam, one of

Fort St. George from which modern India grew seen in a drawing from the 1670s. The inner walls and 'the Governor's Castle' were foundationless constructions dating to the 1640 beginnings. The stronger outer walls were raised in the 1670s. Beyond the walls, on the right, is the Indian town. Many of the homes in the Fort belonged to Portuguese. (Photo: SM Collection)

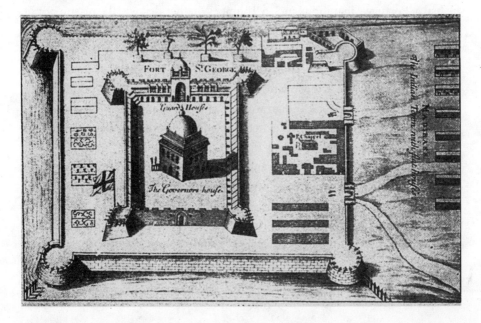

the last vestiges of the Vijayanagar Empire, for three square miles of no-man's-sand a couple of miles north of Portuguese San Thomé. By 1640, on this spit of beach, with water on three sides and no proper anchorage on its east where lay the Bay of Bengal, Day and his superior Andrew Cogan from Masulipatam raised four foundation-less walls around a modest foundation-less building and a few thatched huts and grandiosely called the settlement Fort St. George.

When they established on this barren strip just beyond the northern walls of the 'fort' an Indian settlement of weavers brought from textile manufacturing villages south of Masulipatam, the White Town that was the Fort was called Madraspatam and the Indian town Chennapatam. From these small beginnings there grew Madras that is the Chennai of today, a town founded 20 years before the acquisition of the site of Bombay and 50 years before the founding of Calcutta.

It was from Madras that modern India was to grow; it was Madras that was the chief settlement of the British from the Red Sea to the Philippines till Calcutta became the capital in 1776 of what was developing into the Indian Empire. It was also in Madras and other southern coastal settlements where the Company established factories that a community was born that could more accurately be called Anglo-Indian if you accepted Anglo as being Anglo-Celtic fathers.

From the earliest days, the Anglo-Celts and other Europeans of Fort St. George married or established relationships with the 'Portugee' women of San Thomé, almost all of them certainly *casados* or *mestizos*. Legend has it that Francis Day accepted that barren stretch of beach to establish an English settlement because he had a 'Portugee' inamorata in San Thomé. Whether that was the reason or not, there is reason to believe the liaison; his successor, Henry Greenhill, succeeded to Day's 'Portugee' lady love, and that's on record. Besides those Anglo-Celts who established relationships with 'Portugee' women, others, especially the rank and file of the militia as well as those who ran establishments like taverns, hostelries and stables in Black Town, took Indian women as wives or mistresses. The offspring of these liaisons were the second 'generation' of Euro-Indians, a description I will favour for the nonce, after the Luso-Indians and Ollondaise.

As much to establish a permanent foothold in India as to prevent a growing Roman Catholic population that would result from increasing liaisons with 'Portugee' women, the Company issued a directive to its Council in Madras in 1684: "The soldiers' wives shall come to their husbands, if they can find the means to satisfy or pay the owners for the passages, and for such soldiers as are single men, prudently induce them to marry Gentoos[10] in imitation

10. Telugus, the dominant Indian population in Chennapatnam, but presumably meant to mean both Tamils and Telugus.

of ye Dutch politics and raise from them a stock of Protestant Mestizes."

Three years later, the Court of Directors even more determinedly pursued the idea of raising a mixed community born of Anglo-Celtic fathers and Indian mothers. It wrote to the President of Madras in 1687 "that the marriage of our soldiers to the native women of Fort St. George is a matter of such consequence to posterity that we shall be content to encourage it with some expense and have been thinking for the future to appoint a pagoda to be paid to the mother of any child who shall thereafter be born of such marriage, upon the day the child is christened if you think this small encouragement will increase the number of marriages."

A few years later the Company was encouraging "their humbler servants to make their permanent abode in India," offering a Rs.5 monthly allowance for every child born to a soldier in the ranks.

St. Mary's in the Fort in Madras, the oldest Anglican church built in Asia, was consecrated in 1680. In its early marriage and baptismal records, in several instances, the wife or mother's name has been left blank or filled with only a common English Christian first name. The wife/mother in

St. Mary's in the Fort, the oldest purpose-built Anglican church in Asia, was the scene of many an Anglo-Celt taking for his wife a nameless Indian woman or a one-named Christian woman of Indian descent. (Photo: SM Collection)

such instances was always Indian. Children of such unions would in turn marry Anglo-Celts from the lower ranks or others of similar heritage. And so the Anglo-Indian community grew. Children of such unions, except those abandoned by their fathers, would bear the father's Anglo-Celtic name and would be brought up speaking English (many also spoke their mother's tongue) and according to his customs and practices.

Cases of abandonment were not infrequent both among the Portuguese as well as the Anglo-Celts and other Europeans, who were generally mercenaries serving in the militia. Thus, a large number of Euro-Indian children vanished over the years into the mainstream and became Indian. But there were also many abandoned children who grew up as Anglo-Indians, a large number of them in orphanages where their mothers had left them. Significantly, however, of the Anglo-Indians born in the 17th and early 18th centuries there appear to be few records; in fact, I have come across or heard of only very few Anglo-Indians who could trace their beginnings to even the second half of the 18th century when the Company focused on trade began to look at India with more imperial eyes.

There were, however, several noteworthy liaisons in the pre-19th century era between Europeans and Indians. They produced many Euro-Indians who, in turn, were worthy of being recorded in history. As early as the 1670s, Job Charnock, later to found Calcutta, married an Indian woman who remained Hindu. Their three daughters, baptised in St. Mary's in Fort St. George, Mary, Elizabeth and Catherine, married respectively Charles Eyre (not Eyre Coote as many have it) who succeeded the founder as Agent in Calcutta, William Bowridge, a senior merchant, and Jonathan White, Secretary to the Bengal Council. The Whites had a daughter and the Bowridges a son, both of whom Elizabeth Bowridge took back to England and they, like many others to follow, would have passed into the Anglo-Celtic mainstream.

The well-known 18th century dreamer of an empire, Joseph François Dupleix, married a Euro-Indian from San Thomé whose maiden name was Jeanne Albert. Her first husband was a Vincens and one of their daughters married a Charles Barneval, a member of the Fort St.George Council. When Dupleix captured Fort St.George in 1746, it was believed that Mrs.Barneval had a hand in negotiating the surrender of Madraspatam to the French. Then there was Catherine Noele Grand (née Worlee) of Tranquebar, who was to become a great courtesan in Europe before eventually marrying (in 1802) Count de Talleyrand, the first Prime Minister of France.

Like Jeanne Albert, Catherine Worlee's mother too was Euro-Indian and she married a Frenchman from Pondicherry. And Thomas Parry of Madras, who

founded what is described as the
second oldest business house still
in existence in India, left bequests
in his will prepared in 1823 to
sundry Indian women with whom
he had associated on the southern
Coromandel coast, wherever Parry's
had business establishments, and
their children.

Joseph François
and Jeanne Dupleix,
who first dreamed
of an Indian empire.
Jeanne Begum was
a metisse from San
Thomé, many of whose
children by her first
marriage married
well in Madras and
Pondicherry. Dupleix
was the Governor of all
French settlements in
India. (Photo: Library,
French Institute,
Pondicherry)

*

The list can go on and on, especially till the end of the 18th
century. Many of the Anglo-Indian offspring born during
this period were sent to England if their fathers could afford
it and, if they were fair, they returned to India as convenated
servants of the Company or commissioned officers in
the Company's army or passed into the Anglo-Celtic
mainstream at 'Home'. If the fathers could not afford it, the
offspring generally passed into the Indian mainstream on
the death or desertion of the fathers, either as Anglo-Indians
or as Indians. These Anglo-Indians, educated in India in
the English medium, were recruited by the Company or the
merchant houses as uncovenanted employees or as artificers
and warrant officers in the Company's army. Few identifiable
Anglo-Indians or Euro-Indians with lineage dating to this
period, when miscegenation was as its peak, can be traced
today. As Stark puts it, "In general terms it may be said that
the Anglo-Indians of the period between 1600 and 1775 have
merged either with the British or Indian peoples. Those of
the years following 1775 are divided perhaps equally into
(1) those who have merged or are merging into the British
nation, (2) those who have merged or are merging into the
Indian nation; and (3) those who exist as the Anglo-Indian
race of today." By the 1780s, the Anglo-Indian population
in India was much larger than the British population in the
country. It was to cause the British concern.

*

It was the Battle of Plassey (1757) that led the British—a description more accurate only after the formal union of England and Scotland in 1707—to dream the dreams of Dupleix and his Jeanne Begum and to make their initial focus of nearly 150 years on trade secondary to a new focus on expansionism. The East India Company depended on Anglo-Indians to play a significant role in the military, in governance and in commercial activities. These country-born sons, mainly of Anglo-Celts employed by the Company, were better suited to the climate of the country and knew the languages of their mothers as well as local practices, making them more able to deal with Indian employees of the Company or Indians the Company did business with. Stark, one of the first to point out the importance of his community to the rulers in the 19th century, wrote, "But for the presence in India of successive generations of those sprung from British fathers and Indian mothers, it may well be questioned whether in India England would ever have passed from the market place to the forum, from the factory to the council chamber, from merchandise to empire, from Company to Crown."

It was the heyday of the community. But its relative prosperity was also to grate with the increasing number of shareholders of a successful Company; they sought these positions for their sons and other kin in a land where the pagoda[11] tree was being shaken successfully. Their pressure on the Court of Directors led to an order in 1786 that prevented Euro-Indian orphans from being sent to England for higher studies. The Standing Order applied only to Anglo-Indian orphans and those whose fathers had died. If, however, a child's father was alive, it could be sent to England by the father. But to judge by the uproar over the order in Anglo-Indian circles there would appear to have been not too many such fathers around. The Company issued these orders in the belief that "the settlement and education in England of such orphans involved a political inconvenience because the imperfections of the children, whether bodily or mental, would in process of time be communicated by intermarriage to the generality of people in Great Britain, and by these means debase the succeeding generations of Englishmen." That persons of mixed descent would inherit the worst characteristics of both races was a view held by many on both sides of the racial divide even to recent times. But in this instance it was being reflected as national policy. This was the first signal of discrimination against those of mixed blood in India. Five years later, even more discriminatory orders were issued: East Indians, as Anglo-Indians were called at the time, could not serve as officers in the civil, military and marine services of the Company or on its ships.

---

11.   Pagoda: an Indian unit of currency at the time.

The orders of 1791 received encouragement in their passage, when the mulattos and Blacks in San Domingo (now Dominican Republic) and Haiti revolted (1791-94) against the Spanish and the French and the call to establish a Black Republic was made by Toussaint L'Ouveture, a mulatto. That the revolt in the West Indies was a factor in the 1791 decision was indicated in 1804 when Lord Valentia, on an inspection visit (1802-06) on behalf of the Company's Court of Directors to all its settlements in India and Ceylon, wrote in his diary (published in 1811), "The most rapidly accumulating evil in Bengal is the increase of half-caste children ... This tribe may hereafter become too powerful for control.With numbers in their favour, with a close relationship to the natives, but without an equal proportion of pusillanimity and indolence which is natural to them, what may not in future be dreaded from them ... I have no hesitation in saying that the evil ought to be stopped ..."

The third step to curb East Indian development was in 1795 when the Company decreed that all persons not of 'pure' European descent on both sides should not be allowed to serve in the military except as "fifers, drummers, bandsmen, and farriers". They could not serve even as privates! Subordinate posts in the Judicial, Revenue and Police Departments were also not open to them. Like the Europeans, they too could not own land or live more than ten miles from a Company settlement. Which meant they could not also be farmers or establish businesses where there was no competition from European commercial ventures. There was no civil law they could look to; in fact, in certain parts of the country, Muslim law governed them. In a period of less than ten years the East Indian community's relative prosperity diminished to near poverty. Furthermore, its social status from being virtually European had been made that of an Indian in minor employment. In fact, an Indian could even own property, go to Britain to study if he had the money, and serve in Indian regiments. The Anglo-Indian was effectively deprived of the opportunity of an education abroad and of earning a livelihood.

It was inevitable that, in these circumstances, East Indians with military experience would become mercenaries in the service of numerous Indian rulers at war with each other and seeking European officers to train their forces in the more effective military practices of Europe. Many of them were to rise high in these armies. But when the Company was threatened by the Mahrattas from 1803, not only were the East Indians in the British settlements called to arms, but so were those serving in the armies of the various princely Indian States. The latter were summoned under threat of being declared traitors! But no sooner the Mahratta and other threats were blunted, than the East Indians in the Company's service

John William Ricketts of Calcutta who first gave voice to the discontent among the East Indians over their being treated as 'second class citizens' by the British. (Photo: SM Collection)

were discharged in 1808-9! This could have had not a little to do with Lord Valentia's views. And, so, the East Indians were to remain second class citizens for the next 25 years.

Second-hand citizenship, understandably, caused discontent among the East Indians, particularly among the educated who were increasing in number after the Company opened up the country to the missionaries from Britain early in the 19th century and these missionaries, Protestant as well as Roman Catholics, began to open up schools for the community. First giving voice to this discontent was John William Ricketts who on March 1, 1823 organised a meeting of interested East Indians in his house in Calcutta to establish a school—later named the Parental Academic Institution—that would make it unnecessary for Anglo-Indian youths to be sent to England for higher education. Five years later, he founded the Commercial and Political Association whose aim was to encourage East Indian youth to enter the fields of agriculture, trade and commerce. A Marine School was also established. Calcutta's lead was followed in other parts of the country. None of these, however, improved the lot of the East Indians, for many areas of gainful employment remained closed for them. Their's was a life in limbo, with an East Indian at times considered 'a native subject', at other times British!

Meeting in each other's homes in Calcutta, some of the leaders of the community—and always Ricketts—regularly discussed the political, social and economic disabilities the East Indian community faced. At a meeting in November 1825, it was decided to draft a petition to be presented to the British Parliament. The drafting itself dragged on in debate. It was on this scene that there arrived Henry Derozio, only 18 at the time but acclaimed for his scholarship, poetry, and radicalism that fired even Indian thought in the leading educational institutions in Calcutta. As publisher of *The East Indian,* he passionately championed the cause of those of mixed heritage. His house became a regular meeting place of those like Ricketts who sought emancipation of the East Indians. In 1829, a petition was drafted by a committee of

Henry Derozio, the poet and Indian nationalist who was in the forefront of the East Indians' clamour for rights. (Photo: SM Collection)

East Indians stating their grievances, and Ricketts was funded to sail for England in December that year to present it to Parliament. But given the political turmoil in England in 1830—including the death of the King—Parliament had little time for Ricketts and though the petition was presented to both Houses and Ricketts was examined three times, he had to return a disappointed man in March 1831. A second petition was sent to a new Parliament through an East Indian settled in Britain. Nothing came of that too. The East Indian Movement began petering out by 1830 and, with several of its leaders including Derozio dying thereafter, it came to an end before long. A revival, however, became unnecessary with the promises the Charter of 1833 held.

The Company Charter, when renewed in 1833, put an end to the Company's monopoly and opened up trade to any British subject. It stated that any British subject, including any "natural born" in India, "shall NOT by reason of his religion, place of birth, descent, colour, or any of them be disabled from holding any place, office, or employment under the said Company." Any British subject in India could own land anywhere in British India and trade within and without India in countries thrown open for this purpose to all British subjects. But if the East Indians thought this was going to give them what is now called a level playing field to compete with the British being recruited in England, they were to be disillusioned.

With the years preceding this 'liberalisation' impoverishing them, the East Indians were unable to go to Britain for education and offer themselves for employment in covenanted positions in India. So it was for middle-level functions in uncovenanted positions in those areas vital for British expansionism, such as the Railways, Posts and Telegraphs, Police, Customs and Excise, Survey, Irrigation and Roads (PWD), and the Military, that they were recruited, favoured over the Indians, though even in these departments they were to often find the more senior positions in the middle levels being filled by favoured recruits from Britain.

With English supplementing Persian as the language of the courts and governance and with government departments totally English-oriented, the East Indians were at a distinct advantage. But with Macaulay's Minutes on Education and Jurisprudence, and the consequent positive response of Indians to education in English, the East Indian advantage was nullified and they had to face the challenge of the new English-speaking Indians. At the same time, the East Indians, enticed by the senior uncovenanted positions in government services, ignored the opportunities the private sector offered either for entrepreneurship or as skilled craftsmen. Also, with the opening of the overland route to India in 1835, linking the Mediterranean and the Red Sea, young educated British men with their wives began to arrive in great numbers to seek their futures in India and pose another challenge to the East Indians, a challenge which again diminished their opportunities for progress, with senior British officers and executives preferring the young from 'Home'. There was also arrival in greater numbers of young women from Britain in search of husbands among British officialdom and the officer class. With this, and a Victorian morality, the links of the European men of position with Indian women virtually ceased.

The majority of these British, who went into the same government facilities as the East Indians, settled in India and became the Domiciled European community setting up 'pure' European homes. They, however, as Stark candidly later put it—no doubt to the chagrin of many a Domiciled European—"by the passage of years, by exposure to the same disabilities, by sharing the same permanent interests, and by being eligible for the status of Statutory Natives of India, have merged into the Anglo-Indian community to form with them a political and social unit officially designated by government 'the Anglo-Indian Constituency'." In these circumstances, it would have been almost impossible for any Domiciled European family to have remained 'pure', with no links at all through marriage with East/Anglo-Indians.

By the 1880s, the Public Service Commission created the Imperial and Provincial Services which reserved provincial appointments only to those who were Statutory Indians. The fifty-year influx of those who were to become Domiciled Europeans came to an end. And those culturally Anglo-Indian, but as much nationals of India as Indians, could compete for these posts unchallenged by those from Britain.

The East Indian population grew during this fifty-year period and the increase had much to do also with the growing number of British troops coming out to garrison India and the immediate superiors of the East Indians whom the Company and, then, post-1857, the Raj, brought out for the services the East Indians had joined. Expatriate bachelors chose as marriage partners, more often than not, East Indian women, if they did not fancy the young women from 'Home'—'the fishing fleet'—who were arriving in greater numbers. On the other hand, if the older British recruits brought out wives with them, many settled in India on retirement, wooed by the comfort they could enjoy, and called themselves Domiciled Europeans; but at some point in time just about every Domiciled European family married into East Indian families. The largest number of those emphasising their Anglo-Indianness today comes from this post-1857 lineage and they, in turn, have married into those from the Portuguese line. These are the fourth generation, their lineage that of a large part of the Anglo-Indians of today.

Virtually the only other 'Anglo-Indians', apart from those born of marariages within the community, or to Domiciled European and British soldiers, were the result of the opening of the indigo, tea, jute, and rubber plantations in jungle areas far from urban settlements and where, in the early years, the British planter's only female company was a woman estate worker or her daughters. Tales of *droit de seigneur* were legion.

Dr. Graham's Homes in Kalimpong, founded as a home for the 'orphans' from the tea plantations born of British fathers. (Photo: AITW)

Close to plantations throughout the subcontinent were 'Little Englands' where mothers, deserted or ignored by the British lords of the manor, struggled

Another home once meant for such 'orphans', this one, St. George's, is in the South, now located in Ooty. (Photo: AITW)

to bring up children of mixed descent. Many a planter looked after his offspring, most did not. A proprietary planter called Leslie in South India was a bit of a legend; he was happy to claim his four sons and three daughters he had by a Tamil woman estate worker as his, educated them in a leading Anglo-Indian school in Bangalore and set them all up well in life. On the other hand, most of the children in 'Little Englands' in the past either became wards of orphanages like Dr. Graham's Homes in Kalimpong and St. George's Homes in

Ketti (Ooty) or passed into the mainstream as Indians, surprising strangers with their light eyes. No different from this situation was that of the slaves in European and Anglo-Indian homes. Many a female Indian slave bore a 'Master's' or, more often, 'Little Master's' child till the abolition of slavery in 1833 and the end of the practice in the 1850s.

On the whole, however, the period from 1833 till Independence could be considered a period of prosperity for the Euro/Anglo/East Indians with employment in government service or a British mercantile establishment virtually assured. But in these services, they entered a no man's land or, rather, a uniquely isolated land, looked down on by the British as subordinates despite their upbringing in their fathers' European lifestyle, rather unfairly shouldered aside by the Domiciled Europeans with whom they had to compete for the service jobs, and resented by the Indians whom they tended to lord it over. The separation from the people of their mothers' lineage was to widen, but the divide with their fathers' people was not to become less wide, despite the role they played in the Revolt of 1857 when they wholeheartedly threw their lot in with the British, from the moment telegraphist Brendish stayed at his post and informed British cantonments in the North of the Indian storm that threatened to overwhelm them. When the lines of communication and the forces of law and order were substantially increased post-1857, they were rewarded with middle-level jobs in these services that were assured in perpetuity, offering them a life of some comfort in, by and large, specially established enclaves that were their very own to all intents and purposes till Independence.

The Census of 1911 finally cleared the air, defining the 'Anglo-Indian' as a permanent resident of India of paternal European lineage. With that pronouncement, a distinct community was officially born, its uncertain status of earlier years a thing of the past and the community now firmly proclaimed as one of India's many. This definition was reiterated in 1935 and 1949 and survives till today. This is a communtiy that has made a significant contribution to India through its food, its schools, its service in the railways, hospitals, various other government departments and the military, and in sport.

The Third Generation

If the first generation of Euro-Indians had been sired to the greatest extent by the Portuguese, the second generation owed its genesis to the Dutch, the Danes, the French and the Anglo-Celts in the numerous coastal settlements from Surat to Cochin and from Nagapattinam to Chittagong. The third generation was born of those who first dreamed of empire and of those who led various armies as rajah battled rajah, nawab challenged nawab in the dust of the Deccan, the ravines of Central India and the plains of the Indo-Gangetic north from 1746 to 1857.

It is a period of fairly finite chronological definition. It begins with Joseph François Dupleix's and his wife Jeanne Begum's dreams of an empire born of their decision to support the claims of Chanda Sahib to the Carnatic, which stretched from what is northern Andhra Pradesh today to Cape Comorin and to the Ghats in the west, against an English East India Company supporting Muhammad Ali's counterclaims. When the French captured a virtually defenceless Madras (Fort St. George), the English began raising an Indian army for the first time—its nucleus was what became the Madras Regiment—and decided that whatever the French could do they could do better. And there in the plains of the Carnatic, the British and the French battled each other for forty years during which period was also born the first of the third generation of Euro-Indians in the large support trains that followed the soldiers.

French troops led by Jacques Law and de Bussy (who married Dupleix's *metisse* stepdaughter) and the troops led by Comte de Lally (an Irishman who fought for France), as also British forces led by Stringer Lawrence and Eyre Coote, and mercenaries led by de Meuron and Reinhardt and others from all the countries of Europe who fought for one side or the other, all of them fathered Euro-Indians among the camp followers. But they also gave rise to guns-for-hire, offering to train the armies of numerous Indian rulers warring against each other or the rising power of the British. These trainers—and there were political advisers too—were to rise high in the ranks of these princely states and were sought as husbands for many a minor princess or a favoured maid-in-waiting to tighten their bonds with their benefactors.

It was a practice that continued as, after the Battle of Plassey, the British established themselves as the new rajahs and nawabs in large parts of India and determined the destinies of princely states through the Residents they placed in them. In the early years, many of these representatives of the British were of humble origin. In later years, they were the younger sons of more affluent, better educated families. But many of them took to the grand style of Indian princes and lived in a regal manner complete with harems. In many such families the children often vanished into the mainstream like those of the soldiers Alexander the Great left behind—but there are several families that remain to this day Euro-Indian by birth and name, but seen by many as outside the Anglo-Indian mainstream and virtually Indian, particularly in cases where there are large zamindari holdings.

Hosting such European 'princes' during this period were Hyderabad in the south, the Mahratta Confederacy—including the Peshwas-led Mahrattas in and around Poona and the princely states of Baroda, Gwalior, Indore and Nagpur—Oudh (Avadh), the Punjab and, in later years, Delhi, among many other principalities.

James Kirkpatrick played a major role in Hyderabad politics and William and John Palmer founded the most successful business house in the Deccan. Reinhardt Sombre served the State well, before moving to Sardhana near Delhi and becoming Somroo. Another French General was Perron who fought for Oudh. In Bhopal, the Bourbons of French lineage still thrive as did, in Gwalior, the Filoses of Italian descent, known for their Urdu and Persian scholarship. In Oudh, Claude Martin and Polier, both Frenchmen, left their

Bottom: William Fraser of Delhi was another official with a harem. He like many of his ilk favoured Indian clothes when day was done. (Photo: Internet)

Many a European of standing in the 19th century took Indian women as one or more wives and were responsible for swelling the Anglo-Indian population. Perhaps the best known of them was David Ochterlony of Calcutta who took the Maidan air with his 13 Indian wives or held court with them present. (Photo: Internet)

mark, the former in business, politics and education, the latter in the State's army. Up in the north there were George Thomas, the Irishman who founded Haryana, the green land, and Gen. Henry van Cortlandt, a Dutchman, who led the Sikh armies of Ranjit Singh.

Yet another British officer with a harem, most of it comprising concubines, was Philip Meadows Taylor. (Photo: Internet)

Amongst the British there were administrators like the legendary David Ochterlony in Calcutta who had 13 Indian wives and paraded them in style on the *maidan* every evening and William Fraser in Delhi who only stopped short of the daily parade. In the south, there was Philip Meadows Taylor who also hosted a harem. The three models of rectitude in governance who saw Britain's role in India as only a temporary one, Thomas Munro of Madras, 'Boy' Malcolm of Bombay and Charles Metcalfe of Delhi, had 'bibis' and had children by them. Then there were the soldiers who founded irregular military units that remain revered names in the Indian/Pakistan Army even today, men like James Skinner of Skinner's Horse, William Gardner who raised the Shekhawati Brigade, Hyder Jung (Young) Hearsey, and James Warburton, a legend in the North-West Frontier region.

With so many generations of it having served in India, the Roberts family could not be anything but Domiciled European, even if an Indian maternal line is glossed over. Sir Abraham Roberts' first wife, however, was an East Indian and her son had to be Anglo-Indian. Sir Abraham's second wife was British and her son, to become Lord Roberts of Kandahar, could not be anything but Domiciled European by descent. (Photo: Internet)

One of Robert Clive's contemporaries in Bengal was William Watts, whose grandson became Lord Liverpool, a Prime Minister of Victorian Britain. Another descendant from William Watts, was General Sir Abraham Roberts, the father of Lord Roberts of Kandahar. General Wheeler of the Cawnpore siege was another who married an Indian. And there were hundreds of more such soldiers and administrators descended from various nationalities who contributed to the Euro-Indian population of the period through marriages to East Indians and Indians. It was a time when many of them sent their sons, if fair of colour, to England for education and upbringing. Some stayed on there and became Europeans. Others returned to serve India in covenanted positions. On the other hand, if the boys were dark-skinned or the children were girls, they were raised in India, supported by their fathers who settled in the country and became Euro-Indians or, if raised by their Indian mothers, became Indian.

Despite the loss of thousands of Euro-Indians to the Anglo-Indian community from this time when records were not particularly well kept, if kept at all, many who descended from the third generation survive into present times in India where the Skinners, Gardners, Bourbons and Somroos are names greatly respected. Sadly, search for ancestry among the third generation is hardly pursued. The search is almost always for those from the fourth generation, the post-1857 era of the greatest Anglo-Celtic presence, and dominance in India. It is the search for the Anglo-Indian, not the Euro-Indian, which too often misses the roots of the community.

An Era of Uncertainty

The Anglo-Indians of today are, by and large, of the fourth generation. Meet them as I've done in India and in the UK and Australia, read what several late 20th century Anglo-Indian writers have said in an effort to leave an indelible record of their community before, what some fear, it "vanishes", and it is the stories of their roots in the Raj years, in the post-1857 era, that you hear. The great majority of them are of Anglo-Celtic lineage. They may have over the years married into other national lineages, but this community of Anglo-Celtic lineage dominates, even in recollection. Of the four generations of Euro-Indians, this one, the fourth and the closest to Anglo-Celtic roots, is the one that grew in India as a community plagued with the greatest uncertainty.

The first generation—the Portuguese-Indians—was born of those who planned to settle in India. The second too consisted of those whose sires, mainly from different parts of Western Europe, saw themselves as settlers whose familiarity with local practices would ensure the permanence of their commercial activities and the roots they sank in the coastal settlements they had been granted by local rulers. The third generation, pushing into the interior of the subcontinent, saw themselves as heirs to zamindars, administrators and commanders of armies, and, therefore, rooted in an India where their sires, Indianised to a considerable extent, were men of position and held in respect if not reverence. But a large number of those descended from the first two generations in the coastal settlements began during this third period to feel the first pressures caused by uncertainty, pressures that were to increase in the fourth generation which spread throughout India wherever the Union Jack was planted and the Raj spread the tentacles of modern communication to ensure that flag flew high.

Whenever the British wanted them to defend their territories, they called for the Euro-Indians, wherever they were, to supplement the British regiments and the Indian forces they had raised. Most answered what has been described as "the call of the blood", many responded lest they be branded "traitors", and some, if they were powerful enough, did so on their own terms; Skinner, for instance, refused to fight Gwalior, whose "salt he had eaten". But whatever the circumstances under which they volunteered to protect the English East India Company, the Company was only too ready to discard them when the threat was over.

Company orders from 1786 to 1795 pushed the East Indians—a nomenclature derived from those who served the East India Company and still in use on the west coast amongst those with Portuguese-Indian connections—into limbo. It was a time many of them joined the ranks of Indian potentates and trained their armies, soldiered with them, and even led them. But the threats posed by Mysore and the Mahratta Confederacy from 1798 brought the first call to arms of the East Indians "on pain of death". No sooner the Mysore and Mahratta wars were over, than, the Commander-in-Chief in 1808-09 discharged all East Indians from the British regiments and barred the army to take them again; they were now even asked to get Company permission to join the armies of Indian princes.

Called to defend British interests whenever it suited the Company and discarded whenever not needed, hamstrung by various laws that hampered neither the British nor the Indians, there couldn't have been a greater period of uncertainty for the community. But emigration was not seen as an answer in the early 1810s. Petitions were seen as the answer. And in the 1820s Ricketts, Derozio, Pote and Kyd of the Kidderpore docks, led the petitions movement. Whether the East Indians' petitions had anything to do with it, or whether it was due to British officials like John 'Boy' Malcolm urging "this body of our subjects in India (needs) every measure which can raise it from its equivocal condition and render it useful and respectable," the Act of 1833 gave the East Indian the opening he needed. But an early linguistic advantage was lost when Macaulay's Minute on Education gave the Indian the opportunity to catch up with English. Sadly, Indians taking like fish to water in the English medium did not spur the East Indian to do educationally better in his own schools that had put down roots long before the post-Macaulay Indian ones. And he began to lose out on appointments to administrative positions in government.

Fortunately for the East Indians, new avenues of employment opened out to them in the 1850s. Laying the wires for telegraphic services from 1851 and the rails for the Railways shortly thereafter, they found their technical adaptability, their physical hardiness to cope with the varying terrains in India, and their ability to linguistically deal with local workforces as supervisors more sought after by the Company and the private British firms involved in this work than men from Britain or the Indians themselves. From here it was but a hop, skip and a jump for the East Indians to monopolise the middle levels and technical positions in the Railways and Telegraphs. By the 1940s, over half the Anglo-Indian population was dependent on these two services, with the Government, in turn, dependent on them to keep these lines of communication open. Apart from these two services, they sought employment in such transferable services as Customs and Excise, Survey, the Public Works Department, and the Police and the Military where hardship postings were virtually the rule. The indigo, jute and tea plantations and their factories in isolated wildernesses also attracted East Indians in the supervisory grade. It was a comparatively few who sought employment in the mercantile or educational services.

With the Railways offering comfortable residential enclaves at every railway junction, with life in these rural areas inexpensive, with plenty of recreational opportunity, particularly in the outdoors, with a close-knit community sharing common interests and with much time spent in the railway yards from childhood, the Railways became virtually a hereditary occupation for many an East Indian. There was little incentive for higher education and the moment a boy finished high school, or reached 16, he was ready to join the Railways as a fireman to start the journey that would one day take him to senior mail train driver. This lack of higher and wider education in families dependent on the private-run railway companies, that virtually guaranteed East Indians employment, was to contribute significantly to the community's uncertainty when the guarantees were removed. This was so in every one of the popular government services East Indians opted for.

This is not to say that there were no East Indian officers in the senior grades in the railway companies and workshops, in government services and the police and the military. Or that there were no well educated administrators and professionals, well trained teachers, nurses and secretaries. But with the focus on early employment in avenues that preferred Anglo-Indians, the family's focus was on comparative comfort and keeping the family together, not in pushing the talented upwards.

There can be no more inspirational story of a family that bucked this trend than that of the Straceys of Bangalore and Madras. Daniel Stracey was a District Forest Officer serving in the mofussil and dogged by ill health. Ethel Stracey was a housewife who taught a little music to add to what was a far from modest kitty. Yet she saw her four sons and two of her three daughters through college. Patrick Stracey went on to gain an international reputation as a forestry expert and wild life conservationist. Ralph Stracey joined the Indian Civil Service and, after retirement, became a Director of Imperial Tobacco. Cyril Stracey was selected by Nehru to join India's fledgling Foreign Service and retired as an Ambassador. Brother Eric who joined the Police went on to become Tamil Nadu's (former Madras Province) first Director-General of Police. Doreen Stracey became a doctor and served in hospitals in the central Indian wilderness, Winifred became a well-qualified teacher and Margaret became a nurse who married well into a planting family, the Leslies. There were no uncertainties in such families; the Straceys repeatedly stressed they were Indian, belonging to one of the hundreds of communities in India, the Anglo-Indian community. Education had led them out of uncertainty. A community which lived in uncertainty was one that did not educate itself or move into the wider Indian world the Straceys had done in college.

Uncertainty in the community was to grow from yet another step it took. When the Revolt of 1857 began, the East Indians again volunteered their services to the British and took part in many an action. Memorable among these actions was the role the boys from La Martiniere College, all East Indians, played at the siege of Lucknow. Aged below 13, they fought side by side with the rest of the defenders, manning a post throughout the siege. The school became the only school in history to be awarded battle honours as a result of the role its boys played in Lucknow. Apart from battle honours, they and their descendants were rewarded with education free at the College. The last of the line had enjoyed the privilege till the new millennium. But while this role of the Anglo-Indians could be understood by many an Indian—particularly as Anglo-Indians too had fallen victims at the outset of the Revolt—hard to understand was voluntary military service of another kind by Anglo-Indians. A condition of Railway service was becoming a member of a supplementary military unit, the Auxiliary Force (India) established in 1931. In various government services too, Anglo-Indians were encouraged to become members of the local AF(I) unit. When riots broke out, the AF(I) was often called out to maintain law and order and their methods were rather rough and ready—neither meant to win friends among the Indians nor influence them. But Anglo-Indians saw it as duty; Indians saw it as beyond the call of duty. In later years, when there were Railway and other strikes, the Anglo-Indians again did not participate, winning no Indian friends in the process. It must, however, not be forgotten that one of

Both: An armoured train and the detachment manning it from Lillooah Railway Colony's AF(I) unit. (Photos: AITW)

the first railway strikes in the country, affecting the Madras & South Mahratta Railway in 1911, was led by an Anglo-Indian mail train driver, Alexander.

Back to work after the Revolt, the East Indians were once again forgotten by the British and, by then, further distanced from the Indians. But if they thought the Public Services Commission's creation of the Imperial and Provincial Services in 1880 would prove helpful to them as a consequence of a ban on recruiting in Britain for the Service, they were mistaken. They were recognised as Indians and had to compete with fellow-Indians, generally doing better only in the lower-middle cadres that often involved hardship postings, as in the Forestry, Survey and Public Works Departments.

The greatest uncertainty, however, began with the founding of the Indian National Congress in 1885 and the first firm steps being taken by Indians towards achieving freedom. The British response was to offer several social and political reforms. The Morley-Minto Reforms of 1909 were followed by the Montagu-Chelmsford Reforms of 1919 and the Gandhi-Irwin Pact (1931). Little was offered to the Anglo-Indians in these agreements to bolster their confidence; on the other hand, their uncertainty was increased as Indian response to these British gestures were the Non-Cooperation Movement in 1920 and the Quit India Movement in 1942 during both of which the Anglo-Indians weakened their relations with the Indians and gained little by offering armed support to the British. No doubt the Services Sub-Committee and the Communal Award gave the community some security—"Special consideration … for employment in the services" in the case of the former and 12 seats for Anglo-Indians in seven legislatures in the case of the latter—but that was not enough to bolster Anglo-Indian confidence.

Henry Gidney, the first truly national leader of the Anglo-Indian community, was, in a rare gesture of recognition of the community by the British at the time, invited to participate in the First Round Table Conference (1930-31). He got it partially right when he admitted in 1931 that "the introduction of the Reforms and the whirlwind-like speed with which it has advanced has caught the community unprepared to meet effectively the suddenly developed and altered conditions and we fear our position will be worsened when India is given Dominion Status." He sought an area of about 200,000 acres in India to establish a separate Anglo-Indian Province/State. He was to inspire with his concept William Edward Thompson, who had started in Bombay a journal he called *The Review* in the 1920s that became, and remains, the community's all-India voice, and E.T. McCluskie of the Brit-Asian League, Calcutta, a successful realtor. Thompson suggested the community, together with the Anglo-Burmans and Anglo-Malays, establish a home in the Andaman and Nicobar Islands.

Sir Henry Gidney, the first national Anglo-Indian leader. (Photo: AITW)

McCluskie looked for a homeland in the heart of the sub-continent. Between Thompson's and McCluskie's dreams was David S. White's one to establish an Anglo-Indian settlement centrally in South India.

David S. White, who led the All-India Association in the South but broke away and founded the Anglo-Indian and Domiciled European Association of Southern India. (Photo: AITW)

Even while separate settlements for Anglo-Indians were being talked about, the voice of the community was beginning to be heard a little louder through Col. Henry Gidney, IMS (RTD.) who, with some success, began to draw the different Anglo-Indian associations together and forge unity. After the early attempts by Ricketts and his cohorts, the first serious attempt to establish an Anglo-Indian association was in Calcutta, where the Eurasian and Anglo-Indian Association was formed in 1876 with E.W. Chambers as its President. A Madras branch was founded the same year by D. S. White and then a Bombay branch. White, however, broke away from the Association for not very clear reasons and in 1879 established the Anglo-Indian and Domiciled European Association of Southern India, which has its own branches and is still active. No longer surviving, though, is its newsletter, *The Anglo-Indian*.

The Eurasian and Anglo-Indian Association further split in 1898 and the breakaway faction was led by Dr. J.R. Wallace, who then founded the Imperial Anglo-Indian Association later that year. The other faction called itself the Anglo-Indian and Domiciled European Association, Bengal, with its headquarters in Calcutta. In an attempt to bring all these associations together, Charles Palmer established the Anglo-Indian Empire League in Allahabad in 1908 with John Harold Abbott a major player in it. Abbott, who was nominated to the Central Legislative Assembly and who was to lead the League as the Great War got underway, was a staunch Empire man. During the Great War he travelled all over India and raised a volunteer Anglo-Indian force of 6000 men that served overseas. His son Roy was the first volunteer. It was the League's Bombay branch that Gidney joined in 1918 after he returned from the War and began taking a greater interest in the difficulties of his community. He was elected President of the branch in 1919.

John Harold Abbott, an Empire man, who was closely involved with Anglo-Indian associations in Calcutta and Allahabad. (Photo: Internet)

In 1921, Gidney took over the reins of the Anglo-Indian and Domiciled European Association in Calcutta and, determinedly working towards unification, amalgamated five other provincial associations with it and absorbed the Empire League. He added the words "of All-India and Burma" to 'Association' in 1926, by when 19 more Anglo-Indian associations had joined the fold. Gidney then had the Association's name changed to the All-India Anglo-Indian Association. Gidney was no Empire man. He recognised the Anglo-Indian community as an Indian community and had little patience with the Domiciled Europeans who lived in India like Anglo-Indians and could not escape inter-marriage with Anglo-Indians but styled themselves differently.

When Sir Henry died in 1942, Frank Anthony, a leading barrister, became the head of the Association and moved its headquarters from Calcutta to Delhi. *The Anglo-Indian Review,* going back to the Association's earliest days, is its voice. The Madras Association that White founded has, however, stood firm against amalgamation, seeking federation. For its part it formed in 1992 with other associations, mainly in South India, a federation called The National Forum of Anglo-Indian Associations.

Right: Frank Anthony, who succeeded Gidney, and emphasised even more than Gidney that Anglo-Indians were Indians first. (Photo: AITW)

Stephen Padua who led the Travancore-Cochin revolt against Anthony who held that Feringhis were not Anglo-Indians. (Photo: AITW)

This federation had its genesis in the Federated Anglo-Indian Associations of Cochin, North Travancore and South Malabar (now Kerala) which had its roots in an association founded by Stephen Padua in 1930 that germinated branches throughout the two princely states—Travancore and Cochin—by 1939 to represent mainly Anglo-Indians of Portuguese lineage. These branches federated in 1939, with Joseph Pinheiro as President, and the Federation was amalgamated with the All-India Anglo-Indian Association in 1947 by S.P. Luiz. But with Frank Anthony never willing to consider the Malayalam-speaking 'Feringhis' as Anglo-Indians, A.A.D. Luiz led the Federated Anglo-

Indian Associations out of the All-India fold in 1953 and formed the Union of Anglo-Indian Associations of Travancore and Cochin, federating in 1992 with the Anglo-Indian Association of Southern India. The All-India Anglo-Indian Association and the Southern India Association still do not quite see eye to eye, but the Constitution of India is clear; if European (not necessarily British) paternal lineage is provable by a person whose family has been permanently residing in India, he or she is Anglo-Indian, whatever language now spoken. Certainly the Euro-Indians of Portuguese lineage, who are the major element in southern India, have shown a greater degree of certainty as a distinct community than other Euro/Anglo-Indians.

Whatever the differences between the two major associations, the attempts at resettlement within India, or staying put where they were in the country, only reflected the views of Gidney, and, later, those of Anthony and those leading the southern federation. Namely, that the Anglo-Indians were natives of India—as the Stracey brothers were to still later say, "We are Indians"—that they were one of India's minority communities and, therefore, were only seeking rights and not favours. Gidney repeated these views at three Round Table Conferences and out of all of it emerged the Government of India Act 1935, which recognised the Anglo-Indians as a distinct minority community in India, defined who an Anglo-Indian was, gave the community representation in legislatures and reservations in some government services, and provided for educational grants to its schools.

This should have removed uncertainty for the community, but the Quit India Movement in the 1940s, the disturbances that ensued—in which the Anglo-Indians were noticeable in leading police action against the unrest nationwide—and Sir Stafford Cripps telling Gidney that only the Congress, and not the British Government, could help the community, revived uncertainty again.

Anthony's efforts after Gidney's death and his personal equation with Mahatma Gandhi, Jawaharlal Nehru and, particularly, Vallabhbhai Patel brought the community considerable concessions. He obtained two seats for the community in the Constituent Assembly—totally out of proportion to its numbers, and got concessions, not given to any other community in India, embodied in the Constitution in 1949. What was stated about the community in 1935 was reiterated in the Constitution; under Article 331 two nominated seats in the Lok Sabha were allotted to the community, under Article 333 nominated representation in the legislatures of States (Andhra Pradesh, Bihar, Jharkhand, Karnataka, Kerala, Maharashtra, Tamil Nadu, Uttarakhand, and

West Bengal) with Anglo-Indian populations of over 2000 each, was provided, and job reservations for the community, in the Railways, Customs and Post and Telegraphs Departments were included in Article 338(3). Educational grants to its schools were also promised by the Government. All this was for a period of ten years, during which the number of job reservations alone would decrease every year during the period. Today, long after the ten-year period provided for the community to catch its breath, all the concessions continue, with the exception of job reservations.

Despite these unique concessions, uncertainty remained and Anthony was unable to convince about half the community that its future lay in India after Independence. This had a lot to do with several factors. Many in the community saw themselves as being culturally 'British' and feared inability to be comfortable in what was likely to be an increasingly Indian cultural milieu. Several holding such views had strong anti-Indian biases. Britain itself provided entry post-Independence for those Anglo-Indians able to provide proof of male British ancestry. And some Indian States themselves stoked Anglo-Indian fears by their linguistic policies in schools (making the local tongue compulsory and witholding grants to Anglo-Indian schools that did not teach local languages and did not reorient syllabuses to develop a more Indian focus). And as the pace of Indianisation increased in employment, competing Anglo-Indians felt discriminated against, thinking they were passed over to make way for less competent Indians, but ignoring the fact that the latter were educationally better qualified. Together, all this triggered emigration of large numbers of Anglo-Indians to Britain, even though Anthony fought and won the Anglo-Indian battle for education in the courts. Initially, about 200,000 Anglo-Indians left in the 1950s and 1960s. Many of them, however, not particularly comfortable in the UK, where colonial views died hard at the time, moved on to Canada, the US and Australia when opportunities arose.

The battles Anthony won for Anglo-Indian education have seen English retained as a medium of education and this was later to help in the growth of an appreciation in the country that the NEW India needed English. Anglo-Indian schools now offer compulsory Hindi classes, a local State language in many of them, and a syllabus that is more India-oriented. But even this acceptance of an Indianness failed to stop the exodus. A feeling of insecurity in employment and an uncomfortableness in adjusting lifestyles to those of others in India were more powerful than all Anthony's attempts to convince his people of the need for "cultural friendship with our Indian brethren". The time has come, he said, when "Anglo-Indians must realise that India is their motherland and that India is fertilised by the fruits of their labour." Many an emigrating Anglo-Indian thought Anthony was a traitor to the community, his complexion leading to even snider remarks.

Staying on in India were three classes of the community: the middle-class and upper middle-class in senior positions in the public or private sectors and who led a comfortable life in India; the lower middle-class in middle-level supervisory and technical positions who did have emigration in mind but were not sure what their skills would get them abroad; and the rest, about half the total population, who were poor or did not have the wherewithal to emigrate and awaited a relative abroad to sponsor them. Some of that sponsorship did happen in the 1970s and 1980s when migration became easier. But in the 1990s, India after liberalisation was beginning to look a different India, an India that was slowly being Westernised and growing an upwardly mobile middle-class. Now Anglo-Indian uncertainty was over whether it might not be better to stay put in India. This was a tempting prospect and increasing numbers of the Anglo-Indian young began going beyond high school and getting degrees that qualified them for a whole range of employment in the 'New India' where their English language skills were an asset.

Despite increasing focus on education and greater opportunities for employment, the community still has a large number of persons, perhaps about 40 per cent of the community, who would be considered poor—either because they are unemployed or are underemployed despite a modest level of education. This may be no more in percentage than the country's 40-45 per cent, but considering its economic status pre-Independence when it was largely a middle-class, salaried community, living in a modest degree of comfort, this number today is a matter of concern for the community's leaders. However, helping hands from abroad who have set up various help-the-community NGOs, some support from better-off members of the community in India, scholarships and, in many cases today, parental willingness to pay for their studies, even if it is a struggle, have helped improve the lot of the community, but much more needs to be done to elevate the less-well-off section of the community to its pre-Independence status when only few in it were considered poor. What is needed is much greater financial support for ensuring higher education for the less-well-off in the community. There needs to be much greater discussion in the community, at home and abroad, on this issue, particularly in the light of how other English-speaking minority communities in India, like those from the northeast, are determinedly seeking education and, then, being sought after and employed all over India. As Neil O'Brien, the President-in-Chief of the All-India Anglo-Indian Association, says,

Neil O'Brien, the President-in-Chief of the All-India Anglo-Indian Association in 2012. (Photo: AITW)

Anglo-Indians must realise that "the days of finishing Class 8 and getting jobs have gone."

That is something the community has begun to realise and large numbers in the community are in comfortable jobs in the information technology, hospitality, tourism, and audio-visual entertainment industries, in advertising, public relations, journalism, in banks and multinational companies, in the professions and in teaching at all levels, in the armed services, in fact in every profession other young Indians are making headway in. And if emigration is on their mind, it is for the same reasons as any other Indian: brighter prospects, and not because he or she is uncomfortable in India or uncertain of his or her future.

Neil O'Brien, a fluent speaker in Bengali and Hindi like all his children—his son Derek is a Member of Parliament representing a regional Bengali party—once said, "India has a glorious tomorrow; the Anglo-Indian community must be part of that tomorrow." He was echoing Frank Anthony: "Let us always remember that we are Indians. The community is Indian. It has always been Indian. Above all, it has an inalienable Indian birthright."

Such identification has become greater with greater numbers of the community employed in more cosmopolitan workplaces that employ well-educated persons from all over India, belonging to various faiths, communities and cultures. The secret of this has been the increasing number of Anglo-Indians going in for higher education, particularly in colleges run by Christian denominations.

With this move into such workplaces there has also been a diminishing of what Frank Anthony once called "an anti-Indian complex", particularly among the less-educated in the community. Many Indians for their part saw the emigration of Anglo-Indians immediately after independence as "disloyalty" to India. These assessments have virtually vanished with the years, particularly after the 'New India' began emerging in the 1990s.

Post-2000, young Anglo-Indians look no different from their young colleagues in cosmopolitan workplaces with a

Anglo-Indian secretaries in Calcutta, just as the times changed and a pan-Indian attire began to be considered by Anglo-Indian women, one of whom here opts for a saree. (Photo: Richard O'Connor)

Both left: *Today, the saree and the salwar-kameez have become everyday wear to work for Anglo-Indian girls as it is for other young Indian women. (Photo: AITW)*

pan-Indian population; they look the same, dress the same, talk the same (whether in English or the local language or a mixed patois) and eat the same, except perhaps at home where beef or pork might be cooked.

As one Anglo-Indian said in a survey, at the beginning of the 1990s, "An Anglo-Indian age is coming as Anglo-Indian values are becoming the values of the elite in India. More and more people are doing the things we do—drinking, dancing and going to clubs ... We are absorbing them; they are adopting our lifestyle."

It may be an exaggerated view, but in 21st century India, Anglo-Indian culture and the social culture of educated,

Westernised Indians have begun to appear the same; only in religion are separate practices followed.

This in itself raises in the community a new cause for concern. A community that was endogamous is beginning to increasingly marry outside, the women in particular finding non-Anglo-Indian husbands. With the offspring of the latter not considered, by definition, Anglo-Indian, the concern is whether the community will, over time, slowly vanish in India. Looking at the positive side of the issue, many Anglo-Indians point to the ways through which the community has tried to preserve its identity, such as community literature, reunions, NGOs, church organisations, old boys' and girls' associations, Anglo-Indian associations, social networking and other websites, etc. However, a closer look shows that most of this has been generated by those who were children of the Raj, those who decided to emigrate in the 1950s and 1960s, and the community in India.

Overseas, the young born to Anglo-Indian parents have for the greater part married 'outside' and become more stoutly British or Australian, Canadian or American, particularly from the second generation. Amongst the poorer Anglo-Indians in India, too, many married into the local community and their children vanished into it in the 1960s and 1970s, though helping hands have made this less of a practice in the 1990s. Nevertheless, the debate over whether the community will vanish by the end of this century is a concern of many Anglo-Indians. Those who fear this point to the fact that with the emergence of linguistic States in India, a common language has helped to bind to an extent many regional communities in each such State, but with the Anglo-Indian community scattered all over the country there is little opportunity for binding; in fact, with their language, English, there is a greater likelihood of them forging links with the 'New Indian', the Westernised one whose numbers are burgeoning. But as a member of a community fewer in number than the Anglo-Indians and one which is also emerging only in the last couple of decades from a traumatic setback, I see hope of both the Anglo-Indians and my community surviving till the day when a 'New India' emerges sans communities. Our respective cultural roots run too deep, particularly if we accept our Indianness in India.

Cooking up a Feast

A nglo-Indians as a community are a most gregarious people and informal hospitality is very much a part of their warmth. Anyone dropping into an Anglo-Indian home will be served a drink and a snack or can be sure to be invited to sit down for a meal if s/he arrives close to lunch or dinner time. But Anglo-Indians are at their most sociable on festive occasions or at functions connected with life-cycle rituals. Baptisms, christenings, first Holy Communions, Confirmations, birthdays, betrothals, weddings, baby showers, wedding anniversaries, even deaths are all marked by gatherings served with a lavish spread of food and drink. Every occasion—even death, when Irish style wakes are not unknown—is a time to celebrate with the smallest of spaces needed to dance in and even smaller spaces for the harmonium or guitar or piano player and the singer/s who'd drive Karaoke to shame.

The community is strongly religious, be its members Roman Catholic (the majority) or Protestant (usually Anglican). Anglo-Indian festivals are closely connected with their faith, particularly the life of Jesus Christ. Thus, going to church on these occasions is the first

Christening the newborn in church is one of the first lifestyle rituals in an Anglo-Indian family and it is a joyous occasion for all friends and relatives who gather for the occasion. (Photo: AITW)

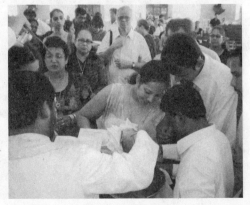

Christmas is a time for the whole family to get together both at home and at parties. Carol singing gives choirs, informal groups and families (as in this photograph) a chance to demonstrate their talent as well as enjoy themselves. (Photo: AITW)

Christmas is also an occasion for institutes, clubs and church groups to hold children's parties where every child waits with bated breath wondering what Santa Claus is going to bring him or her. (Photo: AITW)

priority. But after church, most festival days are occasions for families to gather together ('and bring your friends'), enjoy a table laden with food, drink well if not wisely, and sing along as loudly as possible. Shaking a leg is not ruled out in many a home even on some of these occasions.

Christmas, the festival most celebrated, begins at least two weeks before December 25th, when the Christmas Tree is put up and decorated, and ends only the day after New Year's Day or, in many a home, when the Christmas Tree is taken down 12 days after Christmas. This is a season for partying, dancing, eating and imbibing. But it is also a time for the

Long before Christmas, members of the family and friends get together to make the goodies for the Season. Getting elbows-deep into mixing the ingredients for the Christmas Cake is an annual ritual. Making kulkuls *is also an occasion when the whole family lends a hand, as in this photograph of the D 'Souza family of Trichy. (Photo: AITW)*

whole family to pitch in to decorate the house and make the goodies to serve guests who come a-calling. *Kulkuls,* shaped marzipans, chocolates, rose cookies and a variety of wines are made with all hands contributing. But the highlight is the mixing of the ingredients for the Christmas Cake—with the whole family getting elbows deep into it, particularly if it is a large one.

New Year's Eve is a time for merriment with dance parties high on the agenda at which the New Year is rung in. But there are many who choose to attend the midnight church services rather than those attended on New Year's Day by the revellers of the night before. New Year's Day lunch, like Christmas lunch, is truly a feast that starts late and goes on well into the evening.

Lent (in March/April) may have involved fasting from Ash Wednesday to Holy Saturday, the day before Easter Sunday, but now fasting is expected only on Ash Wednesday and Good Friday. Preparing for post-church Easter Sunday begins weeks before with the making of Easter eggs, shaped often bunny-like—marzipan sweets, and other goodies. And after these are enjoyed on coming back from church, it is time for the Easter Feast.

Life-cycle rituals are marked by solemnity in church and wining, dancing and merry-making at home or in a hall arranged for the occasion. Perhaps the liveliest of these

One of the highlights of the post-church celebration of an Anglo-Indian wedding is the cutting of the wedding cake—an elaborately designed masterpiece—by the bride and bridegroom. Seen here Barry and Tanya DeRozario. (Photo: AITW)

Both bottom: *Another post-church ritual at the reception is an ancient tradition that Anglo-Indians alone seem to continue. The Grand March in which everyone joins in is the most enjoyable part of the occasion for everyone at a wedding. (Photo: AITW)*

celebrations is the wedding reception. After the solemnity of the church ceremony, the banter-mixed felicitation speeches and toasts, and the cheers when the wedding cake is cut, it's 'let the dance begin' when the newly married couple take the floor. And then it's foxtrots, waltzes and jive even in this day and age when these are virtually forgotten ballroom forms, interrupted only by a few minutes of an even older

past revived: The Grand March, an Anglo-Indian tradition that is still a deeply embedded part of the community's culture, in which everyone joins in. On such occasions, it is a treat to see even the tots joining.

Very much part of Anglo-Indian culture is song, music and dance. Anglo-Indians seem to be born with a special talent for all three. Almost from the time they can walk, Anglo-Indian children become a part of every festivity, which makes song and rhythm come to them almost naturally and contribute to the *joie de vivre* that's an intrinsic part of the Anglo-Indian character. So is food, especially the enjoying and sharing of it.

*

The first decade and a half of my life included travelling several times a year on the Indo-Ceylon Boat Mail from Madras to Colombo. That journey included a ferry sea-crossing and two railway operators. But my fondest memories of those journeys was Spencer lunches on the Indian side and Victoria[12] dinners on the other. Both served unforgettable fare that became a favourite of mine. 'Butler food' is what the elders called it and 'Butler Cuisine' is what I did when I, many years later, became aware of the word 'cuisine'. But by then I had also become aware that 'Butler Cuisine' basically derived from 'Anglo-Indian Cuisine', that also became known as 'Raj Cuisine', one of the earliest fusion cuisines in the world, now a bit over 500 years old.

Anglo-Indian fare, like the community, derived from the Portuguese to the British, including along the way the influences of several other European nations. With few European women coming out in the early days of European settlement in India, Western dishes as envisaged by the settlers were prepared by Indian cooks or *khansamahs* or 'butlers' as many Westernised Indian households in later years called them. And with the Indian cooks came Indian flavouring—resulting in the same Anglo-Indian dish tasting different in different parts of India because of local cooks using the regional flavourings with which they were most familiar. At the same time, the Indian cooks introduced their 'Masters'/'Sahibs' to rice and curry, the latter often made blander or with Western inputs like meat stock or tomatoes or wine. By the early 19th century, with the memsahibs arriving and 'Whites Only' clubs being established, where culinary experts like Col. Kenney-Herbert in Madras held sway, what was Euro-Indian fare became more refined—though *khansamahs* were often too wily for the likes of the Colonel and went, at least partly, on their own way, creating

---

12.   Victoria Hotel, Colombo, the caterer.

what became 'Butler Cuisine'. Anglo-Indian Cuisine, meanwhile, became progressively more Indian, though the regular use of beef or pork or wine gave it a character of its own. This Indianisation was further helped with more Anglo-Indians being able to afford cooks and the ladies of the house—usually excellent cooks—concentrating only on cakes and bakes, pastries, sweets and wine, and festive fare, and wistfully hoping their cooks would follow their instructions when it came to regular meals.

Soups seasoned with cumin and red chillies, roasts cooked in whole spices like cloves, pepper and cinnamon, rissoles and croquettes (cutlets) flavoured with turmeric and garam masala, omelettes and scrambled eggs in their masala versions, and stews, bland or flavoured with Worcestershire Sauce (itself an Anglo-Indian creation), are all part of regular Anglo-Indian fare and many of these have passed into Indian Cuisine as well.

While Anglo-Indian Cuisine was influenced by the various European settlements in India, it was the English who left an indelible mark on it. Roasts, stews, bakes, sandwiches are a legacy of the British, as are fish and chips, cutlets, sausages, egg dishes, puddings, custards, cheese, etc. Once, English roast dinners complete with steamed vegetables, roast potatoes, Yorkshire pudding and gravy, English sausages, pies and puddings, especially bread pudding, were common in Anglo-Indian homes. In those leisurely times, English 'Teas' too became an Anglo-Indian ritual, with dainty cucumber sandwiches, cakes, scones, butterfly cakes, and pastries served and tea sipped from miniature fine bone china tea cups.

There was also a strong Scottish influence on Anglo-Indian Cuisine. Scottish dishes such as treacle pudding, pancakes, Scotch eggs, shortbread, oats porridge, beef pepper mince and potatoes (mince and tatties), hotch potch, potato, leek and onion soup, hot toddy, steak and kidney pie, cottage (or shepherd's) pie, sheep's head, etc. were all given a distinctive Anglo-Indian taste over time.

The French left a legacy of baguettes, croquettes, quiches, crêpes, mousses, éclairs, etc. Crêpes became Anglo-Indian pancakes and pan rolls with a variety of sweet and spiced savoury fillings. 'Coq au Vin' locally meant rooster cooked in tomatoes with a dash of red wine. Crumb fried chicken or Poulet Goujans, French onion soup, and lightly batter-fried fish (fish meunière) are other examples of French-based Anglo-Indian dishes.

The Dutch introduced baking dough that made use of yeast, curried beef steak (that they called 'Smore') and potatoes, and 'Fricadelles' or 'forced meat' ball cutlets of minced beef, chicken or fish.

The Portuguese influence began with the introduction into India of various ingredients and condiments, such as coriander, red and dried chillies, garlic and vinegar, and vegetables such as potato, tomato, pumpkin, and cashew. They left the Anglo-Indians their famous 'Vinha de Alhos', or vindaloo, pickled fish and prawns known as 'balachao', 'chacuti de frango' or chicken xacuti, chicken and meat 'buffards', and sour and spicy fish dishes. Portuguese food makes good use of vinegar, so most of these dishes have a slightly tangy taste. Sweet dishes such as *dodol, bebinca, kulkuls, fritters*, and coconut cookies are all legacies of the Portuguese.

Vindaloo, the best-known of the Indo-Portuguese dishes, is a curry dish, its name derived from the Portuguese 'vinha de alhos'. *Vinho* is 'wine' or 'wine vinegar' and '*alhos*' is garlic. It was originally a 'vinegar and garlic'-based watery stew made with pork or meat. With the addition of spices and chillies, it is now one of the spiciest and most popular curry dishes in Anglo-Indian homes. It is today also made with fish, poultry and even vegetables, with potatoes added to absorb the extra vinegary taste. With the addition of potatoes (Hindi: *Aloo*) it became known as vindaloo instead of the original 'vinha de alhos'.

Authentic Anglo-Indian vindaloo is not a curry but more of a thick sauce-based dish, which tastes better as it ages. The authentic taste of vindaloo comes from a unique blend of the fat in the meat mixed with the garlic, vinegar, cumin powder and chilli powder. The blend of spices for vindaloo varies from person to person and place to place, but the basic ingredients are the same. Many other Anglo-Indian dishes have a unique history behind them—and many of them are told in the many cookbooks Anglo-Indian authors are now compiling, books that enjoy a popularity wherever the Union Jack flew.

There is a certain glamour about Anglo-Indian cuisine with its quaint names like Railway Lamb or Mutton Curry, 'Dak Bungalow' (Travellers' Bungalow) Curry, Country Captain

Vindaloo, derived from the Portuguese kitchen, is a favourite in every Anglo-Indian home. (Photo: Bridget White-Kumar)

Chicken, Pork *Bhooni*, Chicken/Meat *Jalfrezi*, Devil Pork Curry, Fish Kedgeree, Double Onions Meat Curry (*Dopiaza*), etc.

Despite all this variety, beef roast and pork roast are all-time favourites and prepared practically every week in an Anglo-Indian home. So is an almost standardised Sunday Lunch, whose recipes are included at the end of this chapter, courtesy Bridget White-Kumar, a Bangalore expert on Anglo-Indian Cuisine.

The typical basic Anglo-Indian Sunday Lunch consists of yellow (coconut) rice, ball (kofta) curry, a cutlet, a *foogath* or some other vegetable dish, devil chutney, and bread pudding. To the Anglo-Indian's favourite lunch, I have added a mulligatawny soup[13] (said to have been invented at the Madras Club, which was for 'Whites Only' in the days of the Raj), and a wine—there are few Anglo-Indian families which do not produce a home-made wine.

Another Sunday option could be a *pulao* (a savoury rice dish), chicken korma (a coconut-based 'white' curry), *raita* (chopped vegetables marinated in curd), masala fried fish, and *papadams* (a large, crunchy savoury wafer).

A typical combo lunch on an average day is Anglo-Indian pepper water with steamed rice and a *jalfrezi* or a meat fry which would normally be beef, lamb or pork. The fry is usually with pepper or red chilli powder in combination with a few other ingredients. This is a sautéed dish, which can be prepared also with poultry, game, seafood, etc.

Anglo-Indian pepper fry or its variation, *jalfrezi*, is the perfect dish to have when suffering from a cold or while feeling blue. The word *jalfrezi* comes from *jal,* meaning spicy or pungent, and *frezi* meaning fried. What started out as an insipid fried meat concoction is now spiked with a variety of spices. It's an ideal dish to prepare with leftover roasts. Today, it is a dish synonymous with the cuisine of West Bengal. It could also be substituted for the cutlet. A modified version of the *jalfrezi* is the devil curry. As its name suggests, it is a rich and fiery hot dish, prepared with beef, mutton, lamb, chicken, pork or eggs and lots of chillies. This could be served instead of the ball curry.

*

---

13.   Patricia Brown, another Anglo-Indian cookery expert, calls this "Dol Soup (made with lentils, a hearty beef stock and spices)" and starts her typical Sunday lunch with it, supplementing yellow rice and ball curry with a "fiery Bhaji or Charchari" and a salad. Her dessert is a Bread and Butter Pudding.

Here are recipes for an Anglo-Indian Sunday Lunch by Bridget White-Kumar.

MULLIGATAWNY SOUP

This soup is the anglicised version of the Tamil *milagu thanni* (*milagu* is 'pepper' and *thanni* is 'water'). So it was, in fact, 'pepper water', which, in South India, with additional flavouring and thinner stock, is called *rasam*.

The original mulligatawny soup made in the English clubs was with chicken or mutton/lamb stock seasoned with pepper. Later, other spices were added to give it a different flavour. Anglo-Indians in the South, however, prefer the more watery 'pepper water' which is closer to *rasam* than the thicker mulligatawny.

Ingredients
(to serve six)
½ kg soup bones and pieces of meat (beef, mutton) or ¼ kg chicken chopped into medium size pieces
1 tsp chilli powder
2 tsp pepper powder
1 tsp cumin powder
1 tsp coriander powder
1 tsp crushed garlic
2 big onions sliced
1 cup coconut paste or coconut milk
1 sprig celery (optional)
Salt to taste
2 cloves
2 small sticks cinnamon
1 tbs oil or butter

Mulligatawny may be very much part of British club cuisine but it is also an Anglo-Indian favourite, the pepperier the better. (Photo: Bridget White-Kumar)

Method
Cook the bones, meat and all the ingredients with 6 to 8 cups of water in a large vessel on high heat till it reaches boiling point. Lower the heat and simmer for at least one hour till the soup is nice and thick. Garnish with mint leaves and serve with a spoonful of rice in each bowl.

Many a British diner in the clubs likes to add a teaspoon of sweet mango chutney in his helping or squeezes a bit of lemon juice into it.

YELLOW (COCONUT) RICE

Ingredients
(to serve six)
1 pack of coconut milk diluted with water to get four cups of milk, or one fresh coconut grated and milk extracted to get four cups of diluted milk
2 cups of raw rice or Basmati rice
1 tsp turmeric powder or a few strands of saffron
Salt to taste
4 tbs butter or ghee
3 cloves
3 cardamoms
3 small sticks of cinnamon

Yellow (Coconut) Rice is the centrepiece of the Anglo-Indian Sunday lunch. (Photo: Bridget White-Kumar)

Method
Heat ghee in a large vessel or rice cooker and fry the spices for a few minutes. Add the washed rice, salt, turmeric and four cups of coconut milk and cook till the rice is done.

Yellow rice is best eaten with ball curry or chicken curry and devil chutney.

BALL CURRY

Ingredients
(to serve six)
3 chopped large onions
1 sprig curry leaves
3 tsp chilli powder
1 tsp coriander powder
3 tsp ginger-garlic paste
3 big tomatoes puréed
½ cup ground coconut paste
1 tsp spice powder or garam masala
Salt to taste
3 tbs oil
1 tsp coriander leaves chopped finely for garnishing
½ tsp turmeric powder

Ball Curry, the traditional accompaniment of Yellow Rice (Photo: Bridget White-Kumar)

Ingredients for the mince balls (kofta)
½ kg fine-minced meat (beef or mutton)
½ tsp spice powder or garam masala
3 green chillies chopped
A small bunch of coriander leaves chopped finely
Salt to taste
½ tsp turmeric powder

Method
Heat oil in a large pan and fry the onions till golden brown. Add the ginger-garlic paste and the curry leaves and fry for a few minutes. Now add the chilli powder, coriander powder, spice powder, turmeric powder and coconut and fry for a few minutes till the oil separates from the masala. Add the tomato purée and salt and simmer for some time. Add sufficient water and bring to a boil.

Meanwhile, mix the spice powder, salt, chopped green chillies, turmeric powder and coriander leaves with the mince and form into small balls. When the curry is boiling nicely, drop the mince balls carefully into it one by one. Simmer on slow heat for 20 minutes till the balls are cooked and the gravy is not too thick.

Serve hot with yellow rice and devil chutney.

FISH CUTLETS

Ingredients
(to serve six)
3 boiled potatoes mashed well
1 kg deboned fresh fish
2 onions minced well
2 minced green chillies
1 tsp pepper powder
1 tsp mint powder or finely chopped mint
1 egg beaten well
3 tbs breadcrumbs
3 tbs oil
Salt to taste

Method
Boil the fish in a little water for five minutes, adding salt to taste. Remove from heat and allow to cool. Crumble the fish with a fork (making sure there are no

bones) and mix together with the potatoes, onions, green chillies, pepper powder, salt and mint. Form into cutlets.

Heat oil in a pan. When hot, dip each cutlet in the beaten egg, roll in breadcrumbs and shallow fry on low heat on both sides till brown. Could also be served as a starter with a salad.

DEVIL CHUTNEY

This is a fiery onion and red chilli chutney that is served as an accompaniment to rice. Its bright red colour often misleads people into thinking that it is very pungent and spicy, but it is actually sweet and sour and only slightly pungent.

Ingredients
2 medium size onions chopped roughly
2 red chillies or 1 tsp red chilli powder
2 tsp sugar
1 tsp raisins (optional)
Pinch of salt
2 tbs vinegar

Method
Grind all the ingredients together till smooth. If chutney is too thick, add a little more vinegar. Serve with yellow rice.

BREAD PUDDING

This pudding was introduced in India by the early British. It can also be made as a savoury dish, substituting sugar and raisins with chopped tomatoes, green chillies, etc. The choice of bread, the addition of optional ingredients, and the details of preparation can make bread pudding into a rich, heavy dessert, or simple light dish, or anything in between.

Another legacy of the British table is Bread Pudding, a favourite Anglo-Indian dessert. (Photo: Bridget White-Kumar)

Ingredients
(to serve six)
8 slices of bread cut into cubes after removing the crusts
3 cups milk
200 g butter
200 g sugar
1 tsp vanilla essence

200 g chopped raisins and cashew nuts

2 eggs beaten well

Method

Take a baking dish and grease it. Spread bread cubes in it.

Heat milk to scalding, and pour over the bread cubes. Set aside to cool for some time, then add all the other ingredients. Add more milk if too dry. The bread should be well soaked. Bake at 350 degrees for 40-45 minutes or until knife comes out clean. Serve warm.

The same pudding can be steamed in a pressure cooker as well.

GINGER WINE

Ingredients

¼ kg fresh ginger

2 kg sugar

6 limes (extract the juice)

3 pieces cinnamon

1 red chilli (remove the seeds)

6 bottles of water

Method

Peel and wash the ginger and cut into thin pieces.

Make lime juice and keep aside.

Put all the above ingredients in a large clean vessel together with 6 bottles of water and bring to a boil. Boil for at least one hour on slow heat. Remove from heat and add the lime juice.

When cold, strain through a thin cloth. Bottle and use whenever required.

✳

Some supplements to this meal served in some parts of India are Fish Kedgeree, a vegetable dish like Cabbage *Foogath*, and a sweet, the Christmas favourite *Kulkuls* being featured here.

FISH KEDGEREE

Kedgeree is an anglicised version of the Indian *kitchri* or *kitchidi*, which was prepared with seasonings, rice, lentils, raisins, butter, etc. In the Anglo-Indian adaptations, fried fish flakes and hard-boiled eggs were added. Fish, either steamed or fried, was a regular item in an English breakfast during the Raj and local cooks began to make a whole meal—and a more flavourful one—by mixing *kitchri* with it and adding whole spices and hard-boiled eggs. Even though originally a breakfast dish, it is a meal in itself for lunch or dinner, and sometimes even a starter.

Ingredients
(to serve six)
½ kg good fleshy fish cut into thick slices
¼ kg raw rice or Basmati rice
4 tbs oil
1 tbs ghee or butter
3 onions sliced finely
3 green chillies sliced lengthwise
100 g (4 tbs) moong dal or toor dal (or any other lentils)
3 cloves
2 small sticks of cinnamon
1 tsp spice powder or garam masala
1 tsp cumin powder
100 g sultanas or raisins (optional)
2 tsp chopped coriander leaves
2 bay leaves
Salt to taste
1 tbs chilli powder
1 tbs lime juice/lemon juice/vinegar
6 whole peppercorns
4 hard-boiled eggs cut into quarters

Method
Wash the fish and cook it in a little water along with bay leaves and salt for about five minutes or till the pieces are firm. Strain and keep aside.

Add sufficient water to the leftover fish soup to get six cups of liquid.

Remove the bones and skin from the boiled fish and break into small pieces.

Wash the rice and dal and keep aside.

Heat the oil in a suitable vessel and sauté the onions, cloves and cinnamon lightly. Add the slit green chillies, whole peppercorns, spice powder, cumin powder and chilli powder and sauté for a few minutes. Add the rice and dal and mix well.

Add six cups of the soup, lime juice/vinegar, sultanas, chopped coriander leaves and salt and cook on high heat till boiling. Reduce heat and simmer covered till the rice and dal are cooked and slightly pasty. Gently mix in the cooked fish, butter/ghee and the hard-boiled eggs. Cover and let the rice draw in the fish for a few minutes.

Serve hot or cold with chutney or lime pickle.

CABBAGE FOOGATH

Foogath is the generic name (but derives from where, no one knows) for dry vegetable side dishes served at lunch. Beans, cabbage, cauliflower, greens, etc. are parboiled, then tempered with chopped onions and spices. No Anglo-Indian lunch is complete without a vegetable *foogath*.

Ingredients
(to serve six)
1 medium size fresh cabbage chopped finely
3 chopped green chillies
1 onion sliced
2 pods (1 tbs) of chopped garlic
¼ tsp mustard seeds
1 sprig curry leaves
½ cup grated coconut (optional)
1 tsp oil
Salt to taste

Method
Heat oil in a pan and add the mustard, garlic and curry leaves. When the mustard starts spluttering, add the chopped onion and green chillies and fry till the onions turn slightly brown. Add the cabbage and salt and mix well.

Cover and cook for about 6 to 7 minutes till the cabbage is soft. Add the grated coconut and mix well.

KULKULS

These are crunchy-fried sweet dough sweets and are a variant of the Portuguese Christmas sweet called 'Filhoses Enroladas'. Making *kulkuls* (always referred to in the plural) is a time-consuming process and requires many hands. Hence, a few days before Christmas, a separate day is designated as 'Kulkul Day' when every member of the family spends a few hours rolling out his/her portion of the *kulkul* dough. Where the name came from is not known, but one theory has that its curled shape contributed to its name. Not a traditional Sunday Lunch 'finisher', but I've included it instead of chocolate because it is very much part of traditional Anglo-Indian fare.

Ingredients
(to serve six)
1 kg flour
6 eggs beaten well
2 cups thick coconut milk
½ tsp salt
½ cup (300 g) sugar
1 tsp baking powder
Oil for deep frying

Method
Mix the flour, salt, sugar and baking powder together. Add the coconut milk and eggs and knead to a soft dough. Keep aside for an hour.

Form *kulkuls* by taking small lumps of the dough and rolling on the back of a fork or a wooden *kulkuls* mould. Alternatively, roll out the dough and cut into fancy shapes with *kulkuls* or cookie cutters.

Heat oil in a deep pan and fry as many *kulkuls* as possible at a time. Drain and keep aside.

To frost the *kulkuls*, melt one cup of sugar with half a cup of water and when the sugar syrup crystallises pour over the *kulkuls* and mix well. Store in airtight boxes when cold.

A Legacy of Schools

The most truly literate community in India is perhaps the Anglo-Indians. Every Anglo-Indian can do more than merely write his name. In English—though, today, there are many among them who could do it in other Indian languages as well.

The beginnings of the modern teaching of the three Rs was in the Portuguese possessions on the west coast where literacy received a further push between 1556 and the early 1600s when the Portuguese on that coast established the first printing presses in India and turned out mainly religious material, successively over this period in Latin, Portuguese, Malabar (Tamil) and Konkani. By the middle of the 17th century, however, Portuguese policy saw the closing down of the printing presses. And printing in India remained dormant till 1712-13 when the Danish-Halle Mission in Tranquebar (on the Tanjore coast), led by Bartholomaeus Ziegenbalg, revived it and Carey, Marshman and Ward took it forward in Danish Serampore (near Calcutta) from 1800. The first book to be printed in English in India was issued by the Tranquebar Press in 1716. It was called *A Guide to the English Tongue* and was by Thomas Dyche.

By this time the seeds for education in English in India were sown in Fort St. George, Madras. Father Ephraim de Nevers, a Capuchin priest, got permission to build St. Andrew's Church in the Fort and from 1642, when it was consecrated, he also permitted Protestant worship in it. In his house adjoining the church he started a school to teach in English the children of Portuguese, British and mixed families—the last-listed the largest number. Rather similar education in Portuguese had been started about three miles down the road, in Portuguese San Thomé, about a hundred years earlier. Portuguese, it should be stated, was the lingua franca of both coasts till well into the 18th century.

The East India Company's Council at Fort St. George, which employed hundreds of Portuguese-Indians, suddenly woke up to the fact that there was a Catholicisation of the Fort's population going on and in 1673 invited a Scottish priest, Pringle, to start a school in the Fort. The student composition was British orphans and children of Indian mothers whose European 'husbands' had deserted them or died. Pringle was succeeded in 1678 by Ralph Ord who in 1692 handed over the management of the school to the Chaplain of St. Mary's in the Fort (consecrated in 1780 and the oldest Anglican Church in Asia that functioned from premises that had been specially built for it). This school, in 1715, under the supervision of the Rev. William Stevenson, took the name St. Mary's Church Charity School. When it merged with the male and female orphanages in 1787, it became the Civil Orphans' Asylum and when it moved in 1954 to what is its present home in Madras it was renamed St. George's Anglo-Indian School and Orphanage—given its roots, the oldest Western-style school established by the British in Asia and the oldest Anglo-Indian school in the country. Schools akin to St. Mary's Charity School

St. George's Anglo-Indian School and Orphanage, Madras, the oldest Western style school in India. Featured here is its hostel. (Photo: AITW)

Barnes School, Deolali, with its genesis in Bombay. (Photo: AITW)

were founded in Bombay in 1718/19 and in Calcutta in 1731. The latter became the Calcutta Free School for Boys and Girls in 1789 and was later renamed the St. Thomas' School. The former, under the leadership of the Rev. George Barnes, was taken over in 1815 by the Bombay Education Society and, later, in 1825, moved to Deolali (Devlali) where it thrives as the Barnes School.

These charity schools, or asylums (orphanages) as some of the institutions that were integrated with them were called, provided, apart from basic education, crafts training for the boys and home-making skills for the girls. The consequence of the latter were regular balls held at the schools to which bachelors—particularly young military officers—seeking wives were invited and many a marriage followed—with some of the girls being as young as 12 years old!

The boys educated at the Madras Male Military Orphan Asylum and Civil Orphans Asylum—which today are St. George's School—were in these institutions trained as carpenters or to work in printing presses. The training Dr. Andrew Bell initiated was by the ancient Indian *gurukulam* system he embraced—an older boy teaching younger boys. This was to develop as the monitorial system after Bell introduced it in Britain and it came back to India with the Euro/Anglo-Indian schools introducing Prefects to maintain discipline. The first formal emigration of Anglo-Indians to Australia was facilitated by Sir William Westbrooke Burton, a judge of the Supreme Court of Madras (1844-1857), who was also the President of the Madras East India Society. Sailing from Madras to Sydney aboard the *William Prowse* (1852) and *Palmyra* (1854) were 168 persons, 143 of them single males. Of these single males, 80 had Madras links. Twenty-four of those from the Madras Orphans' Asylums who had been trained in printing joined Henry Parkes[14] newspaper, *Empire*, as compositors. Some of them also joined the *Brisbane Courier* and a few Cunningham's Press in Pitt Street, Sydney.

The spread of British-style schools after these beginnings was slow. It was only in the early 19th century that the numbers of such schools began to grow, to meet—about which John Ricketts said in a different context—the necessity of promoting the "welfare and interests of the East Indian branch of the rising generation ... including all such youths of European descent as may be destined to be born, to live and to die in this country." The schools that then began to be established also catered to the children of those from Britain working temporarily in India but who could not afford to send their children back to the 'home countries' (Britain) for their education.

This growth in educational institutions also coincided with a liberalisation of the Company's policy that enabled from 1813 the British Protestant missions to establish themselves in India. The Company had placed no restrictions on the Catholic missions and they had had a head start in establishing schools. But it was the schools that the British Protestants established first in the plains and, then, increasingly, in the hill stations that took on the character of the true British/Anglo-Indian school.

Today, there are, not unlike them, hundreds of other educational institutions established later and popularly called 'Convent Schools'. Besides these, there are several elite public schools, like the Doon School, Dehradun, Mayo College, Ajmer, and Daly College, Indore, that owe not a little to the schools founded by the missionaries. But neither the 'convent' schools nor the public schools can claim the heritage of the earlier schools which were set up specifically for British and Anglo-Indian children, though today they have almost entirely Indian student bodies.

---

14. The 'Father of the Commonwealth of Australia', who helped federate what had originally been separate self-governing States.

There are today about 300 schools that could be called Anglo-Indian (erstwhile European) Schools. Nearly 100 of them are a century or so old and almost all the rest date to well before Independence. Among the best-known of these schools are those established in hill stations like Shimla, Mussoorie, Darjeeling, Nainital, Kurseong, Dehradun and Ooty and its adjoining townships. These at Independence were about 75 in number. There are many more with long histories in the plains. Most of them are in today's metro cities and where there were major Anglo-Indian 'colonies', like Jabalpur and Trichy. Once, about 40 per cent of these schools were Roman Catholic institutions and about a quarter were Anglican. About 10 per cent were run by other Christian denominations and about 20 per cent were railway schools but with a low enrolment. The remaining schools were non-denominational or Government-run. Just before Independence, there were about 60,000 children enrolled in these schools, over 80 per cent of them Anglo-Indian The management pattern has not changed too much today, but the enrolment is over 90 per cent Indian. I offer here a purely subjective selection of some of these schools over a hundred years old.

The earliest of the Euro/Anglo-Indian schools are, as already mentioned, St. George's in Madras, St. Thomas' in Calcutta, and Barnes, Deolali. The growth after this was slow, with only the Roman Catholics and the German-Danish missions establishing schools, of which only a few survive. It was only after the opening of Suez, which enabled increasing numbers of British families to come in India to seek work in a country where communication technology was being developed apace and the East Indian population began to grow, that schooling became a compelling need for both communities. It was also around this time, in the early 19th century, that the Company lifted the prohibition of British missionaries coming out to India. It was these missions that established not only 'Anglo-Vernacular' schools but also the Euro/Anglo-Indian schools. And the Roman Catholic missions, with increasing numbers of their faithful among both communities, simultaneously began establishing such schools. It was between the 1840s and 1900 that these began to put down roots in India, particularly in the hill stations.

The first Euro/Anglo-Indian school to be established in this period is believed to be what became the Mussoorie School but was always called 'Maddocks' till it closed in 1900. The school was established in 1835 by John Mackinnon, who had run a school for army children in Meerut. The Rev. Robert Maddocks, who came out to Mussoorie to head it and reorganised it, left a lasting impression that long survived in his name being synonymous with the school.

Top and right: La Martiniere, Calcutta, in the 1930s (Picture: D.M. Alney) and Constantia, *the core of La Martiniere, Lucknow, the legacy of Claude Martin, a 'nabob' of Oudh. (Photo: AITW)*

The earliest of those still going strong appears to be La Martiniere, Calcutta, founded in 1837. Claude Martin, a French 'nabob' of Oudh, had wanted it started in his mansion, *Constantia*, in Lucknow but legal hassles over territorial rights had it opening its doors in Calcutta. La Martiniere, Lucknow, was to follow, being started in 1845, the same year as the Convent of Jesus and Mary opened in Mussoorie.

Then, in 1846, was founded Loretto in Darjeeling and in 1847 the first of the 'military asylums' established by Sir Henry Lawrence, Lawrence in Sanawar (Kasauli). Three other Lawrence Schools were established for children of the British/Anglo-Indians in the Army; Sanawar was followed by other Lawrence Military Schools in Lovedale (Ooty) and Mt. Abu (Rajasthan) in 1858, and Ghora Gali (Murree—now

One of the military schools Sir Henry Lawrence founded. This one is popularly called Lovedale, the name deriving from the area in Ooty where it is located. (Photo: Internet)

in Pakistan) in 1860. Also founding a school that honoured his name was George E.L. Cotton, the Metropolitan Bishop of Calcutta, who also gave an impetus for opening more such schools. Bishop Cotton, Shimla, was founded in 1863, almost immediately followed by Bishop Cotton, Nagpur. Bishop Cotton, Bangalore, opened in 1865.

Other early Euro/Anglo-Indian schools that are still much sought after are:

North: St. George's, Mussoorie (1853), Auckland House, Shimla, a rather exclusive girls' school (1866), Sherwood, Nainital (1869), Christ Church, Jabalpur (1870), and Oak Grove, Mussoorie (1888). Most major railway junctions had railway schools that were, in fact, Anglo-Indian schools, but Oak Grove, started by the East Indian Railway, was the only residential railway school and one situated in the hills. St. Deny's was started in 1882 in Murree, which is now in Pakistan.

Bottom left: St. George's, Mussoorie. (Photo: AITW)

Oak Grove School, Mussoorie, the only residential railways school and the only one in the hills. It was started by the East Indian Railway and is now run by the Northern Railway. (Photo: Internet)

St. Joseph's, Darjeeling, better known as North Point, where it is located. (Photo: Internet)

Top right: *St. Paul's, Darjeeling, whose genesis was in the school Ricketts started in Calcutta. (Photo: Internet)*

East: St. Paul's, Darjeeling (1864), whose genesis was much older schools in Calcutta, namely the Parental Academy (1823) and Calcutta Grammar School (1836). From the Parental Academy there developed Doveton College, Calcutta (1850-1916), which benefitted from the will of Capt. John Doveton, an Anglo-Indian in the Nizam of Hyderabad's army. The will also endowed a school in Madras (1856) that flourishes today as Doveton Corrie Protestant Schools. Other schools in the East are St. Joseph's, North Point, Darjeeling (1888) and Mount Hermon, Darjeeling (1895).

South: St. John's Vestry, Tiruchchirappalli/Trichinopoly (1773), St. Joseph's, Bangalore (1858), Breeks Memorial, Ooty (1874), Stanes in Coimbatore (1862) and Coonoor (1875), Baldwin's in Bangalore (1880) and Hebron, Ooty (1899).

Stanes School, Coimbatore, the legacy of a coffee and tea planter. (Photo: Internet)

Cathedral and John Connon School, Bombay, better known as Cathedral. (Photo: Internet)

West: Christ Church, Bombay (1825), Cathedral and John Connon, Bombay (1860), Bishop's, Poona (1864) and St. Peter's, Panchgani (1904).

There are many other schools of this ilk still successfully running in India and, as I said, mine is a subjective selection based on age and reputation. Two other such schools dating to the early 20th century, however, deserve special mention. The St. Andrew's Colonial Homes was founded in 1900 by the Rev. John Graham in Kalimpong (Sikkim) and renamed after him in 1947. The orphanage that became a school was founded to adopt the numerous children British planters had sired in liaisons with local tea garden workers. Many of these children passed into the mothers' community over time,

Dr. Graham's Homes in Kalimpong. (Photo: AITW)

St. George's School, Ketti (Ooty). (Photo: AITW)

but others were brought to Kalimpong by their mothers or staff of the Homes who persuaded the mothers to give the children a better opportunity in life through education. A school founded in the South for the same reasons was St. George's, first set up in Kodaikanal in 1914 and moved to Ketti in Ooty in 1922. Both institutions today are less of orphanages than they are boarding schools.

These schools functioned as girls only, boys only or as co-ed institutions. But many a girls only and boys only school was there in the same hill station and their was some interaction, like inviting each other for film shows, plays and sports meets. The more liberal even had a dance or two a year. But at the end of the day, the focus was on a sound

Fresh-faced Anglo-Indian schoolgirls in an all-girls' Anglo-Indian school shortly after Independence, when such schools were still the virtual preserve of Anglo-Indian and British children. (Photo: La Martiniere)

education, discipline, and insistence in participating in sports activities: *mens sana in corpore sano.*

Common to all these schools were Western style uniforms down to the shoes—dresses for girls and many a school insisting on ties for shirt-and-trousered boys—a Prefect and House system, Anglo-Indian cuisine, outdoor and extra-curricular activities, and, in many of the boys' schools, a cadet corps that was semi-military. The last-listed activity alone has vanished from the scene in these schools today.

Once, the great majority of students in these schools were Anglo-Indians or the children of Europeans who could not afford to send their children to Britain for their education or who were stuck in India during World War II. Frank Anthony who negotiated the survival of the Anglo-Indian schools said in 1966 that "without our schools and without our language, English, we cannot be an Anglo-Indian community." As though to emphasise this, as the older schools became unaffordable to many Anglo-Indians and sought the Westernised Indians whose affluence could keep them going, Anthony established the Frank Anthony Public Schools—in Delhi (1956), Calcutta (1965) and Bangalore (1967). But despite numerous scholarships, the Frank Anthony Schools themselves have a minority of Anglo-Indians today.

Frank Anthony Public School, Bangalore. (Photo: Internet)

Apart from the schools, there were a few teachers' training institutions established for Anglo-Indian high school graduates. These include two in Chennai, St. Christopher's (1923) and the Anglo-Indian Teachers' Training School (1912), an adjunct of the Presentation schools in Church Park, Chelmsford in Murree (1924), and Mount Hermon in Darjeeling (1972).

Speaking of the changed education pattern in the Anglo-Indian schools of today, Neil O'Brien, President-in-Chief of the All-India Anglo-Indian Association, describes the Anglo-Indian school as "a school that provides a particular type of education.... It uses English as its medium of instruction ... (but) it has a mixed Western-Indian cultural pattern. The Anglo-Indian school of today is not a hangover of the Raj. It has imbibed a great deal of India; in fact, it is very much part of India. It is Indian in its greatest, in its broadest sense. (But it preserves the) character, discipline, and other traditions associated with the Anglo-Indian schools over the years..."

The major re-orientation in the distinctive syllabus in these schools has been in the social sciences—History, Geography, Civics and Environmental Studies. English has begun to look at Indian contribution to the language. And Hindi and local languages have become compulsory subjects. But, as O'Brien says, the culture and traditions of the past remain deeply rooted in these schools and have even been adopted by numerous Indian English-medium schools established after Independence to produce the 'New Indian'. With this educational background, thousands of Indians, including those of the Anglo-Indian community, have significantly contributed to modern India in the same manner earlier generations from these schools contributed to the laying of the foundations for, and the development of, the India of today.

Lifeline of a Community

Asansol, Bhusaval, Itarsi, Jamalpur (Jabalpur), Perambur, Podanur, Trichinopoly, Waltair… they are all towns that for over a hundred years linked a community through an iconic association with what has been called "the lifeline of the Community": the Railways. There were hundreds of these cities and large towns, small towns and places little better than villages all over pre-Independence India, in urban suburbs, parched terrain, on the edges of jungles, many of them far from the better amenities of life, but all home to what they called themselves, "The Railway People", virtually a sub-community in the larger community that called itself

Royapuram, a northern suburb of Madras, was pretty much a railway colony once, home to many who worked on the Madras & South Mahratta Railway whose main terminus was once this station. Royapuram Railway Station, the first station in South India, has been restored but this pre-renovation photograph shows the ornate portico that existed from the time it was inaugurated in 1856. (Photo: AITW)

The Railway Institutes were where the 'Railway People' had fun, like these girls enjoying themselves in the swimming pool of the Institute in Lillooah, near Calcutta, in the 1940s. (Photo: AITW)

Anglo-Indian. Many of them, gypsy-like, moved from place to place, but two things they had in common almost wherever they went: the Railway Colony they lived in, a little neatly kept oasis away from the heat and dust, noise and bustle of India, and the Railway Institute in the Colony where they made the noise, laughed and sang a lot, and made life happy and memorable for themselves. At the time of Independence there was hardly an Anglo-Indian family without a railway connection. Dr. Beatrix D'Souza, a leader of the community, goes further, "nearly every Anglo-Indian alive today has an ancestor who was in the Railways," she states.

The Railway People had their beginnings when Lord Dalhousie suggested in 1843 that India could be best connected by railway. It was Charles Trevelyan, a respected member of the East India Company, who suggested that Eurasians, sturdily built, mechanically inclined, comparatively well educated, and able to get along with one or another of the local languages, would be the best persons to be recruited for laying the railway lines.

As an old railway hand, Ralph N. Moore described it, for the lines to be laid, land had to be surveyed, trees felled in distant forest areas and transported to work sites to be positioned as foundations for the rails that had to be laid on them, earth dug to build high embankments, and the steel rails from England had to be transported from distant parts to work sites and laid for hundreds of miles on the sleepers. Homes had to be built for the railwaymen and their families, workshops and loco sheds constructed for rolling stock, and locomotives imported from England had to be put on the rails in distant places. Thousands of Anglo-Indians were employed at the supervisory level. Many of them were to later move into being engine drivers and firemen, with some even working as *khalasis* ('jacks' in 'Anglo-Indian') normally breaking large lumps of coal for the firemen to shovel, hour after hour, into the fireboxes.

When the Great Indian Peninsular Railway began construction, in 1851, of its first railway line from Bombay—after Madras and Calcutta's earlier proposals failed to get off the ground—3000 Anglo-Indians worked as foremen, supervisors, technical personnel and clerical staff on constructing the line. After India's first train in 1853 first used the broad gauge line from Bombay to Thane, the East Indians became greatly in demand to run the railways, a demand the community was as eager to meet. What resulted in the next hundred years was generations of a family serving the various railway companies of India and, after Independence, those

The Fuller family of Madras seen in 1914. The family has been connected with the railways for five generations, for over 140 years down to today. (Photo: Noel Fuller)

Noel Fuller, now a senior Fitter in the Railways, stands beside the last metre gauge EMU of the Chennai Suburban service. (Photo: Noel Fuller)

Before nationalisation in the 1950s of the numerous privately-run railways in India, each railway company had a first-rate hockey team or two like this, Madras & South Mahratta Railway Rifles team which is seen after winning in 1918, the then premier hockey tournament in South India, the Madras Cricket Club hockey tournament. (Photo: AITW)

of Pakistan as well. From 1951 they were to serve the zonal railways of India (and Pakistan) following nationalisation of the British railway companies.

There were four ways of joining the Railways in pre-Independence days. One way was as a Trade Apprentice who was trained for three years in a mechanical/electrical skill and became a skilled factory worker. The second category was recruited as cleaners and, after training, progressed to Fireman, Shunter, Passenger Train Driver, Mail Driver and Senior Mail Driver. It was a legendary driver of the

Both: At one time, special trains carrying visiting dignitaries and Indian VVIPs were almost always hauled by engines under the charge of Anglo-Indian Senior Mail Drivers. This locomotive hauled the Queen's Special in 1961 and was crewed by Senior Mail Driver Frederick Durham, who received a letter of appreciation from the British High Commission writing on behalf of Queen Elizabeth. He is seen here in suit with Reserve Fireman Francis Weston, First Fireman Ronald Gardiner and second Fireman Ramachandra together with a group of engine cleaners. (Photo: Bryan Mulley)

Eastern Railway, Craker, who took out the first Rajdhani Express in 1969. The third category were high school graduates who were recruited after tests as Apprentice Mechanics and, after four years' training, progressed from Chargemen to Foremen and General Foremen with the best moving on to become Assistant Works Managers, Works Managers or Divisional Engineers. The fourth way was established in 1927, originally for Europeans but later for Indians too. Special Class Apprentices—about ten a year—were recruited from among the educated, trained for

OFFICE OF THE HIGH COMMISSIONER
FOR THE UNITED KINGDOM
NEW DELHI · INDIA

2nd March, 1961

Dear Durham,

        I have been commanded by The Queen to
send you this photograph of Herself and the
Duke of Edinburgh as a small memento of the
part which you played in the arrangements
for the Royal Tour of Her Majesty and His
Royal Highness to India in 1961.

        Her Majesty is grateful for the
contributions of all those who helped to
make the Visit such a happy experience.

(P.H. GORE-BOOTH)
HIGH COMMISSIONER

Mr. F. Durham,
Locomotive Driver,
Western Railway,
Block No. 144/L,
Gangapur City,
Rajasthan.

Senior Mail Driver Edward Selvey (hat in hand) with Eric Streeter, Senior Loco Fuel Inspector (in shorts), and Senior Fireman Vivian Magee (to his right) and First Fireman Eric Tennant (seated to his left). All Anglo-Indian crews like these were common on engines till the 1950s. (Photo: AITW)

four years, put through a London engineering degree course, and appointed Assistant Mechanical Engineers or Assistant Works Managers which Category 3 could only aspire to through the slow process of promotion. The Special Class, however, were in two years promoted to Works Managers or Divisional Mechanical Engineers and could hope one day to become Chief Mechanical Engineers or General Managers.

A record of Anglo-Indian railway officers states that among the little over 400 Special Class Apprentices selected between 1927 and 1969, there were 15 Anglo-Indians. R.D. Kitson, Class of 1951, retired as Chairman of the Indian Railway Board in the 1980s, Norbert de Souza (1958) retired in the 1990s as Chief Mechanical Engineer, Southern Railway, and B.R. Williams (1950) retired as Joint Director, Railway Board, Calcutta, and migrated to the U.S. from where he strongly supports the underprivileged of the community. The achievements of the others—H.V.M. Stewart and C.J. Butler (1927), D.B. King (1928), H.O. Toomey and J.O. Burns (1930), W.C. Britter and E.L.T. Jones (1931), J.B. Rosair (1932), M.A. Plunkett (1943), H.G.T. Woodward (1944), E.J. Kingham (1945) and T.M. Fritchley (1949)—I have not been able to trace but they would undoubtedly have risen high in the Railway hierarchy.

Besides serving in the workshops, loco sheds and on rolling stock, the Loco men, there were those Anglo-Indians in Traffic, as stationmasters and their assistants, guards, ticket

collectors and signalmen. And, in time, the Railways ran their own hospitals and schools which were mainly staffed by Anglo-Indian women working as nurses and teachers.

Almost all of them lived in neat little houses in well-maintained railway colonies set a little apart from the town at railway junctions and terminuses spread throughout the pre-Independence India. In the bigger colonies there may have been areas separated by hierarchy—Running staff, Loco shed personnel, Traffic, and all the junior grades—but the Institute was for everyone and a dance at it was when everyone let his hair down.

In such colonies, there was a similarity to the interior of every railwayman's home. I paraphrase and adapt here a recollection of Caroline D'Cruz that has been published

The Railways ran numerous schools, like this one in Chakradharpur where a class gathers for a performance. (Photo: AITW)

Top left: H.O.D. Brown, a Head Guard on the North Western Railway, Pakistan, shortly after Independence. (Photo: AITW)

Drawing rooms furnished like this were the rule in Anglo-Indian homes in railway colonies. This was Dennis Whitworth's in Lillooah, near Calcutta. (Photo: AITW)

elsewhere but which is so reminiscent of many an Anglo-Indian home I'd been to in the early 1940s. There'd be sofas and chairs in the living room, their quality variable, but in almost every home the centre of attraction would be the head of the family's reclining planter's chair of wood and cane with wooden arms that could be extended for his legs. There'd be a tall rosewood stand for topees and umbrellas, and in many a home a piano—much used—or at least a guitar or harmonica.

Curtains, home-embroidered antimacassars, crocheted doilies, runners and a small carpet would brighten the room as did the framed prints on religious themes—the Sacred Heart was a favourite—or scenes out of the English countryside.

The dining room would always have a dining table and a sideboard or dinner-wagon which would hold the crockery, for table as well as service, cruet stands, sauce boats, and cutlery. Tables were laid for every meal with home-crocheted doilies, English crockery and Sheffield cutlery—even if many, as the years went by, ate with their hands. A meat-safe (a *dhoolie*)—a cupboard with steel mesh 'windows' and its legs in empty Polson butter tins filled with water to keep away insects—would store leftover food. And there'd be an imported 'filter' to store water in.

Under lock and key near the kitchen would be the large wooden Rice Box storing rice, dals and spices. The kitchen itself would always remain soot-covered, the firewood or coal smoke from the clay or iron 'stoves' ensuring that no amount of lime washing could make the kitchen white. And hung on hooks here, or stored in shelves beneath the cooking range, would be aluminium pots, iron frying pans and clay cooking vessels—in which curries cooked best—and a variety of spoons and ladles, some of indigenous wood.

Bedrooms would have high beds with thick mattresses (often filled with coconut coir) on wooden frames and the ubiquitous mosquito nets. At summer's peak, they'd all go out into the gardens that surrounded the house, positioned according to the trees to which the mosquito nets could be tied. There'd also be in the bedroom a dressing table, a chest-of-drawers and/or a cupboard for clothes, and a 'dirty clothes basket'.

The toilet would have zinc bathtubs, metal buckets and mugs (plastic had not come in pre-Independence) and 'thunderboxes'. Till modern plumbing came in, the rear door of the toilet would open on to the garden and the water-carrier and the 'sweeper' would use it to bring in water (including hot water) boiled in drums on makeshift 'stoves' in the garden and take out night-soil. The water carrier had also to ensure water supply for the storage drums in the kitchen—usually from a well in the garden.

Despite such manual facilities, it would always be 'open house' in Railway colonies with neighbours dropping in all the time, relatives and friends from other colonies coming for a few days from time to time, and guests cramming the house for celebrations, family occasions or parties at the Institute.

A Railway Institute or an Anglo-Indian club, like Bowring in Bangalore and Dalhousie in Calcutta, can be as big as the one in Jamalpur or as small as those in such small junctions as Villupuram. There were over 800 of them and over 30 holiday houses located all over India. The Jamalpur Railway Institute—with over 1000 Anglo-Indians using it in its heyday—had a cinema theatre, a six-lane swimming pool, four tennis courts, two billiards rooms, a bowling lawn, a large hall for dances, Housie sessions and cards, as well as catering facilities and a bar. Smaller ones would have just a large hall and furniture, perhaps a pool table, a bar and snacks counter and, of course, a piano. But how they could beat it up or have a lively evening of Housie even with these minimal facilities! Camaraderie—

Both: *Besides the Railway Institutes, the Anglo-Indians also had their clubs in the metros, to which gravitated many of the senior Anglo-Indian railway officials. Two of the best known ones—now with a more cosmopolitan membership—are the Bowring Institute in Bangalore (top) and the Dalhousie Institute in Calcutta. (Photos: SM Collection and AITW)*

Dances at the Railway Institutes were as lively as you could get. As you can see from this picture taken in Guntakal.
(Photo: AITW)

despite the occasional fisticuffs or rumbles over a romance that broke hierarchical lines—was the name of a happy community life in which the whole family figured, from the oldest to the youngest.

As Rudyard Kipling wrote about Institutes in 1899, "Best and prettiest of the many good pretty things in Jamalpur (Jabalpur) is the Institute on a Saturday when the Volunteer band is playing and the tennis courts are full and the babydom of Jamalpur—fat, sturdy children—frolic around the bandstand. The people dance ... they act, they play billiards, they study their newspapers, they play cards, everything, etc. They flirt in a sumptuous building and in hot weather, the gallant apprentice ducks his friends in the swimming bath. Decidedly the railway folk make their lives pleasant."

And Colleen Gantzer, a well-known Anglo-Indian writer, adds, "The Institute was the centre of their (Anglo-Indians') relaxing hours. The men to play billiards or tennis, the women to sit and gossip while the children played around

Top, middle, bottom and previous page (bottom): The Railway Institutes were the centre of Anglo-Indian lives in Railway colonies when they wanted to relax. Many of these Institutes still function in the same buildings whose maintenance varies from renovation to neglect or disuse. Seen here are Institutes in Madurai, Trichy, Agra and Rajamundhry (this one put to other use). (Photos: AITW; Rajamundhry from Glanister Waring)

them. Children were never left at home, not even when the Institute ran its Christmas and New Year Parties. They helped their parents decorate the 'Inster'... then sat giggling on the sidelines while their elders danced.[15]

15. In fact, many a child would take to the dance floor to dance with older siblings or parents or kinsfolk; dancing came natural to Anglo-Indians because they danced from the time they were children.

"Railway Society placed considerable stress on enjoying life without thinking of the future. Why think of the future? Why save? The railways looked after you and when you had to retire you got your Provident Fund and, hopefully, your sons would have joined the Railways and your daughters would have married good Railway men.

"Thus, the social life of the Inster was a very important part of growing up in a Railway colony. And so we went to dances and treasure hunts, and took part in the annual sports organised by the Inster and we learnt, almost instinctively, exactly where to draw the line. These codes of conduct were not enforced by any law makers or Council of Elders. They had evolved and were accepted by everyone as the done thing. Everyone knew what everyone else did: it was a strong, mutually-supportive society. Railway people enjoyed themselves because their society ensured that liberty never deteriorated to license. Your neighbour would not be allowed to harm you.

Both bottom: Call them Railway People or Railway Stock, but it was Anglo-Indian railwaymen like these (seen c. 1900) who kept the wheels of transport moving in India. (Photos: Dr. Beatrix D'Souza)

"But since Railway People had evolved these mores within the tightly structured society of the Railway Colony,

they found it very difficult to adjust to the outside world ...

"Railway People ... lived for the day, assured that the Railway would look after their tomorrows ... They lived life king-size because they had no aspirations outside their contentedly circumscribed lives.

"The Railway colony was a 'colony' in every way. It was a protected outpost of a unique civilisation dedicated to just one aim: to keep those great puffing monsters moving efficiently, uninterruptedly, swiftly..."

Keeping the trains moving is something every Railway Anglo-Indian took pride in. Crews would check-in for duty hours before their train was to leave to check their engine, ensure it was spick and span, that its brass or other metal fittings gleamed, that everything was in order.

He's the lord of all he surveys from the time he takes his train out from his 'home' loco shed. (Photo: Winston Ross)

And as they pulled out of 'home' stations, drivers would blow their own signals on the whistle to tell the families of the three who were the crew that they were on their way. On the journey back, as they neared base, the whistle with its special code would blow, announcing that they would be home in minutes and the pot should be kept on the boil.

Two such drivers, Johanns in 1956 and Percy Carroll of the Bombay Mail in 1994, were awarded the Ashoka Chakra for sacrificing their lives to save their passenger-packed trains.

When the National Forum of Anglo-Indian Associations in January 2003 flagged off the National Anglo-Indian Railway Convention to celebrate 150 years of the Indian Railways, it was the only Anglo-Indian association to organise such a big commemoration. It was a celebration that, during every minute of the two days, demonstrated the Anglo-Indian pride in their railway heritage even if most of them had moved out of the protected railway environment.

Bottom left: Marking 150 years of the Indian Railways, the National Forum of Anglo-Indian Associations organised a National Anglo-Indian Railway Convention in Chennai in January 2003. Dr. Beatrix D'Souza, M.P., one of the organisers, is seen delivering the welcome address at the inauguration. (Photo: Dr. Beatrix D'Souza)

There's been many an Anglo-Indian driver cited for exemplary courage. Percy Carroll was one and he was posthumously awarded the Ashoka Chakra. (Photo: AITW)

Herbert Hart, the legendary safety expert, and his wife Mavis who were honoured at the Convention to mark 150 years of the Indian Railways. (Photo: AITW)

Two things at this Convention in Madras demonstrated this pride to me more than anything else and left such an indelible impression that this book is the result. The two things, I recorded in the following words at the time under the heading 'The Hart of safety':

"The souvenir of the Convention was released by V. Anand, General Manager, Southern Railway and received by H.S. Hart, retired Commissioner of Railway Safety, Southern Region.

"Anand, recalling the era when he started his career with the East Indian Railways, retold the lesson that was drilled into every beginner. It went something like this: 'Make sure you don't break an axle (or whatever it was, he said). But if you break an axle, make sure you don't have to face an inquiry. But if you do have to face an inquiry, pray as fervently as you can that the inquiry will not be conducted by Mr. Hart!' Before coming South, Hart of the East Indian Railway, was with the Bengal-Nagpur Railway, at a time when Mughalsarai was the world's biggest marshalling yard, and there he was a legend in his lifetime, Anand related. Ensuring safe engines was his entire life, just as the Railways were an inextricable part of the life of almost every Anglo-Indian family from the 1850s.

"That singing was as much a part of Anglo-Indian life as the railways, I was reminded of that morning when the 150-or-so present burst spontaneously into the National

Saying farewell is Adrian Baldrey on his last run piloting a suburban electric loco in Bombay. (Photo: AITW)

Anthem at the end of the function. I haven't heard a more rousing rendition of *Jana Gana Mana* in a long time— and it was not accompanying a tape!" Yes, the Railway people were very special Indians.

Beyond Home-making

Almost all the fiction written about the Euro-Indians till recent years—when more Anglo-Indians have begun to write about their fellows than British and Indian writers—have tended to paint the Anglo-Indian woman—always young and beautiful—as a calculating, good-time girl with rather dubious morals whose only aim in life was to snare "a good catch". At best, such writing emphasised only her fun-loving nature, with dating and song and dance the centre of her life. Little recorded and less recognised have been the millions of Euro-Indian women who were the backbone of families and, as model home-makers, made the most out of little and raised God-fearing sons and daughters who grew up to lead stable lives no matter how modest the jobs they entered. Worship, a rare work ethic, integrity and family stability is what Anglo-Indian women passed down to their families from generation to generation.

There could be no finer example of such womanhood than Ethel Stracey whose story has already been told, but what needs to be re-emphasised here is the role she played as a home-maker and how she brought her brood up to help each other till they were all well settled.

Many an Anglo-Indian family had ayahs to help bring up their children and there's many an Anglo-Indian today who fondly remembers these care-givers as members of the family. (Photo: Pirkko O'Meara)

Many such Anglo-Indian women wore two hats, nurturing a home and working outside. There are generations of Indians and British, many of them eminent, from 1900 onward and perhaps even earlier, who owed much to Anglo-Indian 'Nannies' or governesses, teachers, nurses and, in later life, secretaries or personal assistants.

Indeed, till the 1960s, teaching in English-medium schools, nursing in civil and military hospitals, and being a Chief Executive's or Senior Manager's 'Girl Friday' in the leading business houses of the country were the domain of Anglo-Indian women. Their's was work that was not to win them awards or headlines, but as many an old-time manager, in firms like Parry's, Binny's, MacNeill MacGregor, Imperial (now India) Tobacco (which had the biggest contingent of Anglo-Indians), English Electric, Leyland's, Hindustan Lever, Mettur Beardsell, ICI, Best & Crompton, Yule's or Tata's and the foreign banks, still says, "We don't know what we would have done without them." They have also constituted the bulwark of the staff in many a diplomatic mission in the country.

"We don't know what we would have done without them," remembers many a senior executive in the Indian mercantile world. The reference is to secretaries like these seen in a Calcutta office. (Photo: AITW)

But long before all this there were Euro-Indian women who played significant roles in the lives of governors, statesmen and kings. Perhaps the earliest to leave her mark

on history was Hieronima de Paiva, the Portuguese-Indian wife of the leading diamond merchant in India when the Jews of Madras dominated the trade in the late 17th century. After her husband died, she inherited his fortune and then became the mistress of Governor Elihu Yale. She guided him through the trade and helped him become one of the richest men of the Europe of his time. A little bit of that fortune he gifted to a school in the colony of Connecticut and it became Yale College, then University.

Even earlier than the Paivas were the Madeiros or Madra family of San Thomé, a wealthy Portuguese-Indian family whose name, it is stated, was bequeathed to Madras. Antonia de Madeiros during the French occupation of Madras proved so loyal to the British that when the British regained Fort St. George, she was one of only two Catholics allowed to live in the Fort. In later years, whenever the Council of Fort St. George was in financial difficulties—as it was quite often—it would turn to her for a loan to tide the difficulties over. It was her house that became the home of the Governors of Madras Presidency when they moved out of the Fort.

Of the Antonia de Madeiros era was Jeanne Begum, a *metisse* from Pondicherry, whose imperial dreams led to an empire—but not a French one. Jeanne Albert married Jacques Vincens and they had eleven children by the time she was 33, when he died. She remained a beauty and married Joseph François Dupleix, the Governor of the French settlements in India, with whom she had had a long affair. Her knowledge of Indian politics spurred Dupleix into trying to establish a French Indian empire. Together they failed—and paid a heavy price on returning to France. But worse was the fact that they had spurred the British into proving that anything the French could do they could do better!

Another *metisse* beauty, this time from Tranquebar, was Catherine Worlee who went on to become Talleyrand's mistress, then wife, after she left her husband Georges-François Grand and moved to Paris. Her salons there remained famous long after she divorced the legendary French statesman.

Catherine Worlee Grand who became the Countess of Talleyrand and hosted the most famous salons in 18th century Paris. (Photo: Internet)

Anna Leonowens, the 'I' in The King and I, who went on to become a leading suffragette. (Photo: Internet)

A latter-day Anglo-Indian—a heritage she took pains to deny like many others who attained success—was Anna Leonowens, the 'I' of *The King and I*. Born in Ahmednagar to a British sergeant and an Anglo-Indian mother, she travelled a great deal before she was widowed in Penang. She then settled in Singapore where the King of Siam hired her in the 1860s to teach his children English. Her championing of women's rights and her influence with the King led to women's emancipation in Siam. When she left Siam in 1868 she went to Canada and was a well-known suffragette there till her death. Her sister Eliza was the grandmother of the famous actor Boris Karloff, which would have made him Anglo-Indian if he had been domiciled in India.

Of Anna Leonowen's generation were three Anglo-Indian women of whom almost nothing is known today and who are even less remembered. But they were pioneers in their field: medicine. Well-known is the story of Mary Ann Dacomb Scharlieb, an Englishwoman who, refused entry to medical college in England, was allowed to join Madras Medical College in 1875. After graduating, she was admitted for higher studies in London and, returning to Madras, helped found the first major hospital for women in India (in Madras) after which she went on to acquire an international reputation in medicine and a Damehood. What is hardly mentioned is the fact that Scharlieb was joined in that first class to admit women—whom at least one Professor refused to teach or communicate with on his rounds—by three Anglo-Indian girls, the Misses White, Beale and Mitchell. The first two got First Classes, like Scharlieb, but more significantly White topped the class! There have been several Anglo-Indian women after them who became doctors. But in 1878 White, Beale and Mitchell were not only the first Anglo-Indian women doctors but also among the first women doctors in the world, only a couple in the U.S. preceding them by a few years.

One Anglo-Indian woman doctor I'll never forget is Dr. Iverts, who was in charge of a large rural Government maternity hospital and who for years delivered the rich and the poor but who remained isolated in her little home in the hospital campus, respected, acknowledged and remembered by all in the villages around but with none to call a friend. That's dedication for you.

Most Anglo-Indian women achievers of later generations made names for themselves in the more conventional occupations women of the community took to. The field of education brought several of them into the limelight. Amongst them were four who went further than most.

Anglo-Indian experts in Australian Literature with the Australian High Commissioner in India, Penny Wensley, at a conference in Madras. Dr. Beatrix D'Souza, an Anglo-Indian community leader and former Head of the English Department, Presidency College, Madras (second from right) and Prof. Eugenie Pinto, former Principal of Queen Mary's College, Madras (extreme right), are seen together with Dr. C.T. Indra, former Head of the Department of English, University of Madras. (Photo: University of Madras)

Beatrix D'Souza was the first woman (and till date the only person) from Madras to represent the community in Parliament. She was nominated to the 12th (1998-1999) and 13th Lok Sabha (1999-2004). She had earlier represented the Anglo-Indians in the Tamil Nadu Assembly (1991-96) and was the first Anglo-Indian Chairperson of the State's Minorities Commission. She was also a member of the State Commission for Women. But generations of students remember Dr. D'Souza as Professor and Head of the English Department of Presidency College, Madras, one of the first three colleges in India and the nucleus of the University of Madras, where she was recognised as an authority on Commonwealth Literature, particularly Australian writing.

A fellow Australian literature specialist, and also in Government Service, was Prof. Eugenie Pinto. She was the first Anglo-Indian to be appointed Principal of Queen Mary's College, Madras, the third oldest women's college in India. She was also a member of the State Commission for Women for two terms. Two other Anglo-Indian women who made a mark in Government Service as Professors were Yolande Satur and Dr. Anne Mary Fernandez of Tiruchchirappalli. Satur was the first Anglo-Indian in Government Service to be made principal of a college. Anne Mary Fernandez was the first woman to be appointed Registrar of the University of Madras (2003-06). She later became Registrar of Karunya University, Coimbatore.

Dr. Anne Mary Fernandez, the first woman Registrar of the University of Madras, one of the three universities first founded in India (in 1857). (Photo: University of Madras)

Dr. Daphne de Rebello, a pioneering woman in the Indian Administrative Service, and an internationally known educationist. (Photo: Internet)

Bottom right: *Sister Marisa of Calcutta committed to providing a sound education to underprivileged Anglo-Indian children. (Photo: AITW)*

Many an Anglo-Indian girl became a nurse and Indian medicare welcomed them. There are only two non-Anglo-Indians among this team of eight nurses in a district hospital. (Photo: Pirkko O'Meara)

Another outstanding contributor to education but not an academician is Dr. Daphne de Rebello, the first woman Indian Administrative Service officer in Andhra Pradesh and the first Anglo-Indian woman to qualify for the service. She's served in the Government of India's Department of Education, at UNESCO Headquarters in Paris, and with the Administrative College of India. Besides her PhD from Stanford (U.S.) in Comparative Education, she is also highly qualified from the Trinity College of Music, London.

Educational contribution of another kind was from Marisa Robert of Calcutta who, as Sister Marisa of the Carmelites, opened a school to provide an education particularly for disadvantaged Anglo-Indian children. Over 2000 Anglo-Indian children had benefitted from her Marian Education Centre.

In another occupation that Anglo-Indian women favoured, hundreds of them became Matrons of large government and private hospitals from Peshawar to Madurai. But it was in the military nursing service that they gained signal recognition.

Lt. Col. Florence (Flora) Watkins did distinguished service during World War II and in the 1962 and 1965 Wars. She received what were then the two highest awards for nursing, the Royal Red Cross Associate and the International

Lt. Col Florence Watkins, a military nursing officer with a distinguished record of wartime service. (Photo: AITW)

Top left: Successful careers in Nursing and in the Madhya Pradesh Legislative Assembly being over, Florence (Flora) Watkins has had a fulfilling retirement culminating in her being felicitated by distinguished community and military leaders on her 100th birthday shortly before this book went to press. (Photo: Dr. Charles Dias)

Florence Nightingale Medal for her devotion to duty in the Shillong Hospital during the 1962 Chinese incursion. In retirement, she served two terms as a nominated member representing the Anglo-Indians in the Madhya Pradesh Assembly. As these lines were written Florence Watkins celebrated her 100th birthday, with the Army and the Madhya Pradesh Government honouring her at a grand public function in Jabalpur.

Brigadier Dulcie Zscherpel was Matron-in-Chief in the Indian Military Nursing Service in the 1960s, and in 1992 Patna-born Major General Veronica Game was appointed Additional Director General of the Indian Military Nursing Service, today one of the largest military nursing units in the world. Game retired in 1994 after a career during which she was awarded several medals for distinguished service, which included attaining expertise in orthopaedic nursing.

Bemedalled Major General Veronica Game who reached the highest rank in the Military Nursing Service. (Photo: AITW)

A nurse of another era was Helen Rodriguez of Bangalore and Ooty who was the only Indian woman to be awarded the George Medal, the civilian's Victoria Cross. She was the Matron of the Taunggyi Civil Hospital in Burma and refused to leave her post when the Japanese over-ran the country during World War II. She stayed on at the hospital nursing hundreds of the wounded—and even

Helen Rodriguez
who was awarded
the George Medal for
devotion to duty as
much as for heroism
in Japanese-occupied
Burma during
World War II.
(Photo: Internet)

Right: At one time most
air hostesses on air
carriers in India were
Anglo-Indian girls like
this one. It is still a
favoured profession in
the community. (Photo:
Press clippings)

One of those
outstanding air
hostesses was Gloria
Berry of Air India who
was posthumously
awarded the Ashoka
Chakra in 1956 for
courageous behaviour
and devotion to duty
out of the ordinary.
(Photo: AITW)

performing minor operations—till the Japanese forced her to move to the Rangoon Civil Hospital where she was the only one qualified to minister to even more of the wounded, helped only by forcibly recruited aides with no hospital experience at all.

The first Anglo-Indian woman to win an equivalent Indian medal—the Ashoka Chakra—was 20-year-old air hostess (another profession Anglo-Indian women favour) Gloria Berry who died when Air India's *Kashmir Princess* was sabotaged on a flight between Hong Kong and Djakarta. The surviving crew members attested to her courageous actions during the last minutes of the fateful flight. She was the first Anglo-Indian woman to win this prestigious award.

Another field Anglo-Indian women are making their way in is a comparatively new one in India, Communications. And here again there are Anglo-Indians who are high achievers.

Zelma Lazarus from Rajasthan was the first Asian woman to be elected President of the International Public Relations Association. She had worked for 30 years as the Secretary to the head of the Tata company, Voltas, and also

served as General Manager, Corporate Relations, of the Company. After retirement she threw herself into NGO activities and was instrumental in developing the first Braille typewriter to be manufactured in India. But her biggest contribution was as CEO of Impact India Foundation which set up *Lifeline Express*, the world's first hospital on rails. *Lifeline Express* takes modern healthcare to the small towns and villages of India where no medical facilities exist and in nearly 20 years has conducted over 600,000 surgeries. Over one million people have benefited from the services it offers free.

Jennifer (Suares) Arul of Madras is one of the best known faces on Indian television and has also set up news and information channels in Indonesia and Malaysia. She was Bureau Chief in South India for New Delhi Television Ltd., one of India's premier television channels, for over 20 years and has covered major stories in many countries on the Indian Ocean rim. Alice Suares, Jennifer's grandmother, was nominated three times to represent the community as an MLA in the Tamil Nadu Assembly. She also served as Inspectress of Anglo-Indian Schools. She received a gold medal from the King Emperor, for sending her husband and four sons to serve as officers in the Armed Forces in World War II.

Calcutta-born Linda Brady Hawke was Executive Assistant to the CEOs of many multinational companies in Madras, then worked for several international ad agencies before setting up L.B. Associates, a magazine publishing house that brings out *Diplomatist, Creature Companions* (a magazine on pets), and *People and Management*, all of which she edits.

If Zelma Lazarus and Linda Hawke went on to other achievements from a field that Anglo-Indian women had made their own from between the Wars till the 1950s, many others have remained in it and been successful private secretaries, personal assistants, executive assistants, whatever the designations be, to the CEOs of almost all of India's leading corporates. Ever since the bi-annual best secretary competitions started on a national level over twenty years ago, Anglo-Indian women have won the title or finished as runners-up over a dozen times. The very first contest in 1987 was won by Philomena Eaton of Calcutta who was 50-years-old at the time and took part out of curiosity. Eaton headed the team that organised the 9th International Anglo-Indian Reunion in Kolkata in January 2013. Cheryl Millet and Sandra Smith of Madras took the top honours in 1989 and 2004 respectively. Many other Anglo-Indian women have been runners-up in this competition. The National Institute

Jennifer Arul, the voice in the South on one of the most successful television channels in India, NDTV. (Photo: AITW)

Top: From being a secretary to being elected head of the International Public Relations Association, Zelma Lazarus went on in retirement to serve the public, particularly when she started the Lifeline Express, a hospital on wheels to help rural areas. (Photo: AITW)

Bottom: Another successful secretary, Linda Hawke, who went to become an executive assistant to CEOs in the mercantile world and then became a magazine publisher. (Photo: Internet)

Sandra Smith, Best Secretary of the Year in 2004. (Photo: AITW)

Top right: The first winner of the Best Secretary competition, Philomena Eaton, headed the team that organised the 9th International Anglo-Indian Reunion that was held in Kolkata in January 2013. Here she announces the plans for the Reunion with the President-in-Chief of the All-India Anglo-Indian Association, Neil O'Brien, on her left and Dr. Charles Dias, Anglo-Indian representative in Parliament, on the extreme right. (Photo: Dr. Charles Dias)

of Professional Secretaries (now IASAP) which, among other things, organises these contests, was started by a group of secretaries led by Zelma Lazarus (1970-74). In later years, Phil White (1984-85) and Betty Kent (1999-2001) served as chairpersons. There have been several Anglo-Indian women who have been leaders at the regional level and winners of the contests held before the final.

Among Anglo-Indian women who have made a mark abroad are Hyderabad-born Senator Christabel Chamarette (sometimes Christabel Bridge), who was a Greens Senator for Western Australia from 1992 to 1996, Lucknow-born June D' Rozario and Anne Warner. D'Rozario was a Labour member in Australia's Northern Territory Legislative Assembly from 1977 to 1983. She is an urban planner who has served as a Commissioner of the Australian Heritage Commission. Warner was a Labour Member of the Queensland Legislative Assembly and Minister for Family Services and Aboriginal and Islander Affairs in the Goss Government (1989-95). She was the first woman in the Labour Party of Australia to hold a ministerial portfolio. She retired from politics in 1995.

Certainly Anglo-Indian woman have done far more than rock the cradles and instil values in their families.

Right all: Anglo-Indian women who have been successes in Australian politics supporting the Greens, Heritage and the Aborigines include Christabel Chamarette, June D'Rozario and Anne Warner. (Photos: Internet)

Search for a Homeland

The 'Railway colony' mentality of the Anglo-Indians pre-Independence spread way beyond railway junctions and railway towns. In almost every urban area where Anglo-Indians lived they tended to live in little enclaves that were their own, usually not far from a large railway facility. Familiar as I am with Madras and Bangalore, I'd cite such localities as Royapuram, Perambur and St. Thomas' Mount-Pallavaram, which is not far from Tambaram and near a cantonment, and Cox Town, Richmond Town, etc., in Bangalore Cantonment. Going beyond even such Anglo-Indian localities, you would find the aged and poor Anglo-Indians in such 'colonies' as the Friend-in-Need Society homes in Madras and

Residents of the Friends-in-Need Society, Chennai, keep fit with a trainer putting them through their paces daily. (Photo: Internet)

Bow Barracks, inexpensive accommodation created for less privileged Anglo-Indians in Kolkata. (Photo: AITW)

Bow Barracks in Calcutta. Such 'protected' enclaves, nurturing a traditional lifestyle, were not too different from the Brahmin *agraharams* of South India that flourished till the 1960s and which can still be occasionally found.

Given this background and a lifestyle they were reluctant to give up, it was no wonder that Anglo-Indians in the early 20th century began to look for a 'homeland', a 'province' or a 'state' or even a newly-created town they could call their own, away from the British, who looked down upon them unless there was a need for them to answer a call to arms or to supervise the 'natives', and from the Indians who considered them not only lackeys of the British but, worse, in a caste-conscious society, 'outcasts'.

As Blair Williams, an Anglo-Indian engineer who lives in New Jersey, U.S.A., and who did a recent study of the community, states, "Throughout their history they tried to assimilate into the English mainstream, but the English rejected them. The Anglo-Indians (on the other hand) did not accept their Indian heritage, tending to look down on Indians of other communities. This approach of theirs caused Indian communities to resent them and in turn isolated them from the rest of India. And so the Community lived for over two hundred years of British rule not being accepted by either the British or the Indians."

A homeland, therefore, seemed so attractive.

Passing mention has already been made of David White's attempt in the 1880s to establish an Anglo-Indian township near Bangalore and which became known as Whitefield. It was a new settlement that met with some success, particularly with the demand for a skilled workforce in a Bangalore that began slowly industrialising in the public sector from the 1930s. But World War II and the out-migration of the 1950s and '60s virtually emptied Whitefield—though a few of the early families still remain.

Whitefield goes back to April 27, 1882 when the Maharaja of Mysore granted the Eurasian and Anglo-Indian Association of Mysore and Coorg nearly 4000 acres of land for an agricultural settlement in Mysore State, a little east of British Bangalore. The Association was headed by David E.S. White of Madras and was 170 strong at the time.

Whitefield's Anglican, Memorial Church, 120 years old (Photo: Internet)

Starting with 45 families by 1900, the numbers slowly increased and in 1905 the Whitefield Settlers' and Residents' Association was formed. This helped further settlement and, by 1907, 120 Anglo-Indian families had put down roots to be followed by scores of other Anglo-Indian families from the Kolar Gold Fields 50 km to the east. While their families established themselves in Whitefield, the men commuted daily to the KGF by train.

Whitefield legend has it that in the early days of the settlement the young Winston Churchill courted Rose Hamilton, the daughter of the James Hamiltons who ran the only hostelry in town, the *Waverly Inn*. *Waverly* as a garden house still exists. As do some of the homes of the settlers and even some of their descendants. But this Whitefield is quite a contrast to what was once farmland.

Whitefield has today developed as a satellite town of booming Bangalore with the IT industry setting up shop in this once-sleepy suburb in a big way and American-style gated communities for those who work in the industry burgeoning in it. Here, the Anglo-Indian presence is once more to be seen—wherever English is in demand. But it is a much more cosmopolitian Anglo-Indian, one far removed from the 'colonies'.

Not long after Whitefield began putting down roots, a similar settlement was established in the foothills of the Himalaya. John Harold Abbott, a successful land developer in Jhansi, founded Abbott Mount in Lohagar in what is now Uttarakhand, close to the Nepal border, for the "Domiciled European Community". On a spacious estate he built homes for retirees from the community, but shortly before his death there were only a few rent-paying tenants and no prospective buyers. He called it "a white elephant" and lamented, "Everything else I have touched has turned to gold, but Abbott Mount has been my only failure." Today, it is a modest tourist resort.

Other Whitefield-like settlements, but on a smaller scale, included Magra (Clement Town) near Dehradun and Kharagpur in West Bengal.

Referred to earlier has been the Gidney-blessed suggestion by a Bombay Anglo-Indian that island settlements be established in the Andamans and Nicobars. This was a dream of William Edmond Thomson, an elder of the Bombay Anglo-Indian Association, in the 1920s. But this was quickly snuffed out by the climatic conditions and the terrain, which were found unsuitable by a 'recce' party led by an Anglo-Indian civil servant, Norris Cummings. Anglo-Indians, it would appear, were no longer the pioneers they had been in such strenuous activity as railway-building, forest-clearing, land-surveying, and irrigation-developing; the Andamans and Nicobars were found to be a bit overwhelming for those who had got urbanised. There is an unsubstantiated report that, at Independence, Nehru offered the Anglo-Indians a settlement of their own in the Nicobars, long ago a Danish settlement. But once again they decided to have nothing to do with it.

Far more significant than these ventures has been McCluskiegunj, described as "the only Anglo-Indian town" in India and now being promoted as a tourist destination by the Jharkhand State Government. The dying town, now being given new life, takes its name from Ernest Timothy McCluskie, a real estate agent in Calcutta, who wanted to develop a territory the Anglo-Indians could call their own.

E.T. McCluskie of Calcutta, founder of McCluskiegunj. (Photo: AITW)

In 1933, McCluskie founded the Colonisation Society of India and got a local rajah (in what was then Bihar) to grant the Society 10,000 acres of land for an agricultural settlement. The land, which included the tribal villages of Harhu, Duli, Ramdagga, Konka, Lapra, Hesalong, Mayapur, Mahulia and Baseria, was granted with the proviso that already tenanted land could not be encroached on and that settlement could not include ownership of rivers, lakes and hills.

McCluskie sent out letters of invitation to 200,000 Anglo-Indians and by 1943 four hundred Anglo-Indian families had settled in McCluskiegunj after buying shares in the Company the Society had transformed itself into. But with the money necessary to buy land only in the hands of the elderly, it was only older persons, and their children who had been unable to get work in the usual public services that Anglo-Indians got employment in, who settled in McCluskiegunj; the new settlement did not receive an Anglo-Indian population that could ensure the growth of prosperity. But with the fertile soil and their propensity for hard work, the new settlers did develop McCluskiegunj in the 1940s into a town with more facilities than Ranchi, today's capital, 40 miles to the southeast. European style homes, St. John's Church, a club, record stores, cosmetic shops, a bakery, a butchery, a cobbler and provision stores, a school and playground facilities were all established—and the Railways made the town a stop, giving it a railway station. The club would be busy with the Anglo-Indians crowding it, watching plays, dancing, playing Housie or just partying—in fancy dress or otherwise. An

Alfred de Rozario (right), who has been breathing new life into McCluskiegunj with a residential school, restoration of old homes and creating new facilities, the ground-breaking for one of them here being blessed by a priest. (Photo: AITW)

Anglo-Indian Society was formed and still survives. The town even warranted a visit from the Governor of Bihar, Sir Maurice Hallett, before Independence.

Unfortunately, World War II took away most of the able-bodied and decline began to set in. Most of the rest began to emigrate in the 1950s and 1960s from a town that seemed to be dying. Today, there are only around 20 Anglo-Indian families left. But they are beginning to see a bit of a turnaround. Meeting the needs of a small hill station with an equable climate on the Chotanagpur Plateau, some of the homes have become guesthouses. And with Alfred de Rozario, an Anglo-Indian, establishing a boarding branch of Patna's Don Bosco Academy in the town, almost all the houses offer hostel accommodation for the students. It will never again be 'an Anglo-Indian town', but McCluskiegunj is all set to survive with its history well remembered.

Today, the search for a homeland is over. The Anglo-Indian wherever he is has integrated with local communities. But in India, the Anglo-Indian identity survives strong, Anglo-Indians seeing themselves as one more distinct community in the mosaic that is India.

A pictorial portfolio of McCluskiegunj

Past

The first step towards settling in McCluskiegunj was to set up camp as temporary living quarters. This was the Woods' encampment, shared by the Woods, the Ballantynes, Russel, Mahoney and Switzer.

The Woods' bullock cart, essential for carrying materials, equipment and people.

The Woods' cottage comes up in its basic form.

Top right: *Stores got established in due course, like Rogers' Family Stores seen here.*

Bottom and right: *The basic cottages developed into pukka homes like these over the years.*

Anglo-Indian 'farmgirls' tend the cattle.

Left and bottom: *As McCluskiegunj developed, a resthouse was raised. In front of it is the E.T. McCluskie Memorial obelisk unveiled in 1934 and a fountain, both still surviving.*

Right: Experimental agriculture begins under the eye of the colony's Agricultural Superintendent and his team. Here S.A. Bower experiments with cultivating both castor and groundnut simultaneously.

Centre right: As a settler puts down roots, work on his farm begins. Here young Glaskin ploughs the soil in India's time-honoured fashion.

Bottom: The resthouse often served as the McCluskiegunj 'Institute' and this picture of merry-makers at the 1937 Fancy Dress New Year's Ball was taken in front of it.

Left: The Club had a sports ground that was much in use. Here Sir Henry Gidney bats during a Visitors vs. Settlers cricket match.

Centre left: In time, the Gidney Club was established and extensions to it, from time to time, were undertaken by members often offering their muscle.

Bottom left: With the settlement well established by the 1940s it was time for the Governor of Bihar, Sir Maurice Hallett, to visit it.

As in every Anglo-Indian colony in pre-Independence days the members volunteered for service in the A.F.(I) detachment. McCluskiegunj was no different.

Present

A well-kept house with a well-maintained garden. (Photo: Paul Harris)

Several Anglo-Indian houses in the settlement are in this sad state, but some of them are being renovated by new owners. (Photo: Paul Harris)

It's called the 'Doll's House' and is still occupied though in need of improvements. (Photo: AITW)

A house in modest condition midst a large acreage which was once fed by a well. (Photo: Paul Harris)

Another well-maintained house but now used as the Don Bosco Primary School. (Photo: AITW)

McCluskiegunj's Protestant church, St. John's, which was built in 1940 and needs attention. (Photo: AITW)

Dennis Meredith with his daughter Karen, happy to be in McCluskiegunj and see a slow revival of the town. (Photo: AITW)

PART II

Writing a second 'Author's Note' for a book is unusual practice. But as this part of the book deals with the signal contributions Anglo-Indians have made to India and countries abroad, an explanation is necessary, in the light of the history of the community already related, of who are considered Anglo-Indians in the pages that follow.

If a person or a family has, over the years, acknowledged being Anglo-Indian, then there are no problems. Nor if recognised biographies indicate an Indian maternal forebear and a European paternal one. And they are the majority in this part of the book.

But over the years many have considered themselves Domiciled Europeans and, as I have already related, there still exist 'Europeans' who see themselves as being apart from Anglo-Indians. The Constitution of India, drawing from earlier enactments, however, sees them as Anglo-Indians and so they shall be considered as such, be they long settled in India in the dim past or a more recent post-1857 period. Anglo-Indians by this definition, if they are migrants to other countries, are also included here, upto the first generation, that is, the children born to migrant parents either in India or abroad.

There are, however, several achievers who have been listed, particularly by Anglo-Indian writers, as Anglo-Indian on the basis only of their having been born in India. But was the paternal line long settled in India, or was it temporarily settled here? With no solid evidence to meet the residential qualifications of the Constitutional definition, I have *italicised* their names to indicate an element of doubt.

While those I've *italicised* have India as their place of birth, there are several others found in published lists of Anglo-Indians but with no evidence of any Indian residential connection. They could have been born to European (particularly British) fathers and Indian/Anglo-Indian mothers domiciled abroad or they could be descendants of those generations of Anglo-Indian children sent back to Britain in the 17th and 18th centuries and who never came back to India, getting merged with the British population. The permanent residential qualifications writ in the Constitutional definition compel me to add them once again in *italics*, but only as footnotes to Anglo-Indian history, provided there are indications of an Indian maternal connection.

Others in such lists could also have descended from birth during a little remembered piece of history. From the late 17th century, thousands of Indian sailors (lascars), and domestic workers brought back by their British masters, made Britain their home. By the middle of the 19th century there were an estimated 40,000 Indians living in Britain. This was to increase to around 70,000 by the end of the century, when the numbers were increased by the arrival of students and wealthy Indians. The Great War had nearly 150,000 Indian troops serving in Britain and France (from where they were sent to Britain for rest and recuperation). Thousands of children were born of the liaisons/marriages between these Indian settlers/temporary residents in Britain and British women, accounting for a large mixed population. These Indo-British children would have later contributed an Indian lineage in many a British family, making such families, strictly speaking, Euro-Asian, but certainly not Anglo-Indian, having as they did, no Indian residential qualifications. These Euro-Asians have no place in this book.

I appreciate there could be some debate on these decisions of mine, but I felt gilding the lily was not needed by a community which has contributed so much to India that it can be proud of. It's a record that needs no embellishment. I also appreciate there could be many more listed in these chapters, but to trace them, their antecedents, and their records would take a lifetime. So, this may well be a limited selection. But it includes a host of Anglo-Indians the community, nay, India, should be proud of.

S. MUTHIAH

Serving the Flag

The Euro-Indians have served many flags. And every one of them with honour. And valour.

Theirs is a saga that begins with the *topasses* who served their fathers in the defence of Portuguese India from the 16th century. Later, *topasses* served the Dutch, the French and the English East India Companies. From the first days of Madras in the 1640s and for the next hundred years, till the first regiments of the Indian Army were raised in Fort St. David, Cuddalore, by Major Stringer Lawrence, 'Father of the Indian Army' and mentor of Robert Clive, the *topasses* were the bulk of John Company's militia, the leavening agents for the small British contingent drawn in the early days from the retired soldiers who had spent their days in the taverns of London and were brought out to serve in Madras, Bombay, Calcutta and the smaller factories (trading settlements). Many of the officers of the *topasses* were Euro-Indians.

It was only after the French takeover of Fort St. George (Madras) in 1746 and the English retreat to Fort St. David that John Company began to raise an Indian Army, to supplement its European (and Euro-Indian) militia and the occasional Royal regiment from Britain. This expansion of the British military forces after the restoration of Fort St. George in 1749 was to provide many an Euro-Indian—in the more British-specific context, Anglo-Indian—the opportunity of leadership and a path to glory. Many others, capitalising on their experience built on the foundations Stringer Lawrence laid, offered leadership to the forces of the numerous kingdoms of a fragmented India at war with each other. Few reached the higher levels of leadership in the Company's and the Crown's armies in India, but several raised regiments that may have been swords-for-hire but are today proud regiments of the Indian Army.

Two of the earliest to make their mark in the Company's armies were *Lt. Gen. Sir Richard Jones*, who led the Bombay Army in 1808-1809, and *Maj. Gen. Robert Stevenson* of the Bengal Army who in 1833 was in command in Cawnpore and the next year led his forces against the Rajput kingdoms. Little is known about their lineage but for passing references to them being Anglo-Indian.

Better known for the regiments they raised and the survival of the lineage to this day in India are *William Gardner*, James Skinner and Hyder Jung (Young) Hearsey. Gardner, an American-born Colonial, settled in India and married into the Cambay nobility. Disillusioned with service in the Company, be became a military adventurer till 1809 when he rejoined the British on being asked to raise a corps of cavalry. Gardner's Horse—now an armoured regiment— had a distinguished record in several wars, but its home base is Khasgunj, near Agra, where Gardner's estate is still home to his descendants.

James Skinner, son of a Scot and a Rajput mother, was Sikander Sahib to the 3000 men he raised as a much-feared irregular cavalry unit, "The Yellow Boys". Skinner's Horse, a famed armoured regiment today, fought for Gwalior and then, from 1803, for the British, but it was 1828 before he was given a British rank, Lieutenant Colonel. He had a palatial home in Delhi near which he built St. James' Church, still a landmark. But the family's estates are in Hansi. A descendant, Col. Michael Skinner, commanded Skinner's Horse from 1960 to 1966.

The legendary Col. James Skinner, who raised Skinner's Horse. (Photo: Internet)

Born into the Hearseys who had served in India from the early 18th century was Hyder Jung (Young) Hearsey, son of an English father and a Jat mother. Disillusioned with the Company's army, he became a freebooter and served Gwalior as well as George Thomas, another freebooter who founded Haryana. By the time he was 21, Hyder Hearsey had carved himself out a principality, raised an army of five thousand and married into the Cambay nobility. In 1903, he offered his regiments to the British. An explorer, he traced the Ganges from Haridwar to Gangotri and went with Moorcroft into Western Tibet and reached Lake Mansarovar. A kinsman, Major General John Hearsey, was officer commanding at Barrackpore in 1857 when Mangal Pandey fired the first shot of the Great Indian Revolt. John Hearsey, who had earlier dealt with rebellious troops in Wazirabad, is believed to have played a major role in influencing Canning's policy of clemency.

Calcutta-born Col. Henry Forster in 1835 raised the Shekhawati Brigade for the Company to quell recalcitrant Rajput principalities. His son, William Robert Forster, also served in the Brigade which later became what it is today, 13th Rajputs.

Of a slightly later era was Robert Warburton, whose mother was Afghan. After distinguished military service in Afghanistan, he was in 1879 put in charge of keeping the Khyber Pass open and during the decade he was there he raised the Khyber Rifles, a famed paramilitary force that today is a part of Pakistan's Frontier Corps.

Sir Robert Warburton who raised the Khyber Rifles on the North West Frontier. (Photo: Internet)

The Afghan wars are what made the reputation of *Lord Frederick Roberts* of Kandahar. His father, *General Sir Abraham Roberts*, who had fought along the North West Frontier and beaten a track his two sons were to follow, is said to have had a maternal ancestor who was Indian. Abraham Robert's first wife was East Indian and his second was British. It was the latter who was the mother of the man who was to become the Commander-in-Chief of the British Army and a Field Marshal. But if ever there was a family that was Domiciled European, it was the Roberts. For generations members of the Roberts family lived and served in India. Cawnpore-born *Frederick Roberts*, who won a Victoria Cross (1858) during the Great Revolt, was perhaps the first Anglo-Indian to be awarded Britain's highest medal for valour. His step-brother, born to an East Indian mother, Major General George Ricketts Roberts, served with the Bengal Staff Corps.

Top: Col. Henry Forster who raised the Shekhawati Brigade. (Photo: Internet)

Lord Roberts of Kandahar who won the Victoria Cross and rose to become Field Marshal and military head of the British Army. (Photo: Internet)

Another Victoria Cross winner around this period, Gujarat-born Andrew Fitzgibbon, was the youngest to win it. He was a little over 15 years old and a field medic when

he was awarded the medal in 1860 for valour in action in China during the Second Opium War.

Victoria Cross winners during the Great War (1914-18) were Darjeeling-born Reginald Warneford of the Royal Navy Air Service and Coorg-born *William Leefe Robinson*. Warneford, who was the first to shoot down a German Zeppelin over Belgium (May 7, 1915), has a street named after him in Ghent. He was also awarded the Croix de Guerre by France. Robinson, the son of proprietary coffee planters, was a pilot with the Royal Flying Corps when he shot down the first German airship over London (September 2, 1916).

New Delhi-born *Leslie Manser* and Simla-born *Guy Gibson* were awarded Victoria Crosses duing World War II. Manser, after piloting a bomber during the first 1000-bomber raid of the War—Cologne the target on May 30, 1942—sacrificed his life on the way back while enabling his crew to parachute to safety after his aircraft was badly hit. Gibson, who led the 'Dambusters' on May 16, 1943 against the Mohne and Eder Dams in the Ruhr, was considered a

William Leefe Robinson of the Royal Flying Corps who during the Great War won both the Victoria Cross and the Croix de Guerre. (Photo: Internet)

Master Bomber. He was also awarded the Legion of Merit by the U.S. His mother is reported as having been an Anglo-Indian from Bangalore.

The Indian Air Force has been the favourite service of Anglo-Indians from the time Maurice Barker of Bangalore joined it on March 11, 1941 as its first Anglo-Indian recruit. The first of eight Anglo-Indians to reach Air Vice-Marshal rank, he played a significant role in the Bangladesh War. He was, in turn, AOC-in-C Central Command, Eastern Command and Training Command. Another to play an active role in the Bangladesh War was Malcolm Wollen of Bangalore who retired as AOC-in-C Western Command. After retirement, he was chairman of Hindustan Aeronautics Ltd. from 1984 to 1988. A third Anglo-Indian IAF officer associated with Bangladesh was Douglas King-Lee, who was for five years Defence Attaché in that new nation India helped to deliver. King-Lee served as Commandant, National Defence College, and retired as AOC-in-C Eastern Command. He's another airman who retired to Bangalore.

Other Anglo-Indian Air Vice-Marshals of the Indian Air Force were Cecil Parker, Denzil Keelor, J.J. Bouche, J. Greene, K.D.K. Lewis, Sherwin Tully, and Michael

Guy Gibson, the World War II 'Dambuster' and another winner of the Victoria Cross. (Photo: Internet)

Left: Air Vice-Marshal Malcolm Wollen who became Chairman of Hindustan Aeronautics Ltd. (Photo: AITW)

Air Vice-Marshal Maurice Barker, the first Anglo-Indian to join the Royal Indian Air Force. (Photo: Internet)

Air Chief Marshal Denis La Fontaine, the first Anglo-Indian to head the Indian Air Force. He is seen here (right) meeting the head of the United States Air Force. (Photo: AITW)

Bottom both: *The Keelor brothers, the 'Sabre-killers'. Denzil the elder (on top) and Trevor the younger (below) (Photos: Internet)*

McMahon who became Vice Chief of Air Staff 2003-04. But one who went further than them all was Madras-born Denis La Fontaine who became the first Anglo-Indian to head the Indian Air Force. Air Chief Marshal La Fontaine headed the Air Force from 1985 to 1988, moving up from being AOC-in-C Western Command. Gujarat-born Parker built up an enviable record in the Western Sector during the 1971 War. He was awarded the Mahavir Chakra. An earlier (1965) winner of the same gallantry award was Wing Commander Jim Goodman from Guntakal.

Both Keelor brothers, Denzil the elder and Trevor, had the unique distinction of two brothers each shooting down a Pakistan Sabre fighter for which they earned the Vir Chakra. Trevor Keelor's feat was in 1965, making him the first Indian to bring down a Pakistan aircraft. Denzil Keelor in retirement served in the Ministry of Civil Aviation as Advisor and set up the Flight Inspection system. He was President of the YMCA in India for ten years, chairs Special Olympics Bharat and has served as Chairman/Director of a number of other NGOs as well as companies.

John Bouche flew with the Indian Air Force's first Spitfire squadron (in Burma) during World War II and his brother, Air Commodore David Bouche, started the IAF's first night fighter squadron and later headed the Air Crew Examining Board. McMahon, who served in the IAF for 42 years and fought in all of India's wars against Pakistan, was, after retirement, a Director of Blue Dart Aviation and Aero Space India Infra Ltd.

Johnny Greene was AOC-in-C South Western Command. He was, like the Keelor brothers, a vanquisher of Sabres. Keith Lewis was another with an excellent war record but is better recalled for, in retirement, surrendering all his medals—22 in number—in 2009 as an expression of support for ex-servicemen seeking pension parity.

Air Vice-Marshal Michael O'Brian of the Pakistan Air Force. (Photo: Internet)

There were also several Anglo-Indians who served in the Pakistan Air Force, three of them reaching Air Vice-Marshal rank: Eric Hall, Michael O'Brian and Steve Joseph. The first two also served as Deputy Chiefs of Air Staff. And O'Brian was the first Air Force Officer to serve as Commandant of Pakistan's National Defence College. Several other Anglo-Indians in both countries reached high rank in the respective air forces and won numerous decorations for gallantry and outstanding service. Their recognition in terms of proportion could well be the highest of any community.

A rather telling story of pilots in the two warring air forces immediately after Independence is told by Derek O'Brien of Kolkata. A cousin of his father, the daughter of an O'Brien who had stayed on in Lahore, had married an Indian Air Force pilot. Her brother-in-law was with the Pakistan Air Force. The two men had been comrades in the same air force a few weeks earlier but could well have been firing at each other during the hostilities immediately after Independence, given the small size of the two air forces in those days. Fortunately neither died in action. O'Brien goes on to relate that, when he visited Pakistan in 1984, he found a Muslim Anglo-Indian clan of 'O'Briens'.

The Army, on the other hand, has long had the largest number of Anglo-Indians serving in it, particularly as volunteers during the two World Wars. Several thousands volunteered for service during the Great War and there was even an all-Anglo-Indian battalion that distinguished itself at the siege of Kut (Mesopotamia/Iraq). Most of these volunteers had had some military training, for service in the Auxiliary Force (India)—a paramilitary unit—was compulsory for Anglo-Indian railwaymen, who were joined by many other Anglo-Indians from other government departments. During World War II, the Women's Auxiliary Corps (India) and other women's service units played a significant role by freeing thousands of men for active service rather than tying

them down to backroom and headquarters duties. About 80 per cent of the women in WAC (I) and other service units in India were Anglo-Indian and their contribution earned them high commendation.

Amongst the Anglo-Indians who reached command rank in the Army were four Lieutenant-Generals: Pat Dunn, Thomas Henderson-Brooks, Neville Foley and Reginald Noronha. Bihar-born Foley, of the famed Poona Horse, served as Director General of the Mechanised Forces. After retirement, the academically well-qualified General was the nominated representative of the Anglo-Indians in the 12th Lok Sabha. Reggie Noronha of Tangasseri and the Madras Regiment (whose Colonel he became) was commended by all for his leading of the UN forces in civil war-torn Congo in 1965. He retired as Deputy Chief of Army Staff. Henderson-Brooks, the first Anglo-Indian to be made Major General, was appointed by the Government of India in 1963 to inquire into the debacle that followed the Chinese invasion in 1962. His hard-hitting report has still to be released. An Oxford graduate and an IMA gold medalist, Dunn was on leave prior to retirement when he was recalled to serve as Corps Commander in the Sialkot sector during the 1965 war with Pakistan. He was the first Indian to command a battalion and got there starting from the ranks, despite his Oxford degree, being overage when he applied for a commission. He was the Colonel of the First / Third Gurkha Rifles Regiment. The Indian Army's finest victory in the 1965 war has been credited

Lt. Gen. Reginald Noronha, Colonel of the Madras Regiment, retired as Deputy Chief of Army Staff. (Photo: Capt. D.P. Ramachandran)

Top left: Brig. Desmond Hayde (second from right), the hero of Dograi, discussing strategy in the field. (Photo: Anglo-Ink)

Bottom: Rear Admiral Alan O'Leary (Photo: Anglo-Indian Guild, Bangalore)

Admiral Ronald Pereira, the first Anglo-Indian to head the Indian Navy. (Photo: The Pereira family)

to Desmond Hayde's 3rd Jats which stopped the Pakistan Army short of Amritsar and, counter-attacking, captured Dograi and raced towards Lahore, with the ceasefire stopping them short. Hayde was awarded the Mahavir Chakra. Five years after retirement, Brigadier Hayde was posted as Inspector General of Police in Mizoram where he quelled the insurgency and brought peace to the troubled State.

Bombay-born Lt. Col. Arthur R. Peters made a mark in a different military environment. He was a small arms expert and at the Technical Development Establishment (Weapons) in Jabalpur he developed, in 1956, what went into use as the Peters 9 mm semi-automatic pistol.

Fewer Anglo-Indians served in the Indian Navy, but one of them commanded the fleet from 1979 to 1982. Admiral Ronald Pereira, who had commanded the Navy's flagship I.N.S. *Delhi*, served as Flag Officer Commanding the Eastern Fleet, Southern Naval Command and Western Naval Command. He is considered one of the architects of the modern Indian Navy. Two others to reach high rank were Rear Admiral Douglas St. John Cameron and Rear Admiral Alan O'Leary, who both settled in Bangalore when they retired. O'Leary was Chairman of the 6th Services Pay Commission. An earlier contributor to the Indian Navy, Captain Colin McGready, was, in 1951, the first Indian Naval

Officer to command I.N.S. *Venduruthy*, headquarters of the Southern Command and the Indian Naval Academy, the largest training establishment of the Navy. He later served as Director, Naval Training, and President, Services Selection Board. He was one of the pioneers who guided the Indian Navy's growth.

Those mentioned here are just the best-known of the Anglo-Indians who served in India's armed forces. There were numerous others who have contributed, unsung, to making India's military forces one of the best in the world. The story of one is told in the pictures below.

Both right: John Nicholas, a sergeant in a British unit during the Fourth Mysore War, was rewarded for meritorious service during the campaign by being, in 1800, made Superintendent of Seven Wells, the water supply system to Fort St. George, Madras. Uniquely, the post was awarded to him in perpetuity. Thus, for 125 years, a Nicholas was in charge of Seven Wells, as the record shows. The last of the line as Superintendent was Evelyn Nicholas, seen here taking his family out for a drive. He was in charge from 1905 till 1925 when the post ceased with the municipality taking over the facility. (Photos: Zhaynn A. James)

THE SEVEN WELLS NICHOLAS's

		BORN	DIED	AGE (yrs)	HELD POST AS CUSTODIANS OF SEVEN WELLS FROM	TO	NO. OF YEARS
1.	John Nicholas		1812				
	Peter Nicholas		1816				
	Gilbert Nicholas	1794	1816	22	1800	1820	20
	Hammond Nicholas		1820				
	John Nicholas	1795	1820	25			
2.	Sylvester Nicholas	1795	1858	63	1820	1858	38
3.	Joseph Nicholas	1817	1871	54	1858	1871	13
4.	E.A.S. Nicholas	1847	1905	58	1871	1905	34
5.	Evelyn Nicholas	1855	1941	86	1905	1925 (when the appointment ceased)	20

On Government Service

A part from the Indian Railways (which till the 1950s were in private hands), the armed forces and education (again mostly in private hands), the Police was a favoured service of the Anglo-Indians. The 'European' sergeants were a feared force in law and order situations. But there were many other Anglo-Indians who rose to high rank and distinguished themselves.

The most distinguished of them was Bangalore-born Eric Stracey who joined the Indian Police Service in 1943 after topping the All-India entrance exam. He served various Chief Ministers in British India and Independent India and became the first Anglo-Indian to head the Tamil Nadu Police. When the post was upgraded, he became the State's first Director General of Police. Of his years in the Police, he wrote a well-received book, *Odd Man In*, but his *Growing up in Anglo-India* was much the better book, a moving story of an Anglo-Indian family that rose to the top despite all the

Tamil Nadu's first Director General of Police, Eric Stracey, with his senior officers. (Photo: The Hindu)

odds and should be compulsory reading for every young Anglo-Indian.

Another outstanding Police Officer spanning the pre- and post-Independence periods was Ronald Moore of the Calcutta Police who did yeoman service during the communal riots of 1946-1947. A fine boxer, chosen to represent India in the 1948 and 1952 Olympics, he could not make the trips as he could not be relieved of his police duties. In 1956, he was appointed Assistant Commissioner of Police, Calcutta, and in 1964 the first Commandant of the Home Guards. He also raised two battalions of the Calcutta Armed Police. His son Peter retired in 2004 as Director of Prisons, Western Australia.

A third police officer to reach high rank, Calcutta-born Leslie Hart, did distinguished service in Bihar and Orissa, before retiring as Deputy Inspector General of Police in Orissa in 1968.

Pre-Independence, two legendary Anglo-Indian officers who were fluent in the local languages, experts in disguise and who could pass for ethnic Indians were Charles Forgett of Bombay and Francis (Frank) Beaty. Forgett's street-gained intelligence is said to have saved Bombay during the Great Revolt of 1857 when he was the City Commissioner of Police. He was Police Chief from 1855 to 1864. By 1859, he is said to have freed the city of violent crime. He was earlier in charge of the Poona Police and still earlier had brought law and order to the South Mahratta country. Beaty, on the other hand, quelled much of the uprisings in Baluchistan and the North West Frontier Province in the early 1900s, when he was Superintendent of Police, Punjab and Baluchistan. He is said to have been the model for Rudyard Kipling's 'Kim'. A street was named after him in Quetta.

In the 18th and early 19th century, several Anglo-Indians worked in the State and Central Government civil services in middle ranking positions, but few got

Bombay Commissioner of Police Charles Forgett who became a legend for his undercover work in the Maharashtra of the mid-19th Century. (Photo: Internet)

into the prestigious Indian Civil Service (ICS) or, later, the Indian Administrative Service (IAS). It was in the 1930s that, as far as is traceable, the Indian Civil Service appointed its first three Anglo-Indian officers. But before them, it was a law graduate and his father who became known as outstanding administrators.

Maurice Watts, who opted for the Madras Civil Service in 1901, was the Dewan of Travancore from 1925-29 and played a significant role in the affairs of succession. His father, Frank, also of the MCS, was earlier the Chief Secretary to the Government of Travancore. Maurice Watts' sister Dorothea was the second (and first Indian) Principal of the Government College for Women, Trivandrum.

A few years later the first of the three Anglo-Indian ICS officers entered the service of what was called the 'Heaven-born'. He was Ralph, the second of the four successful Stracey brothers. He was appointed in 1932 and was posted in Bengal. Stracey was District Magistrate of Howrah and Collector at Dacca during the worst of the communal riots in the 1940s. He retired in Secretary to Government rank, after 16 years in service, which included serving as Special Officer, Famine Relief. On early retirement he joined Imperial Tobacco as a Director and remained with it till he retired in 1964. He and a few friends founded the non-profit Society for the Advancement of English Education and started the Park English School in Calcutta which still thrives, particularly helping Anglo-Indians. After retirement he settled in Bangalore, his home town, and there, with the help of his brothers and sisters, he started the Stracey Memorial School in their mother's house. Today, however, it no longer has connections with the family.

Hector Brown was the next Anglo-Indian ICS appointee and served in Bihar from 1933. After retirement, he represented the Anglo-Indian community in the Bihar Legislative Assembly from 1969 to 1995. Following him into the Indian Civil Service was Oxford-educated Leslie Johnson who entered the Service in 1939. Known for his contribution to the oil industry in India, Johnson was Chairman of the Oil

Leslie Johnson, one of the first Anglo-Indian members of the Indian Civil Service, contributed significantly to India's oil industry. (Photo: Press clipping)

and National Gas Commission from 1966 to 1970 and laid the foundations for it becoming a successful public sector undertaking. He was equally well-known for his scenic paintings on glass.

The first Anglo-Indian to enter the Indian Administrative Service that succeeded the ICS was A.K. Barren who rose to be Chief Secretary of Orissa in the 1970s. He headed the Orissa Public Service Commission in 1973-74.

Another to get into an all-India service was the oldest of the Stracey brothers, Patrick. He joined the Imperial Forest Service and went on to become Director of Forest Education, Dehradun, and, later, Chief Conservator of Forests, Assam (then undivided). An acclaimed international forest and

Patrick Stracey, a Chief Conservator of Forests and an authority on wildlife and forest conservation, at his wedding, with his brothers Eric standing at the rear, second from left, and Ralph, on extreme right, the first Anglo-Indian to qualify for the Indian Civil Service. (Photo: Michael Stracey)

wildlife consultant, he worked in, or was consulted by, several countries. He was the author of five books on forestry and wildlife and was one of the founders of the Wild Life Preservation Society of India. He is listed in the World Wildlife Fund's Roll of Honour.

The fourth Stracey, Cyril, graduated from the Indian Military Academy and was captured by the Japanese in Singapore. He was perhaps the only Anglo-Indian to join the Indian National Army and, after the War, was a prisoner in the Red Fort before being made Secretary of the INA Relief and Rehabilitation Committee. Then, invited by Prime Minister Nehru to join the Indian Foreign Service, he served in several countries before being appointed Ambassador to Malagasy (1965) and, then, to Finland (1970), the first Anglo-Indian to serve India as an Ambassador.

Another Anglo-Indian to reach Ambassador rank was British-born Noel Jones whose parents migrated from India. When he was appointed British Ambassador to Kazakhstan in 1993 (till 1995) he was the first British

Cyril Stracey, on left, when he was India's Consul-General in San Francisco. The only Anglo-Indian to join the Indian National Army in Southeast Asia during World War II, he went on to become India's only Anglo-Indian Ambassador till date. (Photo: Christine Kurien)

Maurice Baker,
Singapore's first
High Commissioner
(ambassador) to India.
He was later appointed
Pro-Chancellor of the
Singapore National
University. (Photo:
Press clipping)

An outstanding
irrigation engineer
in the late 18th-
early 19th century,
William Willcocks was
responsible for the
building of the Aswan
Dam in Egypt and Iraq's
irrigation network.
(Photo: Internet)

ambassador to come from an ethnic minority. He, sadly, died young.

An Anglo-Indian (but Singapore, where he was born and bred and which he served, would call him an Eurasian) was Singapore's first High Commissioner in India, arriving here in 1967 after a dozen years of teaching English Literature. *Maurice Baker,* the son of a British father and a Tamil mother who had migrated to the Straits Settlements, went on to become one of Singapore's most successful diplomats. He then was appointed Pro-Chancellor of the National University of Singapore.

There were several Anglo-Indian engineers who made noteworthy contributions in India and abroad. Already mentioned have been the Special Class Apprentices who climbed high up the ladder in Railway Service, led by Richard Kitson who became Chairman of the Railway Board, India, 1990-1992.

Among other Anglo-Indian engineers, the high achievers included Dehra Dun-born William Willcocks, a Roorkee graduate. He worked in the Indian and Egyptian Public Works Departments in the late 19th century. Willcocks designed and oversaw the building of the first Aswan Dam in Egypt which was completed in 1902 and for which he was knighted. He advised Bengal on irrigation and, in his most important assignment, drew up plans for the irrigation of 3.5 million acres in Mesopotamia (Iraq) from 1911. He authored two memoirs and two books on irrigation. His brother too was knighted, a rare honour in Anglo-Indian families. Meerut-born General Sir James Willcocks was a distinguished soldier who commanded the Indian Corps in France for a while during the Great War and was later Governor of Bermuda.

In 1949, work on the Snowy Mountains Hydro-Electric Scheme (on the border of Victoria and New South Wales) began with an Anglo-Indian, Ed Patterson, as its chief engineer. The tough, dangerous and unremitting work of taming the rugged geography of the Snowy Mountains became the most complex, multipurpose, multi-reservoir hydro scheme in the world. Over 100,000 men and women, two-thirds of them migrants to Australia, worked on the project over 25 years.

Also making a lasting name for himself abroad was R.O. Preston who, like his father, was a railwayman in India. Preston, between 1897 and 1902, built the Uganda Railways from Mombasa to Lake Victoria Nyanza, targeting a mile a day. He and his 500 Indian workers worked in unimaginable conditions—fevers, lions, food and water scarcity—but the line was built. He wrote two books on his African experience.

Another Indian railwayman who made a name for himself was Bangalore-born Harry Mulleneaux, who was the Chief Electrical Engineer of the Bombay-headquartered Great Indian Peninsula Railway. An inventive engineer, he created several devices for use by the Railways and the Army. He was responsible for the electrification of the railway line from Igatpuri to Poona. Summoned to London by the military during World War II, he had a great deal to do with developing mine detectors and improving mine sweeping equipment for which he was awarded the OBE. A respected figure in Bombay's Anglo-Indian community, he represented it in the Bombay Legislative Assembly.

Also known for his inventions was Stephen Taylor-Smith who served in the Customs and Indian Postal Departments. He was a pioneer in rocket launching, with 270 successful launches to his credit between 1934 and 1944. One of the few Anglo-Indians to have appeared on an Indian stamp, Smith, the Secretary of the Indian Airmail Society, was described on it as the 'Father of Aerophilately'. He launched not only mail and small packages across short distances but also livestock across the Damodar River.

Honoured with a stamp in 1992 was Stephen Taylor-Smith, a pioneer in rocket launching who was called the 'Father of Aerophilately' in India. (Stamp: Indian Postal Department)

A Superintendent in a sister department, the Telegraphs, was designated India's first official handwriting authority. Charles R. Hardless of

Calcutta's writings on the subject made him acknowledged internationally. His sons Nicholas and Richard also became handwriting experts. Far less is known of W.E. de Brunner, a Calcutta engineer, who built and flew his own plane in 1909, not long after the birth of aviation in the U.S.

A much later Anglo-Indian connection with the high blue yonder was Herbert Bouvard (with roots in Pondicherry) who started as an apprentice in Hindustan Aircraft Ltd., India's only aircraft manufactory, and retired as its Chief Superintendent, getting an aeronautical engineering degree along the way. For his work in supervising the production of the training aircraft Pushpak and India's first supersonic jet fighter HF24 Maruti he was honoured with an honorary Air Vice-Marshal rank by the Government of India. Also connected with HAL and its predecessor, the British Aircraft Factory, was Kenneth Anderson, hunter and writer, who retired as the Company's Manager, Planning.

Long before these engineers, the first East Indian to make a signal contribution in a technical field was Joshua de Penning, an alumnus of St. George's School and Orphanage, Madras, and the Survey School, Madras. Both were pioneering Western-style educational institutions in India, the former growing from roots put down in 1715, the latter founded in 1794 and developing into the College of Engineering and, then, Anna University, the world's largest engineering university. Joshua de Penning was a ward of St. George's and like many others there he moved on to the Survey School, many of whose alumni went on to work with William Lambton and then with George Everest on the Great Trigonometrical Survey of India which started in Madras in 1802 and which was described as "one of the greatest scientific exercises of the 19th century".

Initially Joshua de Penning was in charge of the Great Theodolite and supervised much of the triangular work. He was later made Head of the Survey's Drawing and Computation Office in Calcutta. It was this work based on the survey that gave India its shape on paper. de Penning was accompanied by his Madras-born wife Marie all the way from Madras to Nagpur where Lambton died and then to Calcutta when he took charge of the office of the Great Survey which was completed in 1841. One of their children, George, who joined the Railways and could not get a patent for a punkah-pulling machine he had designed, resigned from his job, studied law and established India's first firm of patent attorneys in Calcutta in 1856.

When George de Penning succeeded in getting his patent, it was the first patent issued in India. The firm he established still continues in India and in the family—as de Penning and de Penning—now headquartered in Madras.

Among the many Anglo-Indians who have played notable roles in education in India, one who has been a principal advisor to Government is Prof. Sydney Rebeiro, first Dean of Culture, Delhi University (1985-1992) and Dean of Alumni (1997-2003). With the University from 1961, he was a member of the UGC's first expert panel on Mass Communication Studies and its High Committee on Minorities in Higher Education for the 12th Plan (2012-17). He was also the only non-official member (HRD) of the Planning Commission for the 11th Plan (2007-12). Besides being an advisor to several ministries, professional and educational institutions, and all-India Boards he has been involved with the Fulbright-Nehru Scholarship and Oxbridge India Scholarship schemes. His mother, Mary Isaacs Rebeiro, was Independent India's first woman Postmistress, heading the Mori Gate post office, and his uncle, Theo Isaacs, oversaw the electrification of New Delhi.

And in medicare, Col. A.D. Baptist of the Indian Medical Department contributed significantly to the School

An advisor to the Indian Government on education and human resources, Prof. Sydney Rebeiro has also had an outstanding record as an academician-administrator at Delhi University. (Photo: AITW)

Bottom: *Mary Isaacs Rebeiro, Sydney Rebeiro's mother, was Independent India's first postmistress and was a legend in the Delhi zones in which she headed post offices. (Photo: AITW)*

of Tropical Medicine, Calcutta, and the All-India Institute of Hygiene and Public Health. There were several other Anglo-Indians who served unsung in this Department as doctors in many a place off the beaten track.

Anglo-Indian contribution in Government Service outside the traditional was considerable at the middle levels but recording of further progress has, sadly, been minimal, particularly in the 18th century when many may well have made a mark.

Midst the Boxwallahs

Business, trade, commerce, these were far from Anglo-Indian dreams of building a future in India. Serving the government was seen as the way ahead. There could, however, have been several in the 17th and 18th centuries who did enter this world if only to run guest houses, hotels and taverns and serve as haberdashers, women's couturiers and milliners, furniture makers and provisioners. But there was always the exception. And one of those exceptions was William Palmer of Hyderabad.

Palmer, son of a British general and a Mughal begum, was a senior officer in the Nizam's Army in the early 1800s and for services rendered he received an enormous pension on retirement. Being close to several of the Nizam's Ministers, he, with their support and that of Governor Thomas Rumbold of Madras—one of the archetypal 'nabobs'—and his kin, and his half-brother, John Palmer, "The Merchant Prince" of Calcutta, founded the banking house of Palmer & Co. in 1814. So well did the firm do that it lent Rs 60 lakh to the State of Hyderabad when it was faced with bankruptcy, being unable to settle a debt to the East India Company. But when Hyderabad could not repay a considerable part of the loan, Palmer & Co., Hyderabad, declared bankruptcy in 1820 and the Calcutta firm did so in 1835, both firms taking with them the savings of many an Anglo-Indian family.

More successful was James Kyd of Calcutta, one of the leaders, with John Ricketts and Henry Derozio, of the movement to seek recognition of an Anglo-Indian identity. Kyd, who started as a shipbuilder of the East India Company, fortuitously bought in 1807 the almost eponymously named Kidderpore Docks and in the next 30 years built 25 ships for the Company, including the *Hastings*, a man-o'-war, the only line-of-battleship built in Calcutta.

More significantly, Kyd wrote and published *Thoughts: How to Better the Condition of Indo-Britons* in which he urged the community to enter a variety of professions and "cease staking their all upon government and mercantile offices." This was a time when many Indo-Britons favoured white-collar jobs in Calcutta. In the book he listed 40 trade occupations that Indo-Britons could apprentice for and he showed the way by providing apprenticeships in his shipyard. He also teamed with Ricketts to found the Calcutta Apprenticing Society in 1825.

Henny Derozio himself was the son and grandson of well-to-do Calcutta merchants, Francis Derozio and Michael Derozio, educated Luso-Indians of whom there were many in Calcutta, Dacca and Chittagong. Edward Ribeiro, a jute broker, is a major success story in the jute industry in Dhaka, his home town, in recent years.

By the late 19th and early 20th centuries there were in every major city a few small Anglo-Indian businesses offering a variety of specialised services. In the early 1900s, E.D. Smith, who owned Smith & Sons, 'leading tailors and haberdashers', and Collingwood & Co., 'chemists and druggists', must have been a Madras personality of note for *The Mail* to have paid him special tribute. He was considered a pioneer in advertising by the paper which carried a small front page advertisement from him every day (said to have been the predecessor of the 'personal' advertisements of a later age). This was "looked forward to every evening, much the same way Count Curly was in later years," according to *The Mail's* tribute to him.

Of the same period was Wilfred Pereira who ran well-known pharmacies in Vepery and Mount Road, Wilfred Pereira Ltd. Wilfred Pereira and A.N. Lazarus of Spencer's Pharmaceutical Department together founded the Pharmaceutical Association in 1923, which was to become the Pharmaceutical Society of India two years later. Only qualified chemists and druggists, and diploma holders in pharmacy, could become members. The Society was a major spokesman for them in India till 1949 by when other associations had been founded and a national federation formed.

Another pharmacist, Bengal-born Dennis Amore, developed a successful business career in Bombay and became a close associate of Anglo-Indian leader Frank Anthony. Besides importing pharmaceuticals and high quality wines, he brought in the first equipment to manufacture Aspro in India and pioneered the export of Araldite (some of it used in Sydney's Opera House). He also invented several OTC products.

Contemporaneously, in the first half of the 20th century, Ernest McCluskie was making a fortune in Calcutta as a realtor. Some of this fortune he ploughed into developing McCluskiegunj. Also becoming wealthy in an allied field, contracting and development, was John H. Abbott of Jhansi who, in an earlier period, tried to establish a settlement for the the 'Domiciled European Community'. Several other Euro-Indians of this period also

owned small indigo and jute plantations/manufactories and there was an occasional proprietorial tea or rubber planter.

In the New India post-liberalisation, one Anglo-Indian who made a success of business commensurate with the time was Clyde Cooper, who was one of the founders and Managing Director of Blue Dart Express, a Bombay firm that was a pioneer in logistics in India. He launched India's first airline for express delivery of mail and cargo and, today, three jets operate 300 days in the year linking India's major cities.

One of the community's most successful businessmen in Madras, a medium-scale industrialist, was Denzil D'Monte who also represented the community in the Tamil Nadu Legislature and was active in the Anglo-Indian Association

Dennis Amore, a close associate of Frank Anthony, greeting the then Prime Minister, Indira Gandhi. He was a well-known figure in Bombay's pharma industry. (Photo: AITW)

Bottom left: Denzil D'Monte, a successful manufacturer of auto-ancillaries, was also a leader of the Anglo-Indian community in Madras and was closely associated with hockey administration. Here he presents former hockey star Jimmy Carr (on left) with a token of appreciation for his contribution to the game. (Photo: AITW)

Clyde Cooper, one of the pioneers of modern logistics in India, establishing Blue Dart Express, a flourishing courier firm with its own aircraft. (Photo: Internet)

of Southern India. With Chennai being the automobile capital of South Asia, he served the industry well by running half a dozen auto-ancillary industries in five cities in different parts of India, employing 2000 persons in them. He was also a significant exporter.

After being closely associated with the All-India Anglo-Indian Association, D'Monte branched out to form the Anglo-Indian United Front. He was active in hockey administration in Madras as well as in Catholic affairs in the Diocese for which he was made a Papal Knight. Interestingly, he owned and published a Tamil weekly, *Thondan*, in Chennai.

Another Anglo-Indian businessman in Madras is Maurice Ryan from the Nilgiris who has become a successful player in the IT Industry, his Data Software Research Company Pvt. Ltd. a multicrore business. The firm, offering IT and Consulting Services, has branch offices in California, the U.K. and Singapore. He is perhaps the only Anglo-Indian in India to grab one of the new opportunities India offers in the 21st century. Ryan, described as an IT prodigy, was an outstanding college athlete as well as a good student and went on to make his own way in the IT industry.

In Bangalore, Desmond Pinto, from Trichinopoly, a metallurgist, established Aldan Industrial Products in 1981 to deal in foundry chemicals and consumables and offer technical services to foundries in and around Karnataka. He has a client base of over 200 foundries.

Another Bangalorean, Neil Foley, has been prominent in engineering design. He has made his mark internationally with his designs for sunglasses (Titan), jewellery, bicycles, buses and other products. It was he who designed the torch/baton for the 2010 Commonwealth Games that were held in India.

An outstanding engineering designer, Neil Foley, is making a mark internationally with his work. (Photo: AITW)

Many Anglo-Indian women have over the years supplemented family incomes by running small businesses, such as tailoring, catering, and beauty care. But very few have ventured into significant business investment. One of them has been Elaine Roach, founder and chairperson of the multi-crore Spark Group headquartered in Dubai.

The Group is involved in various businesses including information technology, E-commerce, retail and wholesale, event management, real estate, music productions and travel.

Anglo-Indians who have migrated abroad have shown greater initiative in entrepreneurship. Calcutta-born Basil Sellers started in a stockbroking firm in Australia as a 16-year-old and, before long, was breathing new life into it as well as other ailing companies. Today, he is the chief executive and major shareholder of the Linter Group, leaders in textiles, and Gestetner PLC. He has large investments in other Australian industries such as breweries, broadcast media, and mineral resources. He is listed amongst Australia's 200 richest people, but is based in London these days. One of the founders of the Bradman Museum in Bowral, he is a major supporter of cricket, Aussie Rules football and basketball (in which he once represented South Australia). A serious art collector, he has endowed several prizes for Art. And he is a major contributor to the McGrath, Steve Waugh and Roden Cutler Foundations. In Madras, he supports ANEW, an NGO that trains slum girls for jobs. He has come a long way from the railway colonies of India, demonstrating what initiative can do.

Bert Wallace from Chittagong founded 'Interfrost' in Western Australia in the 1960s and developed a supply chain to provide frozen seafood and vegetables throughout Western Australia. Another succesful Australian Anglo-Indian, Malcolm Prior of Baroda, establised a successful plastic factory, Baroda Manufacturing Pty. Ltd. in Melbourne, and won the Victoria Small Industries Award in 1992.

Joe Tucker from Adra, Bengal, settled in the western United States and became a success in fruit farming, like the Sikhs had done in the early 20th century. He developed a special species of peaches, 'Tucker's Autumn Blush', that stays longer on the trees and extends the peach season. Another Anglo-Indian multimillionaire from the U.S., Dimapur-born Withbert Payne of California who became a chartered accountant at Price Waterhouse after his Oak

Once listed among Australia's 200 richest people, Basil Sellers is one of the world's richest Anglo-Indians and one of the community's leading philanthropists. He is now settled in the U.K. (Photo: AITW)

Top: One of the few Anglo-Indian women to develop a business conglomorate, Elaine Roach, established the multi-crore Spark Group in Dubai. (Photo: AITW)

Bottom: Making a huge success of business in the USA is Withbert Payne of California. (Photo: AITW)

A major player in Canada's bio-industry, Ronald Micetich spread his pharma industry internationally and became an international name in the field. (Photo: AITW)

Grove, Mussoorie, days, founded Starcare International—a hospital financing consultancy—Star Image International, which is into men's fashion, and Starlog in the IT world. He has been at every World Anglo-Indian Reunion from the very first which was hosted in the U.K. in 1989.

Coimbatore-born Ronald Micetich—whose Croatian grandfather developed Micetich Colony for Anglo-Indians in North Madras—parlayed his step-by-step approach to higher studies in chemistry into success in the bio-industry in Canada. From being a research scientist he moved on to setting up SynPharm Laboratories Inc., Edmonton, which he then integrated with NAEJA Pharmaceuticals in 1999. This large pharmaceuticals manufacturer has developed as a major international pharmaceuticals outsource service provider. While developing his businesses, Micetich continued to pursue research and two important drugs, *Tazabactum* and *Mofezolac*, have been credited to him. He passed away in 2006.

Despite the few Anglo-Indians opting for entrepreneurship, those who did get into business did well. Obviously the talent is there; the drive is what is needed.

In Words and Pictures

Till the 1960s most Anglo-Indian schools had an exceptional standard of English teaching. For all I know, they still may, but the beneficiaries in those days, as against today, were to a great extent Anglo-Indians. And with that background, they should have done much better in the world of letters than they did. Sadly, the number of Anglo-Indians who wielded a pen or pecked at a typewriter were much fewer than what there should have been given their educational background.

When I worked with *The Times of Ceylon* in the 1950s, at least a third of the journalists and half the production staff were Burghers (the Ceylon equivalent of the Anglo-Indian). I owe much of my journalistic training to the Francis Ashborns, Stanley Oorloffs and Dick van Cuylenbergs of *The Times*. *The Times* had been British-owned till a couple of years before I joined. There was no such Anglo-Indian numbers in the couple of Indian papers I was familiar with at the time and which had been British-owned, namely *The Mail*, Madras, and *The Times of India*, Bombay. But in the early days of those papers in the 19th century, there must have been a large number of Anglo-Indians working on them. Sadly, there's no record by which to track them. The only one traceable has been Henry Cornish who followed Charles Lawson out of *The Madras Times* and, teaming together, the former Joint Editors of *The Madras Times* founded *The Madras Mail* (later, *The Mail*) in December 1868. Cornish, a barrister, visited Australia in 1875 and on his return published in 1879 an account of his Australian experiences, dismissing its cities as being not on par with his "fair Madras". The book that emerged from that visit, *Under the Southern Cross*, also provided an account of some of the earliest Anglo-Indian migrants to Australia, who arrived there in 1853 and 1854 and got absorbed in printing presses.

Keith Flory, Associate Editor, The Statesman, Calcutta and Delhi, the seniormost Anglo-Indian journalist in India as these lines are written. (Photo: AITW)

In the Cornish era, the second half of the 19th century, there could have been several Anglo-Indians working in British-owned newspapers in India, but as more and more Anglo-Indians sought government jobs and increasing numbers of Indians got university education, the Anglo-Indian presence in Indian newspapers virtually vanished except at the sports desks. The only noteworthy Anglo-Indian journalist of recent times has been Keith Flory, at present Associate Editor of *The Statesman*, Calcutta and Delhi. He is today perhaps the only Anglo-Indian commentator on national affairs. He has in the past been *The Statesman*'s Defence Correspondent and Parliamentary Correspondent. His father, Cyril Flory, was with *The Mail*, Madras, and his grandfather, John Flory was one of the founders of the Anglo-Indian Sports Club, Madras, which played a key role in formalising hockey organisation in India.

Another *Statesman* journalist, Lionel Lumb, left Calcutta in 1963 to work in Britain with *The Scotsman* and BBC Television News. Ten years later he moved to Canada and for the next twenty years made documentaries for the Canadian Broadcasting Corporation and worked as an executive producer in television. He was appointed Associate Professor at Carleton University's School of Journalism in the 1990s and, now, in retirement, focuses on writing fiction. Lumb remembers that when he was at *The Statesman* in Calcutta it had several well-known Anglo-Indian journalists on its staff in senior positions besides others well into the 1970s. These included such well-known journalists as Mervyn Hardinge who edited its Sunday magazine, Charles Tresham its News Editor, and Reginald Maher, who was better known for working with various Anglo-Indian organisations, including the Anglo-Indian Youth League he founded. His *These are the Anglo-Indians* (1962) is one of the early post-Independence looks at the community by one of its own. Contemporary of Maher in Calcutta is the archivist of the Anglo-Indian community, Melvyn Brown. Reginald Maher's son, Gordon, President of the International Federation of Anglo-Indian Associations (2012), is at present Director of the Asian

Pacific Postal College which, from Bangkok, reaches out to 13 countries in the region.

A much- respected Sports Editor, Ron Hendricks, was called 'Governor' by all. (Photo: Internet)

Choosing a different field of journalism, Ron Hendricks became one of the best known sports journalists in India in the second half of the 20th century. He worked with the *Free Press Journal*, Bombay, was made Sports Editor of the *Deccan Herald*, Bangalore, and then moved on as Sports Editor, *Indian Express*, Bombay. So respected was he that other journalists called him 'Governor'. He was succeeded at the *Deccan Herald* by Leslie Wilson, another outstanding sports journalist and a contemporary of Denzil Letoile, Sports Editor of the *Indian Express*, Bangalore. Wilson was also known for his radio commentaries on sports events (all sports!) as well as other State events. His son, Leslie Wilson Jr., followed in his father's footsteps and became Sports Editor of the *Gulf News*. A younger sports journalist, David McMahon, made a mark with the Calcutta *Telegraph's* magazine, *Sunday*, and then with its *Sports World*, which he edited from 1983 to 1988 before emigrating to Australia and doing well in journalism there as Business Editor of *mX*.

Moving on from journalism to fame as an author, one of India's best loved ones, Landour (Mussoorie)-based Ruskin Bond is one of India's most successful storytellers with a range that reaches out from children to adults. He was awarded the Sahitya Akademi[16] Award in 1992 and the Padma Shri in 1999 for his contribution to children's literature. His novel *The Flight of Pigeons* was adapted by Shyam Benegal for the

He could well be called India's favourite storyteller for all ages. For half a century Ruskin Bond has reached out to everyone from children to adults. (Photo: Internet)

acclaimed Hindi film *Junoon* and his *The Blue Umbrella* was adapted for a film that won the National Award for Best Children's Film. At last count, he had written five novels, seventy-three short stories (many which feature in several anthologies and textbooks), and numerous essays, travelogues and poems.

---

16.   India's National Academy for Literature.

Listed among India's best English language writers and highly rated in Commonwealth literary circles is Allan Sealy. (Photo: Dileep Prakash)

Awarded the Sahitya Akademi Award a year before Bond and the Padma Shri in 2012 was Allahabad-born Allan Sealy who is considered the most eminent writer the Anglo-Indian community has produced and is listed among India's best English language writers at a time when Indian writing in English is flourishing. The author of five novels and a book-length travelogue, his first book, *The Trotter-Nama* (1988), a classic on the Anglo-Indians, won the Commonwealth Writers' Prize for Best First Book. In 1998, his *The Everest Hotel* was shortlisted for the Booker Prize.

Two other successful writers of fiction each discovered late in their lives a female Indian ancestor way back in each of their family histories. Calcutta-born John Masters, an Indian Army Officer, came from a long line that had served in the Indian Army and was virtually domiciled here. In 1951, he wrote a bestseller, *Nightrunners of Bengal,* that evolved into a very popular six-volume series on the Savage family, loosely based on his own and which even more loosely—and romantically—traced the history of the British in India. *Bhowani Junction,* the first in this series which went on till 1967, was made into a very successful film but both were, and still are, derided by Anglo-Indians round the world who feel they were misrepresented. Masters followed the Savage series with a successful trilogy on the Great War. In terms of sales he was perhaps the most successful of the Anglo-Indian writers. More recently, Delhi-based *William Dalrymple* has been successful with his fiction and non-fiction. His *White Mughals* is a significant contribution to understanding the genesis of the Anglo-Indian community.

Perhaps the most successful of Anglo-Indian writers was John Masters whose six stories in the Savage series about a British military family that served in India for generations were all bestsellers. (Photo: Internet)

Non-fiction too has had its share of Anglo-Indian writers in India making a significant contribution to the genre. Two hunters who turned conservationists and writers of their adventures were Jim Corbett of Nainital in the North and Hyderabad-born Kenneth Anderson who was involved with aircraft maintenance and production in Banglaore. Anderson wrote eight books, Corbett seven, each of them focusing on not only on man-eaters but also on other jungle denizens, the tribals and the forests.

Top: Travel writers Hugh and Colleen Gantzer have written several books and thousands of articles on their travels in India and abroad. (Photo: AITW)

Writing of travel less dangerous are the prolific travel writers Patna-born Hugh Gantzer and Godhra-born Colleen, who now call Mussoorie home. The Gantzers have, after initial forays into thrillers and detective stories, focused on travel and tourism. They have written over 3000 articles for journals in India and abroad and have nine books on several States (they are authorities on Kerala, where they lived for nine years) to their credit besides several TV features (including a series of 52 episodes). Their latest work is their first novel, *The Year Before Sunset*, and is on the Anglo-Indian community. Another well-known travel writer and photographer is Donald Alney who was for 18 years Principal of La Martiniere, Calcutta.

Bottom: A general knowledge whiz and a leading quizmaster, Barry O'Brien has written one of the country's most successful supplementary textbooks. (Photo: AITW)

After 18 years as a Principal of La Martiniere, Calcutta, D.M. Alney has become a well-known travel writer and photographer. (Photo: La Martiniere)

Also focused on non-fiction has been Barry O'Brien of Calcutta, a leading quizmaster who has conducted over 2000 live quizzes in South and West Asia. Moving on from being a sports journalist to compering and quizzing, Barry O'Brien began writing books focused on General Knowledge. His *Find Out*, an Oxford University Press title, is the largest selling General Knowledge series in India, prescribed in over 1000 Indian schools. He was a nominated Anglo-Indian MLA in the West Bengal Assembly from 2006 to 2011. Brother Derek and father Neil have similar distinguished records and are referred to elsewhere in these pages.

Nicola Marsh, one of Mills and Boon's, favourite writers. (Photo: AITW)

Top: Dr. Jennifer Bayer, an academic researcher in language and communication, is listed as one of India's 400 women noteworthy for writing in English. (Photo: Internet)

An even more academically-focused writer has been Dr. Jennifer Bayer of Mysore who is head of Research, Communication and Literacy, Central Institute of Indian Languages, Mysore, where she has written about Anglo-Indian English and also on the Tamils in London. She has been included in a list of 400-plus noteworthy Indian writers in English in a bibliography titled *Indian Women Writing in English.*

Overseas, authors with an Anglo-Indian heritage include Glen Duncan, born in Bolton in the U.K. in 1965 to Anglo-Indian migrants, Chennai-born Nicola Marsh, whose family moved to Australia, and Bombay-born Russell Lucas. Between 1997 and 2011, London-based Duncan wrote ten novels that a critic said "can't easily be pigeon-holed." Marsh, who has written over 30 Harlequin Mills and Boon's and Modern Heat romances, has had over three million of her books sold worldwide. Her first mainstream romance, *Busted in Bollywood,* was released last year and her first Young Adult novel, *Serenity of the Sun,* will be released in 2013. She started writing in 2001, and her first Harlequin title came out in 2003 and was selected Best Harlequin Romance that year.

Lucas was born Russell Graham Newlands in Bombay where his father, Albert Newlands, was at one time the most highly decorated police officer in the British Empire and a champion boxer, cyclist and swimmer. When the Newlands divorced, his mother married James Lucas and Russell took his surname. The family moved to the U.K. in 1946. Lucas shifted between jobs in the U.K. and Bombay till he settled with Vauxhall Motors in Luton, rising to high managerial rank. His first bawdy romp was a collection of short stories, *Evenings at Monginis[17] and Other Stories* (1990). This was followed by two other novels with strong elements of sex that were translated into several languages.

Besides these writers, several other Anglo-Indians in Australia, the U.K. and North America are writing more than ever before on the community, both non-fiction and

---

17.   Once a renowned Bombay restaurant and night club.

fiction. They include Dr. Gloria Jean Moore in Australia, Margaret Deefholts in Canada, and Sylvia Staub and Blair Williams in the U.S. Moore has focused on the history of

Margaret Deefholts from Canada is a well-known travel writer in North America and an editor of Anglo-Indian anthologies. (Photo: AITW)

the Anglo-Indian community and her best-known work is *The Anglo-Indian Vision* (1986), a comprehensive overview. Deefholts, besides writing fiction, particularly short fiction, and editing Anglo-Indian anthologies, is a well-known travel writer in North America, especially contributing on India. Staub, who worked in Indian Government offices overseas, later joined *Time-Life* as a copy editor and moved on to one of its spin-offs, *Emerge,* as copy chief before retiring into freelance work. And Williams has done a significant study on Anglo-Indians in the 21st century.

Top left: Dr. Gloria Jean Moore, a post-Independence writer who has been focused on writing about her community for the last twenty-five years. (Photo: AITW)

Williams, a senior Railway engineer in India who got into manufacturing engineering in the U.S. in 1976, started, after retirement, the Calcutta Tiljallah Relief Inc., a charity to help indigent Anglo-Indians in three major cities in India. His CTR Publications, which contributes to this cause, has published seven books on the Anglo-Indian community so far. The five anthologies he has published, among them *The Way We Were, The Way We Are, Women of Anglo-India, Voices on the Verandah,* and the latest, *More Voices on the Verandah,* reveal the wealth of writing talent among Anglo-Indians abroad; the contributors to these collections all appear to have a book or two in them. All these anthologies evoke poignant memories of the Anglo-Indian past in India between, say, the 1920s and the 1960s. As Lionel Lumb, who edited the latest *Voices,* says, "While you can take Anglo-Indians out of India, you cannot, cannot, cannot take India out of them." Now there's another Anglo-Indian publisher, Harry MacLure, whose 'Anglo-Ink' was founded in 2012 in Chennai to bring out books on the Anglo-Indians. MacLure

Taking a look at the Anglo-Indian community in India today, Blair Williams has beside his professional work as an engineer started a publishing house in the U.S. that is his philanthropic contribution to the less well-off in his community. (Photo: AITW)

had 15 years ago started, with the help of Founder Publisher Les D'Souza, who had settled in the U.K., the quarterly *Anglos In The Wind*, which now reaches out to Anglo-Indians worldwide.

The first Anglo-Indian to play a major role in publishing was, however, Neil O'Brien, well-known in educational circles, who for years headed Oxford University Press's Calcutta office and then became OUP's All-India Deputy General Manager. Called the 'Father of Quizzing' in

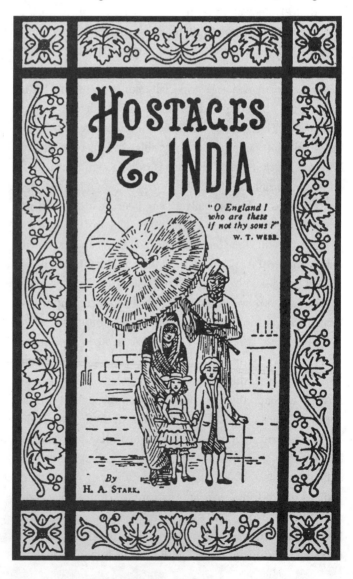

The cover of Herbert Stark's classic that was the first book that focused on the community's history and portrayed how shabbily it had been treated. (Photo: SM Collection)

India, he organised in 1969 in Calcutta India's first quizzing competition.

But the first writers to get the Anglo-Indian voice heard must be Herbert Stark and Cedric Dover, both of Calcutta. Stark, a member of the Bengal and Indian Educational Services, who went on to be a member of the Bengal Legislative Council, was a President of the Anglo-Indian and Domiciled Europeans Association, Bengal. In 1926, he wrote *Hostages to India: The Life Story of the Anglo-Indian Race* and in 1932 *The Call of the Blood: Anglo-Indians and the Sepoy Mutiny*. Both books were heartfelt cries for recognition of the Anglo-Indians by the British and for members of the community not to be treated as second class citizens. Even more strident and angry cries were Dover's *Cimerii or Eurasians and Their Future* (1929) and *Half-Caste* (1937).

A well-known biologist, zoologist and anthropologist in India, the U.K. and the Straits Settlements, Dover refuted the theory of purity of race. Writing about miscegenation he said, "Today there are no half-castes because there are no full castes." *Cimerii* was his first challenge of racist discrimination against Anglo-Indians. In *Half-Caste* he wrote about how wrong it was to forever see a 'half-caste' "as an undersized, scheming and entirely degenerate bastard. His father a blackguard, his mother a whore ... but more than all this, as a potential menace to Western Civilisation, to everything that is White and Sacred...." and how this view needed to be vigorously challenged. In the London of the 1940s he teamed with several Indians who were campaigning for freedom and described himself as "the first Eurasian to ally himself with the struggle for Indian independence". After the War, he joined the faculty of various Negro universities in the U.S., lecturing on miscegenation and its results and learning about African-American culture.

The Rev. Henry Bower, a well-known name in Tamil scholarship and Dravidian studies. (Photo: Internet)

Other Anglo-Indians who made a mark in scholarship and science in the past include Henry Bower, Thomas Beale and Stanley Prater. Madras-born Bower became a missionary of the Society for Propagating the Gospel, but was better known for his Tamil scholarship and the numerous

One of the three Anglo-Indians who served in the Indian Constituent Assembly, Raymond Platel of Calcutta. (Photo: AITW)

Top: *Stanley Prater's writings kickstarted the wildlife conservation movement in India (Photo: Internet)*

Henry Derozio who sang of freedom for Indians and East Indians alike and was one of the few Anglo-Indians honoured with a stamp. (Stamp: Indian Postal Department)

translations he did of Christian writing, including a *History of Christianity in India,* and translations still studied or used (like Bishop Caldwell's *Liturgy*). His children carried on his Dravidian studies.

Thomas Beale was an authority on the Muslims of India and worked with H.M. Elliot on a Mohammedan history. Beale himself compiled *An Oriental Biographical Dictionary* which was published posthumously in London in 1894. Prater was an outstanding naturalist who was curator of the Bombay National History Society and the Prince of Wales Museum, Bombay, for 25 years from 1923. He was the author of a classic, *The Book of Indian Animals* (1948), and Executive Editor of *The Journal of the Bombay National History Society* in which he focused on 'Wild Life Preservation in India' in several issues in 1935, kickstarting the conservation movement in India. He represented the Anglo-Indians in the Bombay Legislative Assembly in the 1930s and 40s and represented the community, together with Frank Anthony, in the Indian Constituent Assembly. A third Anglo-Indian representative in the Assembly was Raymond Platel of West Bengal.

Several Anglo-Indians also contributed significantly to the Urdu world of letters. They included Dyce Sombre, George Puech and Dr. Benjamin Johnston of Hyderabad (the latter two also wrote in Persian as did James Skinner) and Balthasar Bourbon of Bhopal. Sir Florence Filose of Gwalior composed Hindi music and wrote lyrics for his compositions.

The greatest of these wordsmiths, however, was one who lived only twenty-two years and is as much forgotten by Anglo-Indians as Indians for whose freedom he sang. If India had Poet Laureates, he would have been one to be crowned. His name was Henry Louis Vivian Derozio.

His first collection of poems was published in 1827, when he was only eighteen, and was acclaimed in Britain. At 19 he was teaching at the prestigious Hindu College in Calcutta, but his reformist views on caste, idolatry and women, welcomed by students, had the management asking him to resign. He then became a journalist and adopted almost a militant view on nationalism. In his *To India My Native Land* he sang agonisingly of India's fate and in *The Harp of India* he sang of hope.

> *My country! In the days of glory past*
> *A beauteous halo circled round thy brow,*
> *And worshipped as a deity thou wast.*
> *Where is that glory, where that reverence now?*
> *Thy eagle pinion is chained down at last,*
> *And groveling in the lowly dust art thou:*
> *Thy minstrel hath no wreath to weave for thee*
> *Save the sad story of thy misery!*

—From *To India—My Native Land*

> *O! many a hand more worthy far than mine*
> *Once thy harmonious chords to sweetness gave,*
> *And many a wreath for them did fame entwine*
> *Of flowers still blooming on the minstrel's grave:*
> *Those hands are cold – but if thy notes divine*
> *May be by mortal wakened once again,*
> *Harp of my country, let me strike the strain.*

—From *The Harp of India*

He was considered 'the Morning Star of the Bengal Renaissance' that led to a national awakening. Equally, he spurred the Anglo-Indians to seek their rights. Teaming with John Ricketts, James Kyd and others, he was in the forefront of trying to get Britain to stop discriminating against the East Indians. He founded *The East Indian* for this purpose and urged the East Indians to unite with other Indians. But before any of his dreams came true he passed away in 1831. In 1992, Bengal remembered him by re-naming the massive Durgapur Bridge the Henry Louis Vivian Derozio Bridge.

A contemporary of Derozio in school and a fellow member of the East Indian Petition Committee was Charles Pote, the first of three great Anglo-Indian painters. A miniaturist and a portrait painter, he was much in demand in the Calcutta of the first half of the 19th century. His portraits of Sir Charles Metcalfe and David Hare, now in Calcutta, and of John Ricketts, now in Delhi, are described as 'stunning'.

Norman Hutchinson whose paintings of British Royalty might entitle him to be called the Royal Painter. (Photo: Internet)

The second of the great Anglo-Indian artists was Frank Scallan, also of Calcutta. His etchings of various Indian scenes done in the first half of the 20th century are still much in demand. He was a regular contributor to *The Statesman* on literary, historical and artistic topics and was much sought after as an illustrator by the leading publishers in India. But his full-time work for forty years was with the Survey of India.

The third of the trio went the furthest. Norman Hutchinson was a British Royal Painter, painting Queen Elizabeth II wearing the Kohinoor diamond in 1988. He began painting while a ward of Dr. Graham's Homes in Kalimpong, where one of its patrons. Lady Mountbatten, recognised his talent and paved his way to enter art school. He did portraits, seascapes and still-life, generally in oils. His portraits include ones of Nehru, Edwina Mountbatten, Elizabeth the Queen Mother, and Prince Philip. He exhibited all over the world but settled in London in 1959. He never, however, forgot Dr. Graham's and visited every year, always leaving it with a handsome endowment.

A more recent Anglo-Indian artist who has captured international interest with his miniature paintings on silk is Calcutta-born Bryan Feol. Inspired by Mughal art, Bryan (who settled in New York in 1986) is the owner of Artistic Pursuits in Brooklyn. His painting, *Bridges,* to commemorate the centenary of New York (1998), won him rich praise as has his work *Atlantis* on sea horses. *Independence,* which he created to observe India's 50th Anniversary of Independence, was a big draw, and the first limited edition canvas reproduction of it hangs in the Indian Consulate-General in New York.

Focused on a slightly different agenda has been Whitefield's Michael Ludgrove, an expert on rare books and manuscripts. He was earlier with the auction house Christie's and is now the Curator (Collections) of the Royal House of Mysore.

This talent with words and pictures is today found among Anglo-Indians in India mostly in journalism and advertising where they are solidly professional. But the creative stars of tomorrow are still to arrive.

All the World's a Stage

Indeed, all the world's a stage and, given their almost inborn love for music, dance and performance, Anglo-Indians have shone across the world not only in these arts but also in radio, theatre and films as well as modelling.

The 1950s and '60s were an age when Anglo-Indian singing talent took the world by storm. Lucknow-born Harry Webb dominated the pre-Beatles pop scene as Cliff Richard from the late 1950s, accompanied by his band, The Shadows. He went on to become the biggest selling singles artist of all time in the U.K., with sales of over 27 million in Britain and 150 million worldwide. He is the only singer to have had a Number One singles in the U.K. during each of

Left: Cliff Richard an all-time favourite internationally and knighted for his philanthropy. (Photo: Internet)

Bottom both: Music is very much a part of the life of almost every Anglo-Indian family, whether it is pop music, classical or choral. And it's a thought that cannot be better illustrated than by these two groups. Averne Fernandez's father (extreme left) and his three brothers were a popular group at dances and parties and, later, Averne and her three sisters took off as a separate but equally popular group. (Photo: Averne Fernandez)

The second in a triumvirate of pop music legends, Englebert Humperdinck. (Photo: Internet)

The third in the triumvirate who were at their peak between the 1950s and '70s, Tony Brent. (Photo: Internet)

Also of the 1950s-'70s era were the Sarstedt brothers who individually made names for themselves, Richard, seen here, being better known as Eden Kane. (Photo: Internet)

Right: *Pete Best, the first drummer of the Beatles and now in Liverpool's Music Hall of Fame. (Photo: Internet)*

six consecutive decades, from the 1950s to the 2000s. In 1995 he was knighted for his philanthropic work.

Another pop music legend who has sold over 150 million records over the last 40 years is Englebert Humperdinck, born Arnold George Dorsey in Madras. His song *Please Release Me* was No.1 in Britain and in the Top Ten in the U.S. keeping at bay the Beatles' *Strawberry Fields Forever* and *Penny Lane*. His 1967 ballad *The Last Waltz* was No.1 in U.K. and Ireland and in perhaps every Anglo-Indian heart.

The third in this triumvirate of the 1950s and 1960s in the U.K. was Tony Brent who was born Reginald Bretagne in Byculla, Bombay. Between 1953 and 1959 he had seven Top 20 hits in the U.K., but it was Radio Ceylon that made South Asia love him—particularly his version of *Some Enchanted Evening*.

Two others of this era were Delhi-ites Richard Sarstedt, who sang from the 1960s as Eden Kane, and his brother Peter Sarstedt who topped the U.K. charts in 1969 with *Where Do You Go to, My Lovely*, which reached No. 1 in 14 other countries as well. Kane, the eldest of three brothers, spent 74 weeks on the charts between 1961 and 1963. Younger brother Clive had a hit single in the 1970s and the three recorded together on occasion during this period.

Of this period too was Madras-born Pete Best who was the first drummer of the Beatles, playing with them from 1960 to 1962. He then formed his own bands, the most recent one the Pete Best Band. In 2007, Liverpool inducted Best into its Music Hall of Fame and in 2011 two new streets in the city were name Pete Best Drive and Casbah Close. The Casbah Coffee Club was started in the cellar of their house by his mother, Mona Best, and became popular with

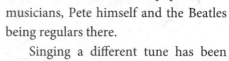

musicians, Pete himself and the Beatles being regulars there.

Singing a different tune has been Ralph Parker from Madurai who is the first Anglo-Indian singer to be signed for a country music record label in Nashville, Tennessee. When not singing or composing country music in Australia, he is a successful businessman.

Also singing in Australia is Calcutta-born Marie Wilson who moved from the Indian Jazz scene to the Australian Jazz circuit in the early 1960s. Her first LP, *I Thought about You*, was the first ever Australian Jazz vocal album to be released in the US. She was named the best New South Wales Jazz Singer of the Year in 1988 and won the Mo Award for Best Female Jazz vocalist in 1995 and 1999.

Country music is what Ralph Parker is known for. (Photo: AITW)

Another Anglo-Indian Jazz singer, called the 'Jazz Queen of Calcutta' in the 1960s and '70s, is Pam Crain, who started singing as a 17-year-old in independent India's first night club, the elite Mocambo. From then, hers was a voice heard all over India and never forgotten. She was the first Indian Western singer to cut an internationally released record. As famous as her were her contemporaries, the guitarist Carlton Kitto and vocalists Rubin Rebeiro and Shirley Churcher. In fact, Churcher's hit song *It's Now or Never* was featured on *Billboard*'s 'Hits of the World' in 1961.

Award-winning Jazz vocalist Marie Wilson. (Photo: AITW)

Another Pam, who cut a record with Pam Crain in 1954, was Pam McCarthy of Bombay, who, seated in her wheelchair, sang with what was possibly the best band in India at the time, her uncle Ken Mac's band. All Bombay's elite, particularly at the Taj, danced to her singing and Ken Mac's music in 1950s and '60s. She was also a good sportsperson and in 1962 won a Gold in Swimming and a Bronze in the Javelin at the Commonwealth Paraplegic Games.

The 'Jazz Queen of Calcutta', in the 1960s and '70s, Pam Crain. (Photo: Internet)

Bombay's favourite singer and band in the 1950s and '60s, Pam McCarthy and her uncle Ken Mac's band. (Photo: Internet)

Once churches reverberated to the voices of enthusiastic Anglo-Indian choristers accompanied by the organ played by such legends as William Alfred Mascarenhas who was the organist at the San Thomé Cathedral from 1904 to 1948 and was a well-known reviser and reformer of church music. (Photo: Simeon Mascarenhas)

Top: *Larry Stellar, singing and drumming his way to an OAM. (Photo: AITW)*

John Mayer, the best known Anglo-Indian Classical musician who moved from Western Classical to fusing it with Indian Classical. (Photo: Internet)

It was in the Governor's Band in Bombay, led by his father, that Larry Stellar got started in the 1940s, playing the drums. When he got to Sydney, his drumming and singing shot him to fame. Forming his own band he played all over Australia as well as in many countries overseas. In 2006, he was awarded the Order of Australia Medal.

If singing comes almost naturally to Anglo-Indians whose homes are full of everyone singing pop songs with varying degrees of success, and whose churches reverberate to the voices of enthusiastic choirs, playing a musical instrument is not far behind in popularity. Almost every home would have a harmonica or a guitar and many would have a piano too in the community's heyday. Not to mention the ubiquitous gramophone and the radio tuned to Radio Ceylon. But for all this love of music, Classical Western music never became a forte. Many a child did take piano or violin lessons, but after a couple of levels were passed chose pop to classical.

An exception was John Mayer who was born into an impoverished Anglo-Indian family in Calcutta and took to the violin when he was just seven. Scholarships took him to Bombay and the Royal Academy of Music, London, where he began exploring the links between Eastern and Western music. He was a violinist with the London Philharmonic for five years and with the Royal Philharmonic for seven, between 1953 and 1965. By then he had begun focusing on compositions fusing Indian and Western Classical music. Writing about him, Yehudi Menuhin said, "Very few musicians make a significant impact on even one sphere of music, but to leave a lasting impression on three vastly different areas—classical, jazz and world music—is an exceptional achievement." It was an impact achieved through an instrumental group he formed, Indo-Jazz Fusions, to record his compositions for albums between 1964 and 1973 and which he revived in 1996 when with the Birmingham Conservatoire where, the next year, he established a Bachelor's degree programme in Indian music.

Many an Anglo-Indian singer sang or played an instrument on local All India Radio stations before the

1960s when Western programmes were offered more air time. But the best known Anglo-Indian voice on the air was that of St. George's, Mussoorie, alumnus Melville de Mello(w) whose name became synonymous with broadcasting in India after he moved into radio from the Army. Reading the news, doing commentary—Gandhiji's funeral was perhaps his best remembered one—heading AIR's Western Music section or producing Doordarshan's acclaimed weekly current affairs and sports programmes, he was the voice of India on the air waves. He was also the author of several sports books. He was awarded the Padma Shri. His nephew Ian Tudor de Mello(w) has been awarded the Order of Australia Medal for his service to aged welfare.

The 'voice' of All India Radio, Melville de Mello(w), interviewing Rakesh Sharma, India's first man in space. (Photo: AIR)

From song and dance to the stage is just a step, and then it's another step to the world of films. The first actresses in both were Anglo-Indians. Mary Fenton from Delhi, to be known as Meherbai, was the first to act on the stage, joining a Parsi theatre troupe at a time when Indian theatre—indeed, South Asian theatre—was dominated by touring Parsi theatre. She was a star on that stage till 1895, acclaimed all over South Asia. She was followed in Parsi theatre by Calcutta-born Patience Cooper who before long moved into silent and sound films to became one of the first superstars of Bollywood. She has also been described as "the first ever female Indian film star" and was the first to play double roles, not in one film but in two. Perhaps her most famous films were *Nala Damyanti* (1920) and *Pati Bhakti* (1922). She starred in 40 films before she retired in 1944.

Bottom: Theatre personality Marcus Murch who long toured with 'Shakespearana'. (Photo: Internet)

Patience Cooper moved from the Parsi theatre to silent and sound films and became 'the first ever female Indian film star'. (Photo: Internet)

More recent Anglo-Indian theatre personalities are Marcus Murch and Joy Michael of Delhi, co-founders with four others of Delhi's leading rep theatre group, Yatrik. Murch toured for ten years with Geoffrey Kendal's Shakespearana throughout South and Southeast Asia before spending three years with rep in the U.K. On his return to Delhi he helped

Joy Michael, co-founder of Delhi's famed rep theatre group Yatrik, receiving the Padma Shri from President Pratibha Patil. (Photo: AITW)

found Yatrik in 1964, rejoined Shakespearana, and then, in 1973, began working with school, college and young theatre groups in Delhi.

Michael, on the other hand, trained with the London Academy of Music and Dramatic Art and has since then stuck with Yatrik directing its plays for over 40 years. She has directed over 250 plays in all for Yatrik and others. She was awarded the Padma Shri in 2012, after earlier receiving the Sangeet Nataka Akademi, Delhi Natya Sangh and Sahitya Kala Parishad Awards.

A theatre personality in the South is Priscilla Corner of Bangalore who has acted in a score of plays, sung for films and acted in them, including a feature film, *The Outhouse*, on the Anglo-Indian community.

Abroad, Russell Peters has made a name for himself as a Canadian-based stand-up comedian who was a few years ago ranked among the top 10 earning comedians in the world by *Forbes* magazine. The son of Anglo-Indian parents from Calcutta, who migrated to Toronto, Peters started his career in 1989. Today, he is known for programmes he has done in the U.K. and Australia besides Canada where he performs to sell-out, record-breaking crowds.

A favourite Canadian stand-up comedian, Russell Peters. (Photo: Internet)

Another famous comedian overseas, Alistair McGowan of the U.K., is the son of George McGowan of Calcutta who emigrated to England. His *Big Impression* TV show (1999) won him five awards. He was popular for his impersonations of celebrities on BBC Radio.

One of the first women to act in Indian films, Renée Smith chose the screen name Sita Devi. (Photo: Internet)

Also a theatre actress in the South is Andrea Jeremiah of Chennai who has moved on to playback singing and acting in films. From 2010 she has been much sought after by Tamil film-makers and in a 2013 hit, *Viswaroopam*, she stars with Kamal Haasan, perhaps the finest actor in the South.

The first women to act in Indian films, whatever the language, were all Anglo-Indians, most of them using Indian names. They included Renée Smith (Sita Devi), Effie Heppolet (Indira Devi), Beryl Claesson (Madhuri) and Irene Casper (Sabita Devi). The best known of this group, however, was not Anglo-Indian; Ruby Myers (Sulochana) was Jewish. In the 1920s she was the highest paid female film star in Asia but once the talkies came, she and the others faded out.

Then came Patience Cooper who received screen credits. After her the best known Anglo-Indian film actress in India was Burma-born Helen Richardson, only 'Helen' in all screen credits. Starting a Bollywood career in 1953, she first caught the attention of the public in 1958 and over the next two decades she was the dancing 'H-Bomb' of India's filmdom, acting in over 700 films. In 2009 she was awarded the Padma Shri.

Top left: From the stage to playback-singing to Tamil films with leading stars has been the progress of Andrea Jeremiah. (Photo: Internet)

Bottom: Moving from modelling to choreographing glamour events has been Marc Robinson, once India's 'No. 1 Male Model'. (Photo: Internet)

Helen Richardson was always 'Helen' to the Indian film industry and the 'H-Bomb' to the millions of her fans. (Photo: Internet)

Three Anglo-Indian men who made it to Bollywood were Delhi's Howard Rosemeyer, Denzil Smith and Bombay's Marc Robinson. A top actor, dancer and choreographer in theatre for several years, Rosemeyer moved to the world of films where he has choreographed movies such as *Parineeta* and *Kucch to Hai*, and acted in a few as well. Smith has acted in 15 Bollywood films as well as two English movies made in India. Robinson, on the other hand, made just one film in Hindi, but for several years was India's No. 1 male model. Since then he has been a model coordinator, choreographer for glamour events, and National Director of the Femina Miss India contests. In Madras, Jeffery Vardon has choreographed

Merle Oberon of
Bombay and Calcutta
became one of
Hollywood's leading
actresses.
(Photo: Internet)

Bottom: Perhaps the
best cameraman ever
of the South Indian film
industry, one of the
world's biggest, Marcus
Bartley. Behind him is
his son and assistant.
(Photo: AITW)

From dancing in
Can-Can Juliet Prowse
went on to become a
popular Hollywood
actress and then a TV
star. (Photo: Internet)

successful Tamil films like *Valli* and *Aalavandhan* as well as several stage musicals. He also features in the recent Tamil film *Poda Podi*.

A few film actors and actresses who became big Hollywood names fought shy of acknowledging Anglo-Indian heritage. *Boris Karloff*, born William Henry Pratt in London, had paternal grandparents who were Anglo-Indians. Edward Pratt Sr and his son Edward Jr, Karloff's father, were in government service in India. Pratt Sr's wife Eliza was the sister of Anna Leonowens. Merle Oberon was born Estelle Merle O'Brien Thompson in Bombay and studied at La Martiniere, Calcutta till she was 17. Her father was British, mother Ceylonese. In time, she became a Hollywood film star and was nominated in 1935 for a Best Actress Academy Award. And *Vivien Leigh* who won two Oscars for Best Actress was Darjeeling-born Vivien Mary Hartley. Her mother was Gertrude Mary Robinson Yackjee. The uncertainty of the Yackjee roots is why she is often described as Anglo-Indian. After a few years of schooling in India, the family moved to London where Vivien Leigh studied Drama before moving into Theatre and Films.

Juliet Prowse's heritage is a little more certain. Born in Bombay to Anglo-Indian parents, she grew up in South Africa to where the family had emigrated after Independence. She became a dancer and was spotted in Paris for a leading role in the film *Can-Can*—and she was on her way. She teamed with Frank Sinatra for a while, then with Elvis Presley. She then moved into American television and in the 1980s into hosting international dancing competitions.

India, with the world's largest film industry, has long had a substantial part of it centred on Madras that is Chennai. The southern film capital has long been known for its technicians and two of the outstanding ones have been Anglo-Indians.

From the early 1940s to the early 1980s Marcus Bartley of Madras was considered the greatest cinematographer of his time in the South Indian film industry. He was a master of black and white photography but it was his work with colour that helped the Malayalam classic *Chemmeen* to win the gold medal at the Cannes International Film Festival in 1978. In 1970 he won the National Film Award for the Best Cinematography in India.

The other Anglo-Indian is Lewellyn Anthony Gonsalves who is at present making his mark in the South Indian film industry as a film editor. Starting life as a courier boy, he learnt his job during deliveries to editing studios. From the cutting and splicing method he moved into the digital when given a chance in 1997 and today is said to have heralded the digital age of editing in the South Indian film industry.

Dancing from a young age, being encouraged to perform even while in school, and a relaxed stage presence have all helped several Anglo-Indian girls to became models, with some of them the best in the business. And the good looks of many of them have had them being chosen beauty queens.

The story of the Bredemeyer sisters from Goa is an amazing one. Indira was Miss India in 1975, Anna in 1976 and Ulrika in 1980. Indira also went on to be Miss International runner-up and Anna Miss Asia-Pacific runner-up. All three have had long modelling stints; Anna, who has been described as "a super model", became a leading choreographer after

Bottom left:
Participants in an Anglo-Indian fashion show in Bangalore on World Anglo-Indian Day, 2 August. (Photo: AITW)

Daphne Stokoe-Sampson, the winner in a Marilyn Monroe look-alike competition held in Bombay. (Photo: Phil Crook)

Miss World 1997, Diana Hayden, now actively involved with a slew of NGOs and charities in India and elsewhere. (Photo: Internet)

Sara Corner, Miss India 2001, now a much sought-after model. (Photo: Internet)

her modelling years as well as a much sought-after Brand Ambassador for lifestyle products, promoting several renowned international brands all over India.

But one who went further than the Bredemeyer sisters is Hyderabad's Diana Hayden, Miss India in 1997 who later that year won the Miss World crown. She went on to become a model, modelling for various international brands, then appeared in films in South Africa and Bollywood, hosted several international events, and has been a goodwill ambassador at venues ranging from the Cannes Film Festival to a White House State Dinner. She now lectures on confidence building and motivation but, most significantly, is actively involved with NGOs and charities round the world focused on women and children. Breast cancer, Spastics and HIV/AIDS, among many others, have benefitted from her support.

Following in Diana Hayden's footsteps, Sara Corner of Bangalore was Miss India-World in 2001 and is a much sought after ramp and advertising model. Another top model since 1996 is Allahabad-born Michelle Innes who, besides ramp and advertising modelling, is one of the most popular choices for music video 'shoots'.

Off the ramp but popular for his designs on it has been Shane Peacock of Bangalore. Starting as a fashion designer, he has, since, in partnership with Falguni, established three designer-label stores in Mumbai (including their flagship *Peacock Brides)* and one in Delhi. While West Asia constitutes their major market, their line is also available in London, New York and Tokyo.

Indeed, all the world's a stage for Anglo-Indians and almost every day you find a new face from among them in the worlds of music and dance, theatre and films and modelling. There seems to be no end to the stream of talent and looks and willingness to work hard in this world emerging from the community.

Winners All

It may be argued that, pre-1952, few countries played hockey and that in the kingdom of the one-eyed India was supreme. But even if you buy that argument, what would Indian hockey have been without the Anglo-Indians? Indeed, pre-Independence, from the time Anglo-Indians took to the game c.1890s they dominated the sport totally out of proportion to their numbers. Teams like Calcutta Rangers, Calcutta Customs, Port Commissioner's, Measurers, Bengal-Nagpur Railway, Madras & South Mahratta Railways, Madras Telegraphs, Bombay's Great Indian Peninsula and BBCI teams won tournament after tournament. The felicity with which they played the game, it was almost as though the Anglo-Indians were born to it. Certainly it was the major sport in every Anglo-Indian school, it was the game nurtured in the Railway Institutes and Anglo-Indian clubs, and it was the game every Anglo-Indian parent urged his sons—and even daughters—to excel in during the first half of the 20th century. Later, when the migration of the Anglo-Indians began in the 1950s, it was they who helped Canada, England and, particularly, Australia to take to the game seriously. And if Australia are world hockey champions today, the foundations for that success were laid by Anglo-Indians settling in Perth and Melbourne and Sydney.

Three years ago, an effort to revive Anglo-Indian involvement in the sport was launched by the quarterly

The Anglos In The Wind *journal's 'Dream Anglo-Indian Team'. (Graphic: AITW)*

Chennai journal *Anglos In The Wind*. In a special issue on hockey it picked an all-time Anglo-Indian team from those who had played for India. Those chosen were:

Goal: Richard Allen (Bengal); *Backs:* (L) Carl Tapsell (Bengal) and (R) Leslie Hammond (U.P.); *Halves:* (L) Joe Galibardy (Bengal), (C) Eric Penniger (Punjab), and (R) Leslie Claudius (Bengal) (Captain); *Forwards:* (LW) Gerry Glacken (Bengal), (IL) Pat Jansen (Bengal), (C) Dicky Carr (Bengal), (IR) Jimmy Carr (Madras & Railways) and (RW) Maurice Gately (Delhi). *Coach:* Rex Norris (C.P.)

Jimmy Carr is the only member of this team who never played for India, but "he was every bit as good as K.D. Singh Babu," according to the selectors of this team.

Three players in this team are players I consider amongst the finest in the world of all-time! Eric Penniger of Saharanpur (U.P.), Richard Allen of Nagpur and Leslie Claudius of Calcutta. Penniger captained India on the field when in 1928 it first entered a hockey team in the Olympics and got it off to a winning streak that ended only at the 1960 Olympics. Penniger, considered one of the greatest centre halves of all time, was given the captainship—which he should have been given in the first place—when Jaipal Singh of Cambridge University, and a Blue, named captain in a bit of social hierarchy one-upmanship, did not play

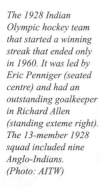

The 1928 Indian Olympic hockey team that started a winning streak that ended only in 1960. It was led by Eric Penniger (seated centre) and had an outstanding goalkeeper in Richard Allen (standing exteme right). The 13-member 1928 squad included nine Anglo-Indians. (Photo: AITW)

a game. Penniger was in the winning 1932 team too and would also have been in the 1936 one, but injury kept him out of that one.

Allen was India's goalkeeper in the three winning teams of 1928, '32 and '36 and would have been there in 1940 too—when he was still the world's best goalkeeper of the time—if World War II had not prevented the holding of the Olympics. His record of allowing only two goals in three Olympics (none in the 1928 Games) still stands.

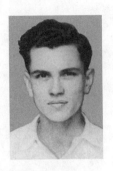

Leslie Claudius as he looked in his youth when he helped India to three Olympic Golds and a Silver and was considered the world's best right-half. (Photo: AITW)

But the greatest of them all must be Leslie Claudius, born in Bilaspur, who, playing right-half, helped India to Olympic Golds in 1948, 1952 and 1956 and to a Silver in 1960, when he captained the team. In the 1960 Games, when India played Australia in the semi-finals, the Australian vice-captain was Kevin Carton, who learned his hockey at St. Joseph's, Nainital. Carton went on to captain Australia. Like Penniger and Allen (who played in an age when the only protective gear was leg pads), Claudius must be one of the all-time greats in the sport.

The first instance of two brothers winning Gold in hockey at the Olympics was recorded by William and Ernest Goodsir-Cullen. Ferozepur-born William was a reserve in that 1928 team that won India's first Gold in hockey, but played in three matches. Ernest, who was a student at Madras Medical College, was chosen in 1936 and played in all the matches when Penniger couldn't make the trip due to injury. Ernest Cullen later migrated to Ireland where he finished his studies, the finals of which kept him out of the Irish hockey team for the 1952 Olympics for which he was chosen.

Other Anglo-Indian hockey Olympians prior to Independence were Michael Roque, Frederic Seaman, George Marthins, William Sullivan, Lionel Emmett, Cyril Mitchie, Arthur Hind and Frank Brewin.

Outstanding Anglo-Indian players in the past included Garney Nyss, Laurie Woodcock, Albert Holder, F.C. Wells, Syd Minto, Meldric Daluz who played in the 1952 Helsinki Olympics, Nigel Richtor, Erman Bastian, Charles Huggins, Roger Magee and Colin Blankley.

In more recent times, Mark Patterson (Bombay), Alan Schofield (Bangalore), Aloysius Edwards who represented Punjab (and captained India in the 1996 Olympics), Leslie Fernandez (Madras) and Adam Sinclair (Coimbatore) have been in Indian teams. While Sinclair has been a forward, the rest were all goalkeepers. Leslie Fernandez was goalkeeper of the Indian team which won the 1975 World Cup at Kuala Lumpur, while Alan Schofield was goalkeeper of the Gold-winning team at the 1980 Moscow Olympics.

'Jimmy' Jameson of the Bombay Police, a good hockey player and sound administrator, umpired in the 1964 and 1968 Olympics. His son John preferred cricket and went on to have a long innings with Warwickshire and played four Tests for England. John also coached Bangladesh during its nascent years in cricket.

Australia's rise in hockey had much to do with the Jamalpur-born Pearce brothers, who learnt their hockey in Nagpur. Three of them played for Australia in the 1956 Olympics—Melville, Eric, and Gordon—and three in 1960 and 1968—Eric, Gordon and Julian. Eric and Julian were in the 1964 team that won Bronze, Australia's first Olympic Medal in hockey. In 1960, Eric had the unique record of scoring all eight goals when Australia beat Japan 8-1. He carried the Australian flag at the Mexico City march past in 1968, the first Australian hockey player to be given the honour. Both he and Julian were elected to the Australian Hall of

Bottom right: The Pearce brothers who put Australian hockey on the road to World and Olympic Championships. All five played for Australia, but Cecil the eldest (front row, left) missed an Olympics call because he had retired by the time Australia had its first Olympic hockey team. The most successful was Eric, standing right. The others are Julian and Mel (standing left and centre) and Gordon (front row, right). (Photo: The Pearce family)

Right: *Eric Pearce, the first hockey player inducted into the Sports Australia Hall of Fame (1984). (Photo: AITW)*

Sporting Fame, Eric in the very first selection in 1985 and Julian in 1990.

Four Australians whose parents were Anglo-Indian migrants played for Australia in the Olympics and in world championships and went on to contribute significantly to the game as coaches. They are Terry Walsh (1976 and 1984), Paul Gaudoin (1996 and 2000), Godfrey Phillips from Burnpur (1968 and 1972) and Don Smart (1964, 1968 and 1972). Phillips, whose hockey home in Australia was New South Wales, unlike the others mentioned who were all associated with Western Australia, was founding President of the NSW Coaches Federation and first Head Coach of the NSW Hockey Academy. Over 25 of his wards have gone on to represent Australia. He was also the convenor of the NSW hockey selectors for over 25 years. He has coached throughout Australia and in New Zealand, USA and Canada. His son Mathew was in the 2008 Australian team before injury forced him out of the highest level. Smart too has coached State and International level teams in Australia from 1981 to 1985.

Walsh, whose parents were from Rawalpindi, coached Malaysia, Australia and Holland post-1986. Gaudoin, whose parents were from Madras, captained Australia at the Commonwealth Games (Gold) and in the World Cup (Silver) in 2002. He then got into coaching following in his father's footsteps and has been Assistant Coach for Australia since 2010 when it won the World Cup in Delhi and the Silver medal at the 2012 London Olympics.

The coach of the 2012 Olympic team was Ric Charlesworth, considered the finest player Australia has produced. As a player he owed much to Mervyn Adams from Bombay who learnt his hockey at La Martiniere, Lucknow. Adams coached Western Australia to eight national championships and in 1976 coached the Australian team to a Silver Medal in the Olympics. In 1978, he coached the Australian women's team for the World Cup.

Other Anglo-Indians who played for Australia in the Olympics were Kevin Carton (1956, 1960), Dennis Kemp

Mervyn Adams, legendary West Australia coach, who coached the national men's and women's teams in 1976 and 1978 respectively. (Photo: AITW)

(1956), Ray Whiteside (1956), Tony Waters (1964) and Malcolm Poole (1976). Among those who were successful as coaches were Fred Browne, Cyril Carton, Ivan Meade, Derek Munrowd and Glen Davis, with Fred Browne being the coach of the Australian hockey team at the 1956 Melbourne Olympics.

English hockey too in the modern era owes much to Anglo-Indian contribution. Neil Nugent from St. George's, Mussoorie, was the first of the contributors, and he played in the 1952 Olympics. Then came John Conroy, possibly the best of them (1952 and 1956), Fred Scott (1956) and *Jon Potter* in 1984.

Another great Anglo-Indian coach on the international scene was Rex Norris from Chikmagalur who learnt his hockey in Bangalore. Norris, who was left-half in that legendary 1928 Olympic team, went on, after Independence, to coach Holland, Italy and Mexico. He was responsible for Holland developing into a major hockey power.

Norris fathered a sporting family. His sons Havelock and Ron boxed for India, Ron reaching the quarter-finals in the 1952 Olympics. His daughters Wendy and Philomena played hockey for India, as did his nieces Yvonne and Dorrell Smith.

Women's hockey, too, in India was dominated by Anglo-Indians till the 1970s. Doreen Stevens and Pansy Thomas excelled in the game in the 1960s, but it was Anne Lumsden of Calcutta who was the first to be recognised for her contribution to the game. She was in 1961 awarded

Bottom right: Anne Lumsden, the first woman to be given the Arjuna Award. She was India's best ever woman hockey player in that era till the mid-1960s when Anglo-Indians dominated the game. (Photo: The Hindu)

Rex Norris, the coach who developed Dutch hockey, seen here with his sporting brood. Rex Norris is in the blazer and from left to right are Ron who boxed for India, Philomena and Wendy who played hockey for India, and Jennifer. (Photo: AITW)

the Arjuna Award, the national award for outstanding performance in a sport, the first Indian woman to receive the award. Before her, Betty Catchick of Calcutta was the most famous Indian woman hockey player.

Another family with an outstanding record in sports is the Boosey family. They made their mark in the sports activity that the Anglo-Indians have fared best in after hockey, namely athletics.

No family has the cumulative record the Booseys from the Kolar Gold Fields have in the triple jump. Father Leslie, who captained Madras, jumped inches short of 50 feet, Derek went over 53 feet and younger brother Allan 48 feet-plus. Derek Boosey represented Karnataka, Maharashtra and, then, Britain 35 times between 1962 and 1972 in the hop, step and jump, including at the Mexico Olympics (1968). From the 1970s, he has at various times headed sports administration at the Sussex (U.K.) and Melbourne Universities, been a coach with Canadian, Saudi Arabian, South Korean, and Chinese national teams, helped coach Australian national decathletes and heptathletes, been a Technical Advisor at the Seoul (1988) and Barcelona (1992) Olympics, was Chief Administrator, Operations, of the XII Commonwealth Games held in Brisbane in 1982, and helped Chinese 10 km walking champion Yueling Chen, the first Asian woman and the first Chinese athlete to win an Olympic Gold Medal. After her stunning victory in 1992, she migrated to the U.S. where, in 1998, she began training again with Derek Boosey, who was her personal coach when she went to the Sydney Olympics (2000), this time with the U.S. team. San Diego (U.S.)-based Derek Boosey also has an amazing record in the World Masters (Veterans) Games. In 1987 he won the hop, step and jump Silver medal representing Australia in Melbourne in the 45-49 age group, in 1991 the Bronze in Japan representing Canada (50-54 years), in 1998 the Gold

Outstanding in the hop, step and jump, Derek Boosey became a coach welcomed by many national teams, a sports administrator and a repeated champion in World Masters' competition.(Photo: SM Collection)

Both top: Leslie Boosey (top) and Henry Rebello (top right) were outstanding hop, step and jump champions in their time. Rebello was a favourite for the title in the London Olympics (1948) till a hamstring did him in. Leslie Boosey's two sons, Derek and Allan, followed in their father's footsteps as triple jumpers. (Photo: The Hindu)

in Oregon representing Canada (55-59 years) and in 2005 the Bronze in Canada representing the U.S. (1960-64). And still he trains—despite the rigours of being the Vice-President of a bioceutical company.

Younger brother Allan followed Derek into coaching at University level in the U.K., Saudi Arabia, Jamaica and Australia. He also followed him into sports administration and was the Chief Administrator in Brisbane when the 2001 Worldwide Games were held there.

Between 1938 and 1952 Leslie Boosey, representing Madras, and Henry Rebello, representing Mysore, dominated the Indian hop, step and jump scene. Boosey was the first Indian to jump over 49 feet and Rebello was the first to cross 50 feet. Rebello was one of the favourites to take the Gold at the 1948 Olympics but injury on his way to his first jump put an end to his hopes.

The first athlete from India to win an Olympic medal was Norman Pritchard of Calcutta in 1900. He competed in the 100 and 200 yards events and the 110 and 220 yards hurdles, winning Silvers in the two longer distances. His medals have been credited to India by the IOC, but the IAAF has claimed that Pritchard had represented Great Britain. Of his, and his family's, domicile, though, there are no doubts. Pritchard migrated after the Olympics and became a well-known actor in Hollywood.

The first to win Olympic medals for India was star athlete Norman Pritchard who went on to work in Hollywood. (Sketch: Internet)

Another hurdler was Jamalpur-born Mervyn Sutton who captained the Indian athletic team in the 1932 Olympics which included sprinters Ronald Vernieux and Dicky Carr, who was in both the 4 x 100m relay and hockey teams. An all-round sprinter, 'Bunoo' Sutton reached the semi-finals of the 110 yards hurdles. Achieving the same feat was James Vickers in 1948, his timing being bettered only by India's best-ever hurdler, Gurbachan Singh, in 1964. Two hurdlers of Madras who participated in the Asian Games (1951) were Carlton Cleur and De Classe in the 110m and 400m hurdles respectively. Ronnie O'Brien picked up the Bronze in the decathlon at the 1954 Manila Games.

One of only two Anglo-Indians to win India's highest coaching award, the Dronacharya Award, was Ken Bosen of Madras who was given it in 2000. The first Indian to throw the javelin over 60 metres (1955), his athletics career was cut short by illness and he turned to coaching, spending forty years of his life in it. He was India's Chief National Coach in 1969-70 and 1985-86. Considered an authority on the throws as well as pole vaulting, he has written several books on these and coaching in general.

India's National Athletics Coach in 1969-70, Ken Bosen was awarded India's highest coaching award, the Dronacharya, only one of two Anglo-Indians to receive it. (Photo: AITW)

Among the women, Barbara Webster of Bangalore won Bronze in the shot put and javelin while Sylvia Gauntlet picked up the Bronze in the long jump at the 1951 Asian Games. Marjorie Suares who captained the Karnataka Hockey, Basketball and Athletic teams, narrowly missed the Bronze in the high jump at the 1951 Asiad. In 1954, Christine Brown won the 100m Bronze at the Asian Games and along with Violet Peters won the Gold in the 100m relay. In 1958, Elizabeth Davenport was the Silver medallist in the javelin and followed it up with a Bronze at the 1962 Asian Games. In the 1966 Games, Christine Forage of Bombay won the Bronze in the Long Jump.

While the Anglo-Indians made hockey India's national game, curiously they did not take to what is the sub-continent's most popular spectator sport today, cricket. Several of them, like Ren Nailer of Kolar and Madras, played first-class cricket—he played for Madras, South India and a record 29 years in Madras's Annual Presidency Match for the Europeans (for whom he played versus the Indians)— but only five made it to the national level, Duncan Sharpe in Pakistan, Roger Binny in India, John Jameson in England and Stuart Clark, born to parents from Madras, and Gujarat-born Reginald (Rex) Sellers in Australia. Sharpe played just a

Bottom left: Roger Binny was the first Anglo-Indian to make it to the Indian cricket team and he proved a key player in that winning combination that brought home the 1983 World Cup. (Photo: AITW)

The first Anglo-Indian to wear the Australian cap in a substantial number of Test matches, Stuart Clark. (Photo: The Hindu)

couple of matches for Pakistan as a wicket-keeper, but Binny, from Bangalore, was an all-rounder who played 27 Tests for India and was a key player in India winning the World Cup in 1983. A cricket administrator in Karnataka and a coach at the national level, he is now a National Selector. Binny represented the Anglo-Indians in the Karnataka Legislative Assembly in 2000-2005. His son Stuart is a key player in the Karnataka team today. Barrington Rowland preceded him in the Karnataka team and played for the State from 1999 to 2007. Stuart Clark represented New South Wales for years before he was called up to represent Australia in 2005-06. He played 24 Tests, 39 ODIs and 26 T20 matches for Australia. Turning out for South Australia in the Sheffield Shield for many years, Rex Sellers was selected for the Ashes tour of England in 1964 but injury prevented him playing any Tests. In 1964-65, he toured India and played in one Test. After his playing career, he has been active in South Australian cricket administration. Another of Anglo-Indian descent who played Sheffield Shield cricket in Australia was Madras-born Mark Lavender, who represented Victoria from 1991 to 1998.

Despite Anglo-Indians giving cricket a secondary place in their sporting preferences, it was one of them who helped launch India on the international cricket scene. Karachi-born Anthony de Mello helped found the Board of Control for Cricket in India in 1928 in Delhi. He was the Board's first Secretary and his boss, R.E. Grant Govan, its first President. They moved the BCCI headquarters to Bombay where they both were instrumental in founding the Cricket Club of India and raising the famed Brabourne Stadium. de Mello, who helped modernise public transport in Delhi, was the organising secretary of the first Asian Games (Delhi, 1951). A modest cricketer, he captained the first 'Rest' team to compete in the Bombay Pentangular.

Bezwada (Vijayawada)-born Neil D'Costa, a good all-round sportsman at St. George's, Ketti (Ooty), became a successful cricket coach in Australia where he helped groom Michael Clarke (the present captain), Phil Hughes, a Test

Bottom: A coach with a fine eye for talent in Australia, Neil D'Costa was the one who groomed Michael Clarke. (Photo: Internet)

Anthony de Mello who helped found the Board of Control for Cricket in India in 1928. (Photo: The Hindu)

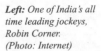

opener, and pacer Mitchell Starc. He is considered one of Australia's outstanding coaches at the grassroots.

Horse racing was a sport that several small-made Anglo-Indians took to in India after Independence, setting several records as jockeys and trainers.

Robin Corner from Bangalore rode 1982 winners at various centres between 1974 and the mid-1990s, being champion jockey 23 times at different race clubs in India from the time he rode his father's horse, *Chief Justice*, trained by his brother, to victory in 1974. He rode for India in International Derbys in Perth and Istanbul, winning in the Turkish capital.

A Bangalore-Calcutta family with a similar record is the Alfords. Arguably India's greatest ever Indian-born jockey till the 1980s, Richard Alford bestrode the racing circuit in India like a colossus in the 1970s. In fact, he spent 20 years at the top in the Indian subcontinent, riding 960 winners when there was much less racing and even less access to its various centres. He rode the winner of the Indian Invitation Cup in 1975 and, as a trainer, saddled the winner of the Calcutta Triple Crown. He has trained close to 800 winners and has won every Classic in India.

Alford comes from a family of jockeys, with his brother Ernest also riding numerous winners in India. His son Shawn is also a jockey, riding in Kuwait. Another son, Rutherford, was badly injured in a racing accident and is now a trainer. His nephew Christopher Alford is one of the few Indian jockeys to have ridden over 1000 winners (between 1994 and 2000). Christopher has won the Calcutta Derby several times.

Both: Richard Alford as jockey and trainer. Many felt he was India's greatest ever Indian-born jockey till the 1980s. (Photo: Press clipping)

The Alfords, connected for four decades with Calcutta racing, are descended from Rutherford Dalrymple-Alford, born in 1906 in Madras and who began the family tradition of riding and training.

Madras-born Sinclair Marshall rode 982 winners in his 35-year-long career, but his most significant achievement was to form the Jockeys' Association of India in 1973 and lead it till he stepped down as President in 2011. He was particularly successful in getting Indian jockeys to be treated on par with foreign ones.

In several other sports, individual Anglo-Indians have made their mark, perhaps the earliest being Kharagpur's Jenny Sandison. The first Indian woman to win a tennis championship in India was her sister in 1925. But from 1927 onwards there was no stopping Jenny who, in 1929, became the first Indian woman to play at Wimbledon. She was there in 1930 too. India's national champion for many years, she won several county titles in Britain too.

India's first woman to play in the Wimbledon championships, Jenny Sandison (second from right), was India's national champion for years in the 1920s and '30s. (Photo: The Hindu)

The first Anglo-Indian to win the Dronacharya Award for coaching, Wilson Jones (left) was the first Indian to win the Amateur World Billiards championship. (Photo: The Hindu)

Bottom: Jennifer (Dutton) Paes who captained the Indian women's basketball team in 1982. (Photo: Internet)

Centre: One of India's finest women swimmers, Nisha Millet, is now into coaching. (Photo: AITW)

The first Anglo-Indian to captain the Indian football team, Carlton Chapman. (Photo: Internet)

But perhaps the greatest Anglo-Indian achiever in sport, another 'Claudius', was Wilson Jones from Poona and Bombay. He was the first Indian to win the Amateur World Billiards Championship (1958) and then he won the title again in 1964. Between 1950, when he won his first national title, and 1966, he won the national billiards title 12 times and the snooker title five times. He then turned to coaching and was in 1996 awarded the Dronacharya Award for nurturing several champions, including some who won world titles.

Two other Anglo-Indian sports stars who made a significant mark in Indian sport are Carlton Chapman and Nisha Millet. Chapman was the first Anglo-Indian to captain the Indian football (soccer) team. Bangalore-born Chapman, between 1992 and 2001, played for some of the leading football teams in the country, led the country in the last couple of years of his playing career, and has gone on to become a leading coach.

Millet, from Madras, went on from the age of 9 to swim competitively for 15 years. In 2000, she was the first Indian woman to be chosen to swim in the Olympics. Moving on to coaching, she has trained hundreds of swimmers of all ages in Bangalore, some of whom have gone on to make Karnataka the country's leading State in swimming. When not coaching, she is a motivational speaker, much sought after by leading multinational and other business houses in India. Jennifer Paes (née Dutton) of Calcutta captained the Indian women's basketball team in the 1982 Asian basketball

Boxing was always a popular sport amongst the Anglo-Indians. This team, Company C in an AF(I) unit, is an all-Anglo-Indian team that won an Army tournament in 1927. (Photo: Zhaynn A. James)

championships. She was a member of the 1972 Olympics team. She is the mother of Leander Paes, of Goan heritage and arguably India's most successful tennis player.

Several Anglo-Indians also led the field in Indian boxing between the Wars, but few went on to higher honours. Gene Raymond, Ronald Cranston and John Nuttall boxed for India in the 1948 Olympics and Oscar Ward did so in the 1952 Olympics where Sidney Greave boxed for Pakistan. Ronnie Moore was selected for the 1948 and 1952 Olympics but police duties prevented his participation. Raymond, many think, was the best boxer India produced till the recent upsurge in boxing in the country. But others claim it was Dusty Miller of an earlier era.

Few communities in India have contributed so much in such a variety of sports in the country and abroad as the Anglo-Indians.

Leaders of the Flock

A flock needs spiritual leadership. It needs leadership of it as a community. And it needs leadership by those who see the community as part of the whole, a leadership provided by men and women who see themselves as leaders in a principality or a nation state.

In the world of Anglo-Indian spirituality there have from the community's beginnings been numerous priests, archbishops and bishops of Euro-Indian heritage ministering to flocks that were Roman Catholic or Protestant, generally Anglican. But few reached the higher rungs of the corridors of the spiritual hierarchy. The first of them was also the first Indian to be bestowed sainthood. Gonsalo Garcias, a Luso-Indian born in Bassein (Vasai), was martyred in Japan in 1597 while on missionary work. He was only 41. He was declared a Saint in 1862. The Feast of St. Garcia is celebrated every year in Bassein and draws crowds from all round the Bombay area.

Saint Gonsalo Garcias, a Franciscan who was martyred in Japan. (Photo: Internet)

Garcia was trained by the Jesuits, but as the Jesuits had not opened up their Order to Indians, he went with them to Japan as a catechist in 1572. He moved to Manila eight years later where he became a successful businessman before being invited by the Franciscans to join their Order. It was as a Franciscan missionary that he returned to Japan in 1592 to work among the lepers. And it was there that he was crucified on charges of attempting to overthrow the emperor.

Cardinal Lawrence Picachy, the first Anglo-Indian Cardinal. (Photo: Internet)

In the centuries that followed numerous Euro-Indians joined the Catholic priesthood or the brotherhood and sisterhood of various international Orders. Their leadership, apart from in the church and mission outposts, was in educational and medical institutions and hospices, many going on to head these institutions. The one who went furthest was Darjeeling-born Cardinal Lawrence Picachy.

Father Picachy, a Jesuit, was Prefect and Rector of Calcutta's famed St. Xavier's College in the 1950s. He went on to become the Bishop of Jamshedpur and Archbishop of Calcutta in the 1960s before being made a Cardinal in 1976. He was one of the Cardinal Electors who chose Popes John Paul I and John Paul II.

In more recent years, numerous other Euro-Indians have contributed significantly to the leadership of the Catholic Church in India. They include Alan de Lastic, an Anglo-Burmese, who rose to become Archbishop of Delhi in 1990 and was Christianity's most prominent spokesperson in India until his death in 2000, and Henry D'Souza who was Archbishop of Calcutta from 1986 until 2002. Earlier, Monsignor Eric Barber had been Bishop and Vicar General of Calcutta for several years. Amongst the Brotherhood, Bro. Jerome Ellens of Madras has been Superior General of the Patrician Brothers of Ireland since 2004, and Bro. Christopher Dawes of the same Order has been its Provincial in India. Sr. Lorraine Delaney of Vishakhapatnam is the Superior General of the Sisters of St. Joseph of Chambery (headquartered in Rome) since 1997.

In the Anglican Church, Madras-born Ivor Smith-Cameron, had his theological training in the United Kingdom when he moved there shortly after Independence and stayed on there to serve as Chaplain in institutions of higher learning in the London area. In 1972, he was appointed Residential Canon of Southwark Cathedral and Diocesan Missioner for the Southwark Diocese, where he became known for his work with refugees and the homeless and in improving race relations. The Queen of England appointed him one of her Chaplains, the first Asian to be so honoured.

Canon Ivor Smith-Cameron, a Queen's Chaplain. (Photo: AITW)

Leadership of a different sort was seen in some Europeans who put down roots in India as well as in some Anglo-Indians who, granted vast swathes of territory by local rulers for services rendered by them, considered themselves virtual rajahs. One who was described as the Rajah of Tipperary, was Irishman George Thomas, linked in curious fashion to a freebooter of an earlier generation, Walter Reinhardt (Sombre/Somroo). French-born Reinhardt fought under several flags, before establishing the principality of Sardhana near Delhi. On his death 21 years after he had married her when she was a teenager, Begum Somroo took charge of the Principality. She left her estate to David Dyce Sombre, descended from Reinhardt's first marriage to another *bibi*. When the British took over Sardhana in 1836 on the Begum's death, Dyce Sombre, with his personal fortune and compensation intact, settled in England. Dyce Sombre was the first person of Asian descent to be elected to Parliament there. Within a year of his election in 1841 he was removed from Parliament being found guilty of bribery. The title to the Sardhana property passed on to other members of the Sombre family from his first wife.

The first person of Asian descent to be elected to the British Parliament, Dyce Sombre belonged to the Somroo family of Sardhana. (Photo: Internet)

The link between Thomas's Hansi and Sardhana was forged when Thomas spread out from his capital and established, to a great extent, what is known as Haryana today and then offered military support to Sardhana. George Thomas became Begum Somroo's lover for a while and then married a girl she chose for him. On his death Begum Somroo brought up his children as her own.

Of the 18th century too was the Marquis de Bussy, to become Governor General of Pondicherry in 1783. In the 1750s, while serving Joseph Dupleix, the then Governor, he married Dupleix's step-daughter, a *metisse*. His victorious campaign in what is Andhra Pradesh today led to him being presented as personal property what became the French enclave of Yanam. Other Frenchmen, freebooters all, who designated themselves Generals, like Pierre Cuillier-Perron, Count Benoit de Boigne and Antoine-Louis Polier, all became *zamin* holders with Indian wives. And there was Claude

Marquis de Bussy, a Governor General of French territories in India from 1783, was awarded Yanam, now a Pondicherry enclave in Andhra Pradesh, as his personal jagir. *(Photo: Internet)*

Perhaps the most successful French freebooter in India was Claude Martin of Oudh, whose contribution that survives is also perhaps the biggest by a person who, in later times, would have been called a 'Domiciled European'. Martin's legacy was three schools, La Martiniere in his Lucknow, La Martiniere in Calcutta, and La Martiniere in his native Lyons in France. Generations of Anglo-Indians benefitted immensely from his two schools in India. (Photo: La Martiniere)

Capt. John Doveton was an Anglo-Indian who prospered in the 19th century, but never forgot his roots. His bequests for schools and scholarships in Madras and Calcutta have helped thousands of Anglo-Indian children improve their lot. (Photo: Internet)

Martin who journeyed from being a soldier in Pondicherry to become the 'Laird of Constantia' in Lucknow where he hosted a harem and owned vast estates.

Then there has been the fascinating, much-debated case of the Bourbons of Bhopal. The family claims descent from the House of Bourbon through Jean-Philippe de Bourbon-Navarre who is said to have arrived in the Mughal Emperor Akbar's Court in 1560, received employment there, and married a lady of the court with his patron's blessings. Obviously he had moved up in the hierarchy and the family retained this stature till the 18th century. In 1775, according to several writers, the family moved to Bhopal and entered the service of the royal family there. In the 19th century Salvador III de Bourbon became General in charge of the Bhopal army and in 1879 Balthazar de Bourbon became a Minister. Whatever the debate about these accounts, the family appears to have been given *jagir/zamin* rights which it lost after Independence. The family became professionals and one of them, Balthazar Napoleon de Bourbon, now claims first place in the Bourbon lineage which goes back to Henry IV.

The first to be seen as a leader of the Anglo-Indian community was John William Ricketts of Kidderpore (Calcutta). It was he who was chosen by the Calcutta petitioners (who included Wale Byrne, James Kyd, Henry Derozio and Charles Pote), to present their East Indians' Petition in 1830 to Parliament in Britain, seeking withdrawal of rules discriminating against Anglo-Indians. Ricketts urged, "If the real interest of India were sought, then these could not be better effected than through those who have been born, educated and are destined to spend their lives in India, namely the East Indians." It was 1833 before the appeal bore fruit and all services in India were opened to anyone resident in India.

Ricketts' leadership began when in 1823 he convened a meeting to establish a public (in fact, a 'private') school for East Indian children which would provide an education that would make them fit for the public services; the other private schools were affordable only to children of wealthy

European, Indian and a handful of East Indian parents. So was born that year the Parental Academic Institution in Calcutta, a non-sectarian Protestant school. In 1836, the Anglicans withdrew their support and established their own school which in due course moved to Darjeeling and is known today as St. Paul's. The Parental Academy, however, benefited in 1885 from a bequest left by Capt. John Doveton (part of which was also for a school in Madras) and it became the Parental Academy and Doveton College (affiliated to Calcutta University). The College was closed in 1916 when it was found that only few Anglo-Indians attended it and it was thought the few would be better benefited by Doveton scholarships to other institutions. Ricketts went on to found in 1828 the Commercial and Patriotic Association (CPA) to train in agriculture, trade and commerce East Indian boys and "such youths of European descent as may be destined to be born to live and to die in this country." As an adjunct to this, he helped to start a Marine School to train any from the CPA who wished to enter the Merchant Marine.

It was the informal group that rallied around Ricketts in these ventures who from 1825 began to meet in each other's homes and resolved to prepare a petition on behalf of the East Indian community to present to the British Parliament. When no immediate action resulting from the first petition, it was decided to send a second petition at the urging of Derozio and Pote. When Ricketts was unable to go to London, Pote agreed to do so. But, for unclear reasons, it was sent to an East Indian in London to take necessary action, but nothing was heard of it thereafter. By then 1833 was on the community and there was hope again.

Wale Byrne, in government service with Ricketts and a close associate of his in all his activities ranging from education to activism, acted for a short time as the Deputy Collector of Calcutta c. 1830s.

The trail Ricketts and his cohorts blazed to establish Anglo-Indian identity was followed by E.W. Chambers and John Harold Abbott in the north and David S. White in the south. Abbott was President of the Anglo-Indian Empire League before Henry Gidney took over in 1921. The Anglo-Indian and Domiciled European Association put down roots in Calcutta in 1876 as the Eurasian and Anglo-Indian Association. It became the Anglo-Indian and Domiciled European Association in 1899 and remained so till Gidney had a resolution passed in 1919 to change its name to the All-India Anglo-Indian Association. The Eurasian and Anglo-Indian Association split in 1898 and the breakaway faction, led by Dr. J.R. Wallace, was founded. In an attempt to unify the associations Charles Palmer founded the Anglo-Indian Empire League in Allahabad in 1908.

Abbott, who was nominated to the Central Legislative Assembly, was a staunch Empire man. During the Great War he travelled all over India and raised a volunteer Anglo-Indian military force of 6000 men who served overseas. His son Roy was the first volunteer.

Leading the Eurasian and Anglo-Indian Association's Madras Branch was David White from its inception in 1876, but in 1879 he broke away from it and founded the Anglo-Indian and Domiciled European Association of Southern India with *The Anglo Indian* as its voice. He then set up its Coorg and Mysore branch in whose name he founded the Anglo-Indian settlement of 'Whitefield' near Bangalore. White, who worked in the Directorate of Public Instruction, Madras Presidency, was a close friend of A.O. Hume who inspired the founding of the Indian National Congress. White spoke at the First Session of the Congress and urged recruitment to the Civil Service of people only from India.

It was an Anglo-Indian scene fragmented by associations that Igatpuri-born Henry Gidney entered in 1918 as a 45-year-old ophthalmolgist with an international reputation. By the time he was 37 he was an FRCS, DPH, MRCP, DO, Lecturer at Oxford and the youngest Fellow of the Royal Society at the time. He saw war service in China during the Opium Wars. In the Great War he was in action in the North West Frontier Province and attained the rank of Lieutenant Colonel in the Indian Medical Service. Disappointed with discrimination in the Indian Medical Service, he quit the Service after the War and established a successful private practice in Bombay. That's when he began to devote himself to all the issues the Anglo-Indians faced, confident that he could contribute to improving their lot.

Sir Henry Gidney was remembered by a stamp in India in 1992 and it reflected the numerous services Anglo-Indians contributed to over the years. (Stamp: Indian Postal Department)

In 1919 Gidney stood for election and was elected president of the Bombay branch of the Anglo-Indian Empire League.

Sir Henry Gidney (seated extreme right) awaiting his train at McCluskiegunj. Waiting around him are other visitors he had brought with him to see the settlement and settlers waiting to see them all off. (Photo: The Colonisation Observer)

And he was on his way, particularly after getting the League to change its name to the All-India Anglo-Indian Association focused more on Anglo-Indians rather than the Empire. He was elected President-in-Chief of the Association in 1921, the same year he was nominated to represent the community in the Central Legislative Assembly. This he was to do till his death in 1942.

Gidney represented the community before the Simon Commission (1928-29) and at the three Round Table Conferences in London (1930-32). At every venue he sought educational safeguards and job reservations, particularly in the Railways. But at the same time he urged the members of the community to think of themselves as Indians, the first Anglo-Indian leader to turn to his fellow-Indians seeking their recognition of the Anglo-Indians as an Indian Community.

Sir Henry spoke bluntly to his kinsmen in Bangalore on one occasion, saying, "Deny the fact you are sons and citizens of India, disclaim it, conceal it in your efforts to ape what you are not, and you will soon be the 'not wanted' at all. The opportunity is yours today to more closely associate yourselves, from early school life, with the rest of India, to realise that you, with all other communities, have a right to live in this your country, and that you are first and last sons of India ... But if there is one thing which you must completely eradicate from yourselves, it is the retention of the 'superiority' and 'inferiority' complexes and you should bring about their replacement with a complex of equality."

Sir Henry Gidney's successor, and a favourite of the Nehru family, Frank Anthony, was another Anglo-Indian who warranted a stamp (2003). (Stamp: Indian Postal Department)

Gidney was knighted in 1931. A man decorated for bravery in action, a flamboyant personality wherever he was, a lady's man in social circles, a *bon vivant*, a warm host and an aesthete, Sir Henry was thought by many to be at his happiest when heading the All India Arts and Crafts Society which has ensured that India's ancient arts and crafts survive and flourish. He is remembered in Delhi in the name of what was once the Anglo-Indian club there, the Gidney Club.

Frank Anthony, an Inns of Court barrister-of-law who succeeded Gidney as the leader of the Anglo-Indians in the run-up to Independence, was even more emphatic when he stated at the very beginning of his tenure, "We are Anglo-Indians by community. Of that fact we have every reason to be proud. We have forged a history, in many way notable, of which any much larger community anywhere in the world could be justifiably proud. Let us cling, and cling tenaciously, to all that we hold dear, our language, our way of life and our distinctive culture. But let us always remember that we are Indians. The Community is Indian. It has always been Indian. Above all, it has an inalienable Indian birthright. The more we love and are loyal to India, the more will India love and be loyal to us."

Anthony, born in Jamalpur, was 34 and a lawyer making his way up when he was elected to succeed Gidney as President-in-Chief of the All-India Anglo-Indian Association. Anthony's call for Anglo-Indians to consider themselves Indian came not as in the case of Gidney's call, which was made when Indians were British subjects, but when India was on the eve of freedom and was the more meaningful for it.

Writing in *The Hindu*, Madras, in August 1948, Anthony summed up his views in an article from which these are excerpts.

"Ever since I assumed the leadership of the Community, several years back, I have made it clear that Anglo-Indians are as much Indians as any other community. The term

Anglo-Indian is merely a communal label. We are Indian by nationality and Anglo-Indian by community.

"I saw clearly from the outset that no community could possibly expect to find a place in India unless it was nationalist in outlook and prepared to support only those policies calculated to promote the welfare and progress of the nation.

"There were not a few in the Community who bitterly opposed my policies. But I realised that when Independence came the Anglo-Indian community, unless wedded to a policy of nationalism, would garner a nemesis not only of resentment but of retaliatory and hostile action from an Independent India.

"Independence meant freedom as much for the Anglo-Indians as for any other section of our people. In fact, for the Anglo-Indians it meant even greater freedom—freedom from a deliberate system of social and economic discrimination.

"After having been deliberately excluded from positions of influence and responsibility till Independence, the Community was canalised into subordinate positions in the key services, such as the Railways, the Post and Telegraphs, and the Customs. This was done for strategic purposes. It was felt that Anglo-Indians, because they were not aware of their true history, were more dependable in these key services. But this policy deranged the economy of the Community which at one time consisted largely of soldiers, administrators and the merchant princes of India and made it artificially dependent on employment in the Railways, the Post and Telegraphs, and the Customs.

"In order that the economy of the Community should be reorganised, and ploughed back once again, into wider and more profitable channels, time is required.

"I am glad and grateful to be able to say that the leaders of India did recognise this need and certain provisions were embodied in the Constitution for a period of 10 years to enable the Anglo-Indian community to readjust its economy...

"There is still a widespread feeling that Anglo-Indians are not nationalist or completely loyal.

"There has always been an element in the Community which insisted on classifying itself as European. This element has not been distinguished by loyalty to the country or to the Community to which they belong.

"They were largely the victims of a system which deliberately encouraged renegadism. Under the British regime an Anglo-Indian who called himself a European was guaranteed preferment over one who refused to deny his parentage or his Community. In fact, no Anglo-Indian, however able or qualified by character, could achieve a position commensurate with those qualifications. If he wished to break through the wall of disabilities built around him by the

British system, he was obliged falsely to declare himself as a European. In this way, many Anglo-Indians became Members of the Viceroy's Executive Council, Governors of Provinces, Surgeons-General to the King, great soldiers and so forth.

"Further, Headships in Anglo-Indian schools were the monopoly of the Europeans. These Europeans purported to look down on everything Indian. In the result, Anglo-Indian children, during the most formative period of their lives, were taught to look away from their country and their Community. It is for this reason that I have been such a bitter opponent of lay Europeans being entrusted with the Headships of Anglo-Indian schools.

"With the elimination of the so-called Domiciled European element from the Community and the reform in the curriculum of Anglo-Indian schools, I am certain that the Community will more than play its part as one of the most loyal and nationalist elements in this Country.

"As Chairman of the Inter-Provincial Board for Anglo-Indian Education on which there is a majority of members of other communities, I have endeavoured to force the pace of curriculum reform. Hindi is now being taught from the 1st Standard. The excessive concentration on British history has to go. Anglo-Indian children will be taught authentic Indian history. I am also hoping that they will be taught this Indian history through the medium of Hindi. In that way, I feel they will be given not only the necessary mastery of what is bound to be the national language, but a natural insight into the culture and heritage of India.

"It is natural that in a period of great change and transition a minority element should entertain certain anxieties. The Community is understandably anxious about the questions of language and culture. I have always maintained that English is as much an Indian language as Gurmukhi, Gujarati and so forth. English is an Indian language because it is the mother tongue of an Indian Community, the Anglo-Indians.

Frank Anthony could let his hair down with the best. Here, in a beachside cottage in Bombay he and his wife trip the light fantastic. (Photo: Priscilla Clements)

"India must necessarily be a composite nation. But this does not mean that it should not be a united nation. Other nations have achieved unity from diversity. In a vast subcontinent such as India it is inevitable that there should be diversities of religion, of language and even of culture. The draft Constitution has recognised the fundamental rights of minorities in the matter of religion, language and culture. In order to give real assurance, however, practice must be squared with precept."

It was not a case to win him approval from Anglo-Indians who, fearing an Indian backlash and finding Britain itself willing to accept them if lineage was proved, were leaving the country. It was not only those leaving the country but many other Anglo-Indians who doubted Anthony's Anglo-Indianness. Was he an Indian Christian, a fifth columnist in the ranks, was a suspicion often bandied about.

Keith Flory of *The Statesman*, Delhi, once pointed out that if Anthony had his admirers and hero-worshippers in abundance there was no dearth of detractors as well. There were those who thought he was a bully. Others said he ran a one-man show. Many accused him of arrogance and being autocratic. Some contended that he did not help the poor. But, said Flory, "there can never be any doubting his commitment to striving for the well-being of his Community, his ensuring Anglo-Indians a secure place in independent India, and his blazing an educational trail that has served as the Community's pathway to prosperity."

Anthony was not to prove as popular as Gidney, but he was to do far more for his community than Gidney. Arguing the Anglo-Indian case before Mahatma Gandhi—not the greatest supporter of the Anglo-Indians as Dr. H.W. Moreno, a leader of a radical Anglo-Indian group, was to find when he in earlier times had several times sought Gandhiji's better understanding of the community—Nehru and, above all, the 'Iron Man' Vallabhbhai Patel, he obtained concessions for the community some of which saw it through a difficult transitory decade and others which still help the Anglo-Indians today through Constitutional provisions.

Anthony, who was a member of the Constituent Assembly, was one of India's principal delegates in the country's first delegation to the United Nations in 1946. He also represented the country in Commonwealth Parliamentary Conferences. All this curbed his practice till 1952 when Nehru requested him to defend an accused Hindu Minister in Pakistan's North West Frontier Province. He was 25 years later to appear for Indira Gandhi before the Shah Commission. He was offered the Governorship of the Punjab and the Vice-Presidency of India by Indira Gandhi but turned both honours down.

Instead, he fought for the language of the Anglo-Indians and their system of education. "Without our language, without our schools, we cannot be an Anglo-Indian community. That is why we have mounted increasing vigil in respect of our schools and our language." He did concede a local language as a second language in Anglo-Indian schools, but their use of English and their system of education still thrive. In 1947, he was elected Chairman of the Inter-State Board of Anglo-Indian Education which laid down standards for the nearly 300 Anglo-Indian Schools in the country. The standards were to be the bedrock of the Frank Anthony Public Schools he started in Calcutta, Delhi and Bangalore. Here, disadvantaged Anglo-Indian children can get the best of education in India.

Of this contribution, Flory has said, "The schools established and administered by the All-India Anglo-Indian Education Institution (a sister organisation of the Association Anthony headed for over 50 years) are the first, and only ones, that are 'owned' by the Community at large. There is no gainsaying the fact that if there has been a significant trend in recent years for Anglo-Indian youth to pursue higher studies and the professions, the Frank Anthony Scholarships scheme has been not only the driving force but more than often the very means to make this possible."

Anthony, however, dismissed the Portuguese-named Anglo-Indians of Kerala, many of them Malayalam-speaking, as 'Feringhis' and paid no heed to them. For years this kept around 50,000 Anglo-Indians out of the All-India Anglo-Indian Association fold.

Joss Fernandez, founder of the Anglo-Indian Guild in Bangalore. (Photo: AITW)

It was this that led to the Union of Anglo-Indian Associations (comprising 36 branches and 70,000 members) being formed by Stephen Padua in Kerala and the Anglo-Indian Guild in Bangalore being formed by Joss Fernandez.

Consequent to this, The National Forum of Anglo-Indian Associations was formed at a meeting of Anglo-Indian MLAs and other leaders in Kerala convened on April 20, 1992 under the chairmanship of Stephen Padua. Its purpose was to bring under one banner all Anglo-Indian Associations in India. The Forum included The Union of Anglo-Indian Associations, Kerala; The Anglo-Indian Association of Southern India, Chennai; The Forum of Anglo-Indian Women, Chennai; The Anglo-Indian United Front, Chennai; The Anglo-Indian Welfare & Development Association, Andhra Pradesh; The Anglo-Indian Service Society, Calcutta; The Dharwad District Anglo-Indian Association, Hubli (Karnataka); and the Anglo-Indian Guild, Bangalore. Former MLA Victor Freitas represents Maharashtra. In 2011, the word 'Federation' was substituted for 'Forum'. Both the All-India Anglo-Indian Association and the Federation recommend names for nomination as MPs and MLAs.

The divide between the Federation and the All-India Anglo-Indian Association has still to be bridged. Joss Fernandez of Bangalore, Stephen Padua, Lawrence Luis and Charles Dias of Kerala, D.V. D'Monte, G.K. Francis and Beatrix D'Souza of Madras and Christine Lazarus of Andhra Pradesh have over the years kept the Federation as strong in its territory as the All-India Anglo-Indian Association is all-India.

Stephen Padua, born in Perumanoor, was a member of the Cochin State Service from 1936. But during his college days he got fellow-Anglo-Indians interested in forming an Anglo-Indian Association in Perumanoor. Lawrence Luiz was its first President and he was its Secretary. Soon afterwards, associations were started in other parts of the State and Padua persuaded them to form the Federated Anglo-Indian Association of Cochin, North Travancore and South Malabar in 1939. Joseph Pinheiro was its first President and Padua its General Secretary. Meanwhile, a branch of the All-India Anglo-Indian Association had been formed in Cochin with C.J. Luiz as President; he was also the nominated Member representing the community in the Cochin State Legislative Council.

In 1947, the Federated Anglo-Indian Association was amalgamated with the All-India Anglo-Indian Association with S.P. Luiz as President. Shortly after the integration of Travancore and Cochin States, a separate Union of Anglo-Indian Associations was formed in 1953.

After his retirement from Government service, Padua was elected Secretary of the Central Board of Anglo-Indian Education, General Secretary of the Union of Anglo-Indian Associations and, then, was its President from 1972 till his death in 1995. He was the guiding spirit behind the formation of the Anglo-Indian Education Fund in 1965 and, in 1969, the All Kerala Anglo-Indian Youth Movement. Between 1970 and 1987 Padua was nominated three times as Member of the Kerala Legislative Assembly. His efforts to coordinate the various Anglo-Indian Associations in the country finally became a partial reality in 1991 with the formation of the National Forum of Anglo-Indian Associations (most of them in the South), of which he became the first President. He was Chairman of the Central Board of Anglo-Indian Education (1991 to 1994) and established eleven Anglo-Indian schools in Kerala. He also founded the Indo-Portuguese Cultural Institute in 1989.

The Anglo-Indian Guild was formed in 1980 by Joss Fernandez to improve the lot of this community in Karnataka. He obtained reserved seats for the community in medicine and engineering as well as fee concessions. He was the nominated Anglo-Indian MLA in the Karnataka Assembly for two terms, from 1984 and 1995. In between, he was nominated to the Lok Sabha to represent the community.

Another Anglo-Indian leader in the South has been Geoffrey K. Francis, the elected President of the Anglo-Indian Association of Southern India for the last 19 years. He is also the President of the Federation of Anglo-Indian Associations. He was nominated MLA (Tamil Nadu), 1985-1988. Dr. Francis is Correspondent of three of the oldest schools in India, St. George's (1709), CSI Bishop Corrie (1836) and CSI St. Mathias (1920). Dr. Francis was a Professor of Commerce at, and then Principal (2004-2012) of, the A.M. Jain College in Chennai. He is the author of books on marketing and management and is working on a book titled *Anglo-Indians—A Contemporary Perspective*, due for publication shortly.

Many of the Anglo-Indian leaders appeared to have had a follower or two very close to them. Frank Anthony's "closest lieutenant" for 40 years was Jhansi-born A.E.T. Barrow who initially taught at Barnes School, Deolali, from 1938 to 1944 and, later, helped set up the Frank Anthony Public Schools. He was an Anglo-Indian member of the Lok Sabha from 1952 to 1970 and 1977 to 1989. He almost single-handedly had the Senior Cambridge Examinations transformed into the Indian School Certificate Examinations administered by the ICSE Board of Education of which he was appointed the Founding Secretary.

Educationist A.E.T. Barrow, Frank Anthony's closest associate. (Photo: AITW)

Barrow would have succeeded Anthony as President of the All-India Anglo-Indian Association had he not predeceased him. Anthony, who led the Association from 1942 to 1993, was succeded by Major Gen. Robert G. Williams who focused on bringing all the associations together. Gen. Williams, a World War II veteran who had been a German prisoner-of-war, played important roles after the War in Indian armaments development. When he passed away in 1998, Neil O'Brien succeeded him.

The All-India Anglo-Indian Association's President-in-Chief as this book goes to press, Neil O'Brien. (Photo: AITW)

Neil O'Brien, publisher, educationist, pioneering quizmaster, columnist and legislator, was chairman of the ICSE Council from 1993 to 2011. He represented the Anglo-Indians of West Bengal in the Legislative Assembly from 1977 to 1992 and, later, the Anglo-Indian community in Parliament. As these lines are written, he is the President-in-Chief of the All-India Anglo-Indian Association.

Playing a leadership role on the wider stage of Indian politics have been only a couple of Anglo-Indians. The first was Lal Chand Stokes, the son of the Rev. Samuel E. Stokes, an American who settled in Himachal Pradesh and became known as the 'Father of the Apple Industry' there. Samuel Stokes converted to Hinduism and became Satyananda Stokes. He was an active member of the Indian National Congress and an All-India Congress Committee member. He went to jail as a freedom fighter. His son, Lal Chand Stokes, became a member of the Party and a Member of the Himachal Pradesh Legislative Assembly for many years. This would make him the first elected Anglo-Indian in the Indian political scenario. He was also a well-known horticulturist and social worker.

The only Anglo-Indian who is an active politician in India as these lines are written, Derek O'Brien, a member of West Bengal's party in power, the All-India Trinamool Congress, which he represents in the Upper House in Delhi. He is also a successful writer of reference books. (Photo: Internet)

Derek O'Brien, the son of Neil O'Brien, is another Anglo-Indian to play an active role in an Indian political party. A Vice-President of the All-India Trinamool Congress rooted in West Bengal, and which he joined in 2004, he represents it in the Rajya Sabha, India's Upper House. He is also the publisher of the Party's official newspaper *Jago Bangla* (all the O'Briens are fluent Bengali speakers). On major issues where the Party has been in confrontation with major

The second Earl of Liverpool, Prime Minister of the United Kingdom for 16 years. Like many in Britain, he had an Indian maternal ancestor generations earlier. (Photo: Internet)

business houses or other political parties, O'Brien has been the spokesman of its leader, Mamata Banerjee.

Derek O'Brien is also a successful businessman, his Derek O'Brien and Associates organising programmes for 3500 schools in India and reaching out to over a million students every year. A quizmaster, like other members of the family, he hosts the longest-running TV Quiz, the Cadbury Bournvita Quiz Contest, and the longest-running corporate quiz show, the Economic Times Brand Equity Quiz. Author of textbooks, reference books and quiz books for several publishers, he is Penguin India's highest-selling reference author.

Apart from these leaders in India, several in high places in England and elsewhere in the 18th and 19th centuries would be considered Anglo-Indian if only they had been domiciled in the Indian subcontinent, having as they did an Indian or East Indian maternal forebear. Perhaps the best-known of them was *Robert Banks Jenkinson*, the 2nd Earl of Liverpool, who became Prime Minister of the United Kingdom in 1812, when only 42 years old. He served as Prime Minister till shortly before his death in 1828. He had earlier served from 1801 as Foreign Secretary, Home Secretary and Secretary for War and the Colonies. His mother was Amelia Watts, daughter of William Watts of the Calcutta Council and his East Indian wife. Watt's second daughter married a Ricketts in Calcutta and their granddaughter Frances was Gen. Sir Abraham Robert's first wife.

Making his mark elsewhere too was Charles H. Champagnac, whose great-grandfather married into a Nawabi family of Avadh in the early 1800s. Charles Champagnac was born in India but moved to Burma (then part of India) c.1890. He became an Inns of Court barrister, practised in Burma and became Mayor of Rangoon. In 1931 he was a member of the Burmese delegation that went to London to negotiate the future of Burma—which led to its separation from India and nationhood.

Another lawyer with Anglo-Indian roots who became a leader outside India was Sir Richard Morgan Jr. His father, Richard Morgan Sr., was an Anglo-Indian who migrated to Ceylon and married a well-to-do Burgher. Richard Morgan Sr. was in the forefront of the campaign in 1816 to abolish slavery in Ceylon. The son, who, curiously, was classified as a Burgher was one of the mid-19th century Burgher Radicals who, together with members of other community leaders sought, under the banner of 'Friends of Ceylon', representative government in the Island. He was also in the van of the reformist movement, seeking abolition of caste consideration in public service. But a move of the successful advocate to the Bench, from where he moved up to the Supreme Court and a knighthood, cooled his ardour in later years.

Yet another who served another flag was Luso-Indian Walter Eugene de Souza, son of Lawrence de Souza of Calcutta. He was first Consul for Portugal in Calcutta and then Consul-General between 1870 and 1884. He was knighted in 1879 for his philanthropy and also received a Papal Knighthood. He later settled in England and was elected Member for Westminister in the London County Council in 1895. Walter de Souza was the great-grandson of Luis Barretto, an 18th century Calcutta merchant and banker, who was known as the 'Prince of Businesses'. Barretto's daughter married Thomas de Souza, who came from another leading Luso-Indian business family in Calcutta known for its contributions to churches, orphanages and schools. Thomas de Souza's son was Lawrence de Souza after whom a home for aged Anglo-Indians in Calcutta has been named.

The Anglo-Indian community has been represented in the Lok Sabha by the following:

1st Lok Sabha (17.4.1952-4.4.1957)	:	Frank Anthony and A.E.T. Barrow.
2nd Lok Sabha (5.4.1957-31.3.1962)	:	Frank Anthony and A.E.T. Barrow
3rd Lok Sabha (2.4.1962-3.3.1967)	:	Frank Anthony and A.E.T. Barrow
4th Lok Sabha (4.3.1967-27.12.1970)	:	Frank Anthony and A.E.T. Barrow
5th Lok Sabha (15.3.1971-18.1.1977)	:	Frank Anthony and Mrs. Marjorie Godfrey
6th Lok Sabha (23.3.1977-22.8.1979)	:	A.E.T. Barrow and Rudolph Rodrigues
7th Lok Sabha (10.1.1980-31.12.1984)	:	Frank Anthony and A.E.T. Barrow

8th Lok Sabha (31.12.1984-27.11.1989)	:	Frank Anthony and A.E.T. Barrow
9th Lok Sabha (2.12.1989-13.3.1991)	:	Joss Fernandez and Paul Mantosh
10th Lok Sabha (20.06.1991-10.05.1996)	:	Frank Anthony and Maj. Gen. Robert E. Williams
11th Lok Sabha (15.05.1996-04.12.1997)	:	Neil O'Brien and Mrs. Hedwig Rego
12th Lok Sabha (10.03.1998-26.04.1999)	:	Dr. Mrs. Beatrix D'Souza and Lt. Gen. Neville Foley
13th Lok Sabha (10.10.1999-06.02.2004)	:	Dr. Mrs. Beatrix D'Souza and Denzil B. Atkinson
14th Lok Sabha (17.05.2004-31.05.2009)	:	Mrs. Ingrid Mcleod and Francis Fanthome
15th Lok Sabha (01.06.2009-)	:	Mrs. Ingrid Mcleod and Dr. Charles Dias

All of them have contributed significantly to the associations they belonged to as well as to the Community. Indeed, the Community has never been short of leaders or voices to speak for it. But the flock might have done better if it had in greater measure grabbed the opportunities the leaders opened out for them instead of depending on concessions alone.

Valedictory

Luso-Indians, Eurasians, East-Indians, Indo-Britons, Anglo-Indians, Euro-Indians, call them what you will, but for 500 years they have made a significant contribution to India and to the countries some of them have settled in since the 1950s. In India it has been a contribution far out of proportion to the community's numbers of 500,000 to 600,000 at its peak. But over the years, this community that is neither of the East nor of the West, or of both, if you will, but very much part of India, has been on the one hand looked down upon by the Europeans—Portuguese, Dutch, British, French and Danes who have each had their moments of governance in territories in India—as being persons with tainted 'white' blood and, on the other, feared by Indians as the strong arm of the ruling powers or seen by the Indian orthodoxy as beyond the pale, being born casteless. This last view is a particularly curious one in the context of history.

Forget the anthropologists' theories that Indians—and everyone else—came out of Africa (not a very happy thought to most Indians who have strong prejudices against the Blacks). More pertinent is the fact that large numbers of Indians refer to Mediterranean roots, Semitic roots, Central Asian roots and Chinese roots, depending on which part of the country they are from. But most curious of all are the proud claims by many, in Northwest India and along much of the west coast, of being descendants of the legions of Alexander of Macedon. Indeed, Anglo-Indian anthropologist Cedric Dover got it right when he said, "Today there are no half-castes because there are no full castes."

Such reality did not stop both Europeans and Indians being prejudiced against Anglo-Indians. The result was the Anglo-Indians being, in many ways, forced into an almost ghetto-like life in their own 'colonies', favoured localities and settlements. Despite this, and all the other legal strictures against them from

Farewell. All the members of the Railway Institute, Guntakal, gather to say farewell to one of its members and his wife. A picture reflecting the camaraderie and unity the Anglo-Indians enjoyed as a community in far-flung parts of India. (Photo: AITW)

time to time till the 1930s, they never lost their camaraderie, their joy of life, their happy-go-luckiness, their work ethic, language, faith or family values. And they not only survived but made contributions ranging from wielding the pen to wielding the sword with equal felicity.

This book is a remembrance of those signal contributions of one of the 4635 communities in India that did more than was demanded of it, a tribute to the few who left a whole subcontinent much that has been little recognised as their contribution. Long may they as a community continue to contribute with greater recognition in an India now emerging as a shining world power.

Retirement was always marked by a round of farewells. This one by his colleagues in Villupuram was for Special A Grade Driver Maxwell Paris and his wife Dorothy on the day he retired in 1970. (Photo: The Paris family)

Bibliography

Allen, Charles: *Raj* (Penguin, UK, 1977)

Anon: *The Anglo-Indian Force*

Anthony, Frank: 'Independence and the Anglo-Indian' IN *The Hindu* (Madras, August 1948)

_____: *Britain's Betrayal in India* (Allied Publishers, New Delhi, 1969)

Arasaratnam, Sinnapah: *Merchants, Companies and Commerce on the Coromandel Coast, 1650-1740* (Oxford University Press, Delhi, 1986)

Banerjee, Ruchira: 'Philippa's Sisters: 'Portuguese' Camp Followers' IN *Indica 49* (Heras Institute, Bombay, 1989)

Barr, P.: *The Memsahibs: the Women of Victorian India 1905-1945* (Secker and Warburg, London, 1976)

Bhargava, Gp. Capt. (Rtd.) Kapil: 'Anglo-Indians in the IAF' IN *Indian Aviation, Civil & Military* (January 2003)

Bidwell, Shelford: *Swords for Hire: European Mercenaries in Eighteenth Century India* (John Murray, London, 1971)

Blackford, Capt. Stan: *One Hell of a Life* (Self, South Australia, 2000)

Boxer, C.R.: *Race Relations in the Portuguese Colonial Empire 1415-1825* (Clarendon Press, Oxford, 1963)

_____: *The Portuguese Seaborne Empire, 1415-1825* (Hutchinson, London, 1969)

Brown, Melvyn: *The Anglo-Indian Quiz Book* (Anglo-Indian, The Newsletter, Calcutta, 1994)

_____: *An Introduction to Anglo-Indian History* (Anglo-Indian, The Newsletter, Calcutta, 1997).

_____: *Social Anthropology of the Anglo-Indian Race* (Anglo-Indian, The Newsletter, Calcutta, 1998)

_____: *The Anglo-Indian Archives* (Anglo-Indian, The Newsletter, Calcutta, 2001)

Brown, Patricia: *Anglo-Indian Food and Customs* (Penguin Books India, Delhi, 1998)

Caplan, Lionel: *Children of Colonialism—Anglo-Indians in a Postcolonial World* (Berg, Oxford, 2001)

Chatterjee, Chandreyee and Das, Mohuna: 'Song Sung Blue' IN *The Telegraph Metro on Sunday* (Calcutta, March 2007)

Chatterjee, Indrani: 'Colouring Subalternity: Slaves, Concubines and Social Orphans in Early Colonial India' IN *Subaltern Studies—Writings on South Asian History and Society,* Volume X (Oxford University Press, New Delhi, 1999)

Clay, John: *John Masters—A Regimented Life* (Michael Joseph, London, 1992)

Craig, Hazel Innes: *Under the Old School Topee* (reprint BACSA, London, 1990)

Dalrymple, William: *White Mughals—Love and Betrayal in Eighteenth Century India* (Viking Penguin Books, New Delhi, 2002)

Dasgupta, Mary Ann (Ed.): *Henry Louis Vivian Derozio (1808-1831)—Anglo-Indian Patriot and Poet* (Derozio Commemorative Committee Memorial Volume, Calcutta, 1973)

Debi, Bharati and Nandan, Anshu Prokash: *The Anglo-Indians of Calcutta—A Community of Communities* (Prashik, Kolkata, 2006)

de Mello(w), Melville: 'Petals on the Ganga' IN *The Illustrated Weekly of India* (Bombay, July 1970)

de Souza, Robert: *Goa and the Continent of Circe* (Wilco Publishing House, Bombay, 1973)

Deefholts, Margaret and Glenn (Ed.): *The Way We Were* (Calcutta Tijullah Relief Inc. Publishing, New Jersey, U.S.A., 2006)

Deefholts, Margaret and Staub, Sylvia W. (Ed.): *Voices on the Verandah* (CTR Inc. Publishing, New Jersey, 2004)

Dodwell, H.: *The Nabobs of Madras* (Williams and Norgate, London, 1926)

Edwardes, Michael: *British India* (Sidgwick & Jackson, London, 1967)

_____: *Glorious Sahibs* (Eyre & Spottiswoode, London, 1968)

Ezekiel, Gulu: 'The Story of a Champion from the East' IN *The Telegraph* (Calcutta, 2008)

Ferdinands, Rodney: *Proud and Prejudiced—The Story of the Burghers of Sri Lanka* (Self, Melbourne, 1995)

Forbes, Earlson: 'The White Australia Policy, Ceylonese Burghers and Alice Nona' IN *The Ceylankan* (Sydney, August 2012)

Gabb, Alfred D.F.: *Anglo-Indian Legacy 1600-1947* (Quacks Books, York, 1998)

Hawes, C.J.: *Poor Relations—The Making of a Eurasian Community in British India 1773-1833* (Curzon Press, Sussex, 1996)

Hayde, D.E.: *Blood and Steel* (Trishul, Dehra Dun, 1989)

Hennessy, Maurice: *The Rajah from Tipperary* (George Thomas) (New English Library, London, 1972)

Jack, Ian: 'The Homeland that Failed' IN *The Independent Magazine* (London, February 1990)

Jarnagin, Laura (Ed.): *The Making of the Luso-Asian World—Portuguese and Luso-Asian Legacies in Southeast Asia, 1511-2011*, Volume I (Institute of Southeast Asian Studies, Singapore, 2011)

Jayawardena, Kumari: *Erasure of the Euro-Asian* (Social Scientists' Association, Colombo, 2007)

Kincaid, Dennis: *British Social Life in India, 1608-1937* (Routledge and Kegan Paul, London, 1938)

Lobo, Ann: 'Introduction' IN *Babette's Pomegranate—Anglo-Indian Cuisine* (Reading, U.K.)

Love, Henry Davison: *Vestiges of Old Madras, 1640-1800—Traced from the East India Company's Records Preserved at Fort St.George and the India Office, and from Other Sources* (John Murray, London, 1913)

Lumb, Lionel and van Veldhuizen, Deborah (Ed.): *The Way We Are.* (CTR Inc. Publishing, New Jersey, 2008)

MacLure, Harry (Ed.): *Anglos In The Wind*, Vol. 1-Vol. 15 (AITW, Chennai, 1997-2012)

Madge, E.W.: *Henry Derozio, the Eurasian Poet and Reformer* (Ed. Subir Ray Choudhuri) (Metropolitan Book Agency, Calcutta, 1966)

Madras Government: *Manual of the Administration of the Madras Presidency*, Vols. I & II and Appendices (Government Press, Madras, 1885)

Maher, Reginald: *These are the Anglo-Indians* (Calcutta, 1962; Print West, Perth reprint 1995)

Maitland, J.C. ('A Lady'): *Letters from Madras during the Years 1836-1839* (John Murray, London, 1843)

Mason, Philip: *The Men Who Ruled India* (Jonathan Cape, London, 1953-4)

Masters, John: *Bhowani Junction* (Michael Joseph, London, 1954) *Memorandum of Association of The All-India Anglo-Indian Association* (New Delhi)

Mines, Mattison: *Public Faces, Private Voices—Community and Individuality in South India* (University of California Press, Berkeley, 1994)

Mitra, Chandan: *Constant Glory—The La Martiniere Saga 1836-1986* (OUP, Bombay, 1987)

Moore, Gloria Jean: *The Anglo-Indian Vision* (Australian Education Press, Melbourne, 1986).

_____: *The Lotus and the Rose* (River Seine Publications, Melbourne, 1986)

_____: *Anglo-Indians—The Best of Both Worlds* (Melbourne).

Moorhouse, Geoffrey: *India Britannica* (Paladin, London, 1984)

Muthiah, S.: *Madras Rediscovered—A Historical Guide to Looking Around* (East-West Books-Westland, Chennai, 2008)

_____: *A Madras Miscellany* (East-West Books-Westland, Chennai, 2011)

Nightingale, Carl H.: *Before Race Mattered—Geographies of the Colour Line in Early Colonial Madras and New York* (American Historical Association, 2008)

Panikkar, K.M.: *Malabar and the Portuguese (1500-1663)* (Voice of India, New Delhi, reprint 1997)

Pearson-Joseph: 'Anglo-Indians of Tamil Nadu—Which is it to be? Survival or...' IN *The Journal of Anglo-Indian & Domiciled European Association of Southern India* (Madras, 1974)

Penny, Frank: *The Church in Madras* (Smith Elder, London, 1900)

Phillips, Zelma: *The Anglo-Indian Australian Story—My Experience* (Zelphil Books, Victoria, Australia, 2004)

Ricketts, J.W.: *Report of Proceedings Connected with The East Indians' Petition to Parliament and Appendix* (Read at a Public Meeting held at the Town Hall, Calcutta,

March 28, 1831) (Baptist Missionary Press, Calcutta, 1831)

Roberts, M., Raheem, I. and Colin-Thomé, P.: *People In-Between—The Burghers and the Middle Class in the Transformations within Sri Lanka, 1790s-1960s,* Vol. 1 (Sarvodaya Book Publishing Services, Colombo, 1989)

Sen, Sumitra: 'Anglo-Indians of Calcutta—Never Say Die' IN *Sunday Magazine* (Calcutta)

Sengupta, Pallab: *Derozio* (Sahitya Akademi, Delhi, 2000)

Spear, T.G. Percival: *The Nabobs—A Study of the Social Life of the English in Eighteenth Century India* (Humphrey Milford, Oxford, 1932)

_____: *A History of India,* Vol. 2 (Penguin Books, London, 1990)

Sta Maria, Bernard: *My People, My Country—The Story of the Malacca Portuguese Community* (Malacca Portuguese Development Centre, Malacca, 1982)

Subrahmanyam, Sanjay: *Improvising Empire—Portuguese Trade and Settlement in the Bay of Bengal, 1500-1700* (Oxford University Press, Delhi, 1990)

Stark, Herbert Alick: *John Ricketts and His Times* (Wilson & Son, Calcutta, 1934)

_____: *Hostages to India, or The Life Story of the Anglo-Indian Race* (Star Printing Works, Calcutta 1926/1936; BACSA, U.K. reprint 1987)

'Stephen Padua Special' IN *Anglo-Indian Journal* (The Union of Anglo-Indian Associations. Kerala, 1995).

Stracey, Eric: *Growing up in Anglo-India* (East-West Books, Chennai, 1999)

Thomas, Edwards: *Henry Derozio, the Eurasian Poet, Teacher and Journalist* (Calcutta, 1884)

Wheeler, James Talboy: *Madras in the Olden Time—Being a History of the Presidency from the First Foundation to the Governorship of Thomas Pitt, Grandfather of the Earl of Chatham, 1639-1702. Compiled from Official Records* (J. Higginbotham, Madras, 1861)

White-Kumar, Bridget: *The Best of Anglo-Indian Cuisine—A Legacy* (Self, Bangalore, 2004)

_____: *Flavours of the Past* (Self, Bangalore, 2006)

_____: *Anglo-Indian Delicacies* (Self, Bangalore, 2007)

_____: *Kolar Gold Fields—Down Memory Lane* (Self, Bangalore, 2010)

Whitworth, Denis: *Lillooah Revisited* (*Anglos In The Wind*, Chennai, 2006)

Williams, Blair R.: *Anglo-Indians—Vanishing Remnants of a Bygone Era* (CTR Inc. Publishing, New Jersey, 2002)

Wright, Denzil Errol: *People of the Raj—The Anglo-Indian* (Ontario, 2003)

Newspapers and Journals:
The Mail, Aside and *Madras Musings,* Madras; *The Hindu,* Madras; *The Times of India* and *Illustrated Weekly of India,* Bombay; *The Statesman, The Telegraph,* and *Sunday,* Calcutta; *The Hindustan Times* and *India Today,* Delhi

Photo Credits:
AITW Collection: Anglos In The Wind Collection
SM Collection: S. Muthiah's Collection

Index

March, 52, 53; Lent (March/April), 51;
New Year's Eve, 50, 51; wedding/wedding
reception, 7, 49, 52, 130
Anglo-Indian Guild, 125, 190–92
Anglo-Indian homes, 30,49, 54–56, 83, 84;
bedroom, 84; dining room, 84; kitchen,
55, 84; living room, 84; toilet, 84
Anglo-Indian 'Nannies', 92
Anglo-Indian artists, 154
Anglo-Indian railway officers, 82
Anglo-Indian Review, The, 42
Anglo-Indians: 1911 definition, 3; Anglo-
Indianness, 28, 189; description of, 1–10;
identifiers, 5–6; identity of, 48, 106, 137,
183; informal relationship with parents,
7; lineage, 3–5, 17, 18, 23, 28, 30, 32, 35;
offspring, 35; period of prosperity, 30;
present times, 34; skin colour, 8
Anglo-Indian localities, 101. *See also*
Anglo-Indian settlements
Anglo-Indian schools, 44, 68–76, 99, 143, 188,
190, 192; 'Anglo-Vernacular' schools, 69;
British-style schools, 68; earliest, 69, 70;
east, 72; Euro/Anglo-Indian schools, 68,
69, 71; headships in, 188; Hindi and local
languages, 76; north, 71; school uniform,
75–76; sought after schools, 71–73; south,
72; west, 73
Anglo-Indian settlements: 41, 104, 184;
in Andamans and Nicobars, 104; in
McCluskiegunj, 105–111; Whitefield,
Bangalore, 103–104, 184
Anglo-Indian spirituality, 179
Anglo-Indian Teachers' Training School, 76
Anglo-Indian United Front, 140, 191
Anglo-Indian Vision, The, 149
Anglo-Indian women, 5, 7, 47, 83, 91–92;
academics, 95, 135, 148; achievers of
later generations, 94–100; actresses, 159,
161, 162; air hostess, 98; in business, 140,
141; in field of medicine, 94–95, 98, 99;
in media, 99; Models, 163, 164; as nurses,
96–98; in politics, 100; in public relations,
99–100; secretarial practice, 99, 100;
significant roles in the lives of governors,
statesmen and kings, 92–93; writings,
147–148

Anglo-Indian Youth League, 144
Anglos in the Wind, 150
Anna University, 134
An Oriental Biographical Dictionary, 152
Anthony, Frank, 42–46, 75, 138, 139, 152, 186,
188–196
Arjuna Award, 170, 171
Article 333, Constitution of India, 43
Article 338(3), Constitution of India, 44
Arul, Jennifer (Suares), 99
Ashborn, Francis, 143
Ashoka Chakra, 89, 98
Aswan Dam, 132
Atkinson, Denzil B., 196
Auckland House, Shimla, 71
Australia, 2, 8–9, 11, 35, 44, 48, 68, 95,
100, 128, 133, 139, 143, 145, 148–149,
157–160, 165, 167–174
Australian hockey, 168–170
Australian Jazz circuit, 157
Auxiliary Force (India), 38
Ayahs, 91

B
Baker, Maurice, 132
Baldrey, Adrian, 90
Baldwin's School, 72
ball (kofta) curry, 56, 59
Bangladesh, 3, 121, 168
Baptist, A.D., 135
Barber, Eric, 180
Barker, AVM Maurice, 121
Barnes, George, 67
Barnes School, 67
Barneval, Charles, 22
Baroda Manufacturing Pty. Ltd, 141
Barren, A.K., 130
Barretto, Luis, 195
Barretto, Moniz, 17
Barrow, A.E.T., 192, 193, 195
Bartley, Marcus, 162
Bastian, Erman, 167
Battle of Plassey (1757), 24, 32
Bayer, Jennifer, 148
Beale, Miss, 94
Beale, Thomas, 151, 152
Beaty, Francis (Frank), 128

Service, 127, 128; in education, 134, 135
Graham, John, 73
Grand, Catherine Worlee (Talleyrand), 22
Great Indian Peninsular Railway, 79
Great Revolt of 1857, 30, 38, 119, 128
Great Trigonometrical Survey of India, 134
Greave, Sidney, 178
Greene, John, 121, 122
Greenhill, Henry, 20
Growing up in Anglo-India, 127
Guide to the English Tongue, A, 65
Gulf News, 145
gurukulam system, 67

H
Haiti revolt (1791–94), 25
Half-Caste, 151
Hall, Eric, 123
Hallett, Maurice, 106
Hamilton, James, 104
Hamilton, Rose, 104
Hansi, 118, 181
Hardinge, Lord, 1
Hardinge, Mervyn, 144
Hardless, Charles R., 133
Hare, David, 153
Harp of India, The, 153
Hart, H.S., 90
Hart, Leslie, 128
Harvey, Robert, 4
Harvey family, 3, 4
Haryana, 33, 118, 181
Hastings, Warren, 1
Hawke, Linda Brady, 99
Hayde, Desmond, 125
Hayden, Diana, 164
Hearsey, Hyder Jung (Young), 33, 118
Hearsey, John, 119
Hebron School, 72
Henderson-Brooks, Thomas, 124
Hendricks, Ron, 145
Henry Louis Vivian Derozio Bridge, 153
Heppolet, Effie (Indira Devi), 161
Hind, Arthur, 167
Hindustan Aeronautics Ltd., 121
Hindustan Aircraft Ltd., 134
History of Christianity in India, 152

Holder, Albert, 167
home-made wine, 56
Hostages to India: The Life Story of the Anglo-Indian Race, 151
Huggins, Charles, 167
Hume, A.O., 184
Humperdinck, Englebert, 156
Hutchinson, Norman, 154
Hyderabad, 14, 32, 72, 137, 152, 164

I
Impact India Foundation, 98
Imperial and Provincial Services, 28
Imperial Anglo-Indian Association, 41
Imperial Forest Service, 130
Indian Air Force, 121–123
Indian Army, 31, 117, 124, 146
Indian Corps, France, 132
Indian Express, 145
Indian Foreign Service, 131
Indian National Army, 131
Indian National Congress, 1885, 40
Indian Navy, 125, 126
indiaticos, 14
Indo-Britons, 1, 138, 197
Indo-Portuguese, 18, 55, 192
Innes, Michelle, 164
International Federation of Anglo-Indian Associations, 144
International Public Relations Association, 98
Inter-State Board of Anglo-Indian Education, 190
Irrigation and Roads (PWD), 27
Isaacs, Theo, 135
I Thought about You, 157
Iverts, Dr., 94

J
jagir/zamin rights, 182
Jago Bangla, 193
jalfrezi, 56
Jamalpur, 77, 85, 86
Jameson, 'Jimmy', 168
Jameson, John, 173
Jansen, Pat, 166
Jayawardena, Kumari, 3, 11
Jeanne Begum (Albert/Vincens/Dupleix), 22–24, 31, 93